Aesthetics
and the Good Life

Aesthetics and the Good Life

Marcia Muelder Eaton

Rutherford • Madison • Teaneck
Fairleigh Dickinson University Press
London and Toronto: Associated University Presses

© 1989 by Associated University Presses, Inc.

All rights reserved. Authorization to photocopy items for internal or personal use, or the internal or personal use of specific clients, is granted by the copyright owner, provided that a base fee of $10.00, plus eight cents per page, per copy is paid directly to the Copyright Clearance Center, 27 Congress Street, Salem, Massachusetts 01970. [0-8386-3336-6/89 $10.00+8¢ pp, pc.]

Associated University Presses
440 Forsgate Drive
Cranbury, NJ 08512

Associated University Presses
25 Sicilian Avenue
London WC1A 2QH, England

Associated University Presses
P.O. Box 488, Port Credit
Mississauga, Ontario
Canada L5G 4M2

The paper used in this publication meets the requirements of the American National Standard for Permanence of Paper for Printed Library Materials Z39.48-1984.

Library of Congress Cataloging-in-Publication Data

Eaton, Marcia Muelder, 1938–
 Aesthetics and the good life.

 Bibliography: p.
 Includes index.
 1. Aesthetics. I. Title.
 BH39.E26   1989   111'.85   87-46420
 ISBN 0-8386-3336-6 (alk. paper)

PRINTED IN THE UNITED STATES OF AMERICA

In Memory
of My Mother and Father

Contents

Preface		9
1	Philosophical Approaches to the Aesthetic	13
2	Locating the Aesthetic	28
3	A Necessary Feature of the Aesthetic	48
4	Applied Aesthetics	66
5	Measuring What Matters	94
6	A Characterization of 'the Aesthetic'	129
7	The Aesthetic and the Ethical	152
Notes		180
Works Cited		194
Index		205

Preface

I believe that having aesthetic experience is a very important part of life, and this work grows out of that conviction. What I hope to do is to provide a characterization of the aesthetic that will enable us to understand what it means to view something aesthetically, or to assess something from an aesthetic point of view, or to know what we must do to help make the lives of others as aesthetically full as possible.

Aesthetic experiences are not simply things that happen involuntarily (although they are sometimes that); people actively seek them. Indeed, one of the things that I hope to show is that part of what it means to lead a moral and rational life is to respond aesthetically to objects, events, and other people. Having aesthetic experiences is thus one of life's central goals. Aesthetic activities and responses enrich life and provide us with what I shall call 'delight' not only by providing pleasure but by sensitizing, vitalizing, and inspiring human beings.

The definition of 'aesthetic' that I propose in this book is as follows: the aesthetic is characterized by delight taken in intrinsic features of objects or events that are traditionally considered worthy of sustained attention or reflection. Just which intrinsic properties are encompassed by this statement and what or whose traditions provide a basis for judgment are a central concern of this study.

In fundamental ways this characterization (I prefer this term to 'definition') is not at all original, but I am not suggesting a radically new way of looking at the aesthetic. Instead, I want to articulate what I think are historically and philosophically shared attitudes about what aesthetic properties, experiences, and evaluations are or entail. I hope to show that this way of understanding the aesthetic is reinforced by both theoretical and practical discussions.

I am grateful to several of my colleagues at the University of Minnesota for their comments and support. Norman Dahl was especially helpful. I am grateful to the University of Minnesota for a sabbatical leave and Bush Fellowship in 1984–85; much of the work for this book was done during that time. Mitchell Charnley, Leslie Foley, and, particularly, Ruth Wood provided invaluable editorial assistance. As usual my husband, Joe, and son, Dennis, were consistently supportive.

I wish to thank Holt, Rinehart, and Winston; Princeton University Press; W. W. Norton & Company, Inc.; Oxford University Press; Prentice-Hall, Inc.; University of Massachusetts Press; John Wiley & Sons; Jones & Jones, Seattle, Washington; United States Department of Agriculture, Forest Service; United States Department of Interior, Bureau of Land Management; and the Saint Paul Chamber Orchestra for permission to reprint published material. I wish to thank Ackerberg and Associates, Inc., Architects, Minneapolis, Minnesota; the Minneapolis Institute of Arts; and the Frans Halsmuseum, Haarlem, The Netherlands for permission to reproduce visual material.

Aesthetics
and the Good Life

1
Philosophical Approaches to the Aesthetic

One way the difficult question of what 'aesthetic' means, or of how the aesthetic and nonaesthetic are to be distinguished, has sometimes been approached is by trying to characterize the aesthetic terms used in descriptions of art works. So let me begin by asking the reader to pick out the "aesthetic words" in the following paragraph.

> Probably composed sometime in the early eighteenth century, Telemann's Suite in A minor, is one of over two hundred works he wrote while he was kapellmeister to the court of Count Erdmann von Promnitz in Sorau, an area that is now part of Poland. In the Suite in A minor, Telemann gives the flute a virtuoso role in the fast section of the *ouverture* while adhering to classic *fugato* texture in the tuttis. The result is a delightful mixture of French and Italian styles, typical of Telemann's undoctrinaire approach to music throughout his life. The procession of dance movements begins with a lively movement that features solo violin as well as solo flute. Some of the other dances will be familiar from their appearance in Bach's suites. These two rather austere minuets are followed by a presto Rejouissance (rejoicing) and then two Passepieds—an old French dance from Brittany, and ancestor of the courtly minuet. The concluding polonaise is in an exotic key—A minor—and, in its harmony and rhythm, suggests Telemann's strong attraction to Polish folk music, another hallmark of the composer's style. [1]

Most people, beginning this exercise, are reasonably confident it will be easy. As they proceed, they often find they move slowly. "Delightful" and "austere" seem clearly to point to aesthetic features; "composed in the early eighteenth century" and "now a part of Poland" just as clearly do not. But what about "solo flute" or "presto" or "undoctrinaire"? Even the reader who felt certain until the end of the exercise will probably find it difficult to convince others that he or she has the one and only correct list. With perhaps weakened confidence, we can now return to cases that seem clear-cut—"austere" or "part of Poland," for example. (I am aware that my confidence in choosing these terms may not be matched by the reader's.) To the extent that confidence remains, how do we explain it? Why pick these out as paradigms of the aesthetic and of the nonaesthetic?

One purpose of this book is to characterize the aesthetic in such a way that its reader can distinguish aesthetic experiences and assessments from nonaesthetic ones and to identify experiences that others will also find aesthetic. The path may seem circuitous at times. This chapter considers current philosophical views with respect to how, if at all, the distinction between the aesthetic and the nonaesthetic can be made.

Philosophical Approaches to the Aesthetic

The issues considered central or most important in distinguishing the aesthetic from the nonaesthetic are matters of dispute even among philosphers. Although their various approaches do not lend themselves to neat categorization, one can, I believe, find three main types: psychological, epistemological, and logical. In my theory I hope to avoid the weaknesses and incorporate the strengths of these diverse theories and at the same time develop a rather different approach, namely a holistic or contextual approach.

Theorists who favor a psychological approach favor an account of the aesthetic based upon the belief that a special psychological or emotional reaction accompanies the claim that some property is aesthetic rather than nonaesthetic. Monroe Beardsley presents such a theory—one in which the crucial element of the aesthetic is what he calls "aesthetic gratification." His paper, "The Aesthetic Point of View," provides a series of refinements on the following more or less introspectively based proposal: To adopt the aesthetic point of view with regard to x is to take an interest in whatever aesthetic value x may possess. He concludes with this definition: To adopt the aesthetic point of view with regard to x is to take an interest in the value it possesses in virtue of its capacity to provide aesthetic gratification when its regional qualities and formal unity are correctly and completely experienced.[2] "Correct and complete experience" is, of course, a problematic notion (or combination of notions). Although Beardsley does not present an argument per se, his emphasis on the role of regional qualities and formal unity in aesthetic experience is one that I shall use later in characterizing the aesthetic.

Where Beardsley requires attention to inherent features (as I will do in my theory), Jerome Stolnitz argues that the aesthetic is marked by a special attitude; the aesthetic for him is characterized by the special mental set of viewers when they have an aesthetic experience. When people approach something aesthetically, he says, they put aside normal, practical concerns and display "disinterested and sympathetic attention to and contemplation of any object of awareness, for its own sake alone."[3] According to such a view we are psychologically different when we ascribe aesthetic properties to things than when we ascribe nonaesthetic properties to them.

Many philosophers have been critical of psychological approaches. J. O. Urmson, for instance, believes they are beset with two sorts of problems. First, if one posits an aesthetic emotion, then there seems to be an obligation to do the same for other kinds of satisfaction—economic, for example. That there is an economic emotion or psychological state does indeed seem absurd. Second, Urmson believes that responses to works of art seem to involve not merely a single emotion, but a whole range and variety of them.

Urmson favors, instead, what I have called an epistemological approach to the aesthetic. Epistemological theories have in common the view that it is a special set of beliefs (perhaps arising from a special cognitive faculty) that results in our claims about the presence or absence of some aesthetic property. Urmson thinks the aesthetic should be located by examining "appraisals distinguished by their concentration on some special sub-set of criteria of value."[4] Aesthetic experience is thus marked by the set of things we pay attention to, not by the way in which we attend. It is what we believe about things, not the mental state we are in that matters. Identifying the criteria of value can be done by engaging in "fieldwork." Urmson suggests that we empirically discover what criteria people apply when they respond in ways that they identify as aesthetic.

There is, I think, a serious problem here. Suppose someone describes an aesthetic experience and goes on to list, as criteria applied, considerations of duty, honor, and loyalty. On what non-question-begging ground can one then say, "But those are not *aesthetic* criteria"?

Another problem revolves around the difficulty of determining the reference of *it* in the question, "What criteria are you applying when you respond aesthetically to it?" How, without independently defining 'aesthetic', can we be sure that the persons questioned are assessing the appropriate object—the sounds created at a concert, for instance—rather than the color of the musicians' clothes, or the social status of the audience?

According to Kendall Walton, another epistemological theorist who considers beliefs of a certain kind to be central to the delineation of the aesthetic, one's belief that an object is of a certain kind makes it possible to judge it on aesthetic terms. In his paper, "Categories of Art," Walton begins with what he calls a "commonplace": "What is important about . . . works of art, as works of art, is what can be seen or heard in them."[5] This has led some theorists, he thinks, to assert that extrinsic information about works is not aesthetically relevant.

But Walton doubts that critical questions about works can be separated from questions about their histories. What we perceive, he argues, depends upon what we know. Aesthetic properties depend not only on nonaesthetic properties (more about this below) but also "on which of its nonaesthetic properties are "standard," which "variable," and which "contra-standard'." These distinctions are among properties all of which are perceptually distinguishable—"features that can be perceived in a work when it is experienced in the normal manner."[6] That a work is in the Italian style is perceptually distinguishable; that it was written in Poland is not. Standard features are those by virtue of which a work belongs to a particular category. Variable features are those that have nothing to do with the category to which an object belongs; contra-standard features are those that tend to disqualify a work as a member of a category.

These classifications can be best understood in terms of an example.

Flatness, or two-dimensionality, is a standard feature of paintings—a painting is always flat. Size is variable—a painting can be huge or tiny. Three-dimensionality is contra-standard for painting.

For Walton, all of this is important for the aesthetic/nonaesthetic distinction in the following way: "What aesthetic properties a work seems to have, what aesthetic effect it has on us, how it strikes us aesthetically often depends (in part) on which of its features are standard, which variable, and which contra-standard for us."[7] For example, the resemblance between a portrait and its subject is a matter of variable, not standard, features shared by the two. The latter (a painting's flatness or two dimensionality, for example) are taken for granted and therefore do not count against the resemblance. The standard features determine the range of possibilities for variable features. Pianos can be played only so fast. Hence, the same speed played on the piano and on some electronic device may result in ones being a brilliant presto passage while the other is merely boring repetition. Which it is will depend upon the category—piano or electronic music—to which the work belongs.

Walton's view is important because it provides a reason for believing that aesthetic properties are not manifest—that is, that they are not always directly perceivable. Fitting an object into a certain category determines what features will be standard, variable, and contra-standard, and, thus, what will count as the aesthetically relevant properties. Since the category to which it belongs is not one of its manifest properties, identification of the aesthetic properties will depend upon more than what is directly perceivable. The position I shall develop later, that traditions influence categorization, is certainly consistent with Walton's view.

Logical theorists maintain that claims of the form 'x is A' (where x is an object or event and A is aesthetic property) have special logical properties. Isabel Hungerland, for example, believes that aesthetic and nonaesthetic features or concepts do not belong to "the same logical category or universe of discourse."[8]

The essential difference between A's and N's (N's are nonaesthetic properties) is indicated, Hungerland believes, by the *fact* that A's are not admitted as evidence in courts of law, by the *fact* that we cannot get our money back because a vase fails to be delicate, by the *fact* that there is no seems/is distinction where A's are involved, and by the *fact* that the notion of standard conditions of perception (for instance normal lighting conditions) makes sense of A's only within cultural subgroups.[9] I am not sure that all of these are facts. If an art dealer advertises a vase as delicate (in *ARTNews*, for instance), and if I order it and it turns out not to be delicate, I may very well try to get my money back—and take the dealer to court for refusal to make the refund. The question of normal lighting conditions seems to be equally true for N's. There is a tremendous difference between normal nighttime room lighting for the United States and third world countries, for instance.

The alleged fact about the seems/is distinction is more interesting. Hungerland thinks that the role of 'x is A' is more like 'x looks N' than 'x is N.' To say, "The sky *looks* blue," does not commit one to say, "The sky *is* blue." One can easily believe the first but not the second. This is not true of "The vase is well proportioned." It is hard to imagine that anyone could believe that the vase *is* well proportioned, but not that it *looks* well proportioned, or vice versa.

So how are *A*'s based on *N*'s? Talk about *N*'s, Hungerland answers, helps us to "take a perceptual viewpoint from which we can see what the critic sees."[10] All descriptive terms (or 'predicates;, to use the philosophic term) have "certain fields of application," knowledge of which is part of their correct use. The fields of application for *table* and *selfish*, for example, differ enormously. *A*'s are terms invented to describe how *N*-featured things look to us from certain perceptual viewpoints under certain conditions, where, Hungerland believes, 'perceptual viewpoint' is best understood by way of an analogy to Wittgenstein's aspect perception. People who fail to notice the proportions of a vase are looking at and seeing the same object as those who do. But they are like people who see a hat, but fail to notice its color, or look at the duck-rabbit figure and see the duck but not the rabbit.

Like Hungerland, I believe that perception plays a crucial role in aesthetic experience. However, I do not think that logical features such as the seems/is distinction work in all cases to distinguish the aesthetic from the nonaesthetic. But before I discuss problems with characterizations of the aesthetic, which turn on logical uniqueness, I wish to turn to another theorist—one whose view combines psychological, epistemological, and logical features.

A Sample Theory

One of the most influential aesthetic theories of recent years is that of Frank Sibley. Because his work combines psychological, epistemological, and logical features, some of it appeals to almost everyone and some of it bothers almost everyone.

Sibley's theory is psycho-epistemological in its inclusion of a special mental faculty—taste—which is supposed to allow us to form perceptions and articulate beliefs about aesthetic properties and their presence in some objects. These psycho-epistemological factors provide Sibley with a basis for his main argument—that aesthetic judgments have special logical features.

Sibley's view of 'the aesthetic' is put forth in a pair of articles, "Aesthetic Concepts" and "Objectivity and Aesthetics." Basically, the view is that aesthetic properties, although objectively real, are not perceived by everyone and are not condition-governed, that is, no set of nonaesthetic properties can act as necessary and sufficient conditions for attributing aesthetic properties to things. Following is a look at the separate points conjoined in his statement:

I. Aesthetic properties are perceived only by people with taste
II. Aesthetic concepts are not condition-governed.
III. Aesthetic judgments are objective judgments.

I. Sibley suggests that we begin by looking at the various sorts of things we say about works of art. These remarks, he believes, fall broadly into two categories:

1. Some properties referred to by the terms in the remarks can be perceived by anyone with normal eyes, ears, and intelligence.
2. Some properties referred to by the terms in the remarks *cannot* be perceived by just anyone with normal eyes, ears, and intelligence, but require an exercise of taste, or special perceptiveness, sensitivity, discrimination, or appreciation.[11]

(Notice that this precludes including as aesthetically relevant anything like smell or touch or mouth-taste; wine tasting, for example, is not then an aesthetic activity. This is debatable, but not crucial, I think, to Sibley's position.)

Aesthetic properties are of the second kind. Taste, "an ability to *notice* or *see* or *tell* that things have certain qualities,"[12] is required to notice that things are unified, balanced, integrated, lifeless, serene, somber, elegant, and so forth. It is not required to perceive that things are red, noisy, brackish, clammy, square, docile, curved, freakish, and so on. Sibley believes that this theory matches people's intuitions about which properties are aesthetic and which are not. (My intuitions do not match Sibley's. I wonder whether being red is not one of thing's aesthetic properties; I am certain that freakishness can be; we will see in the next chapter that "elegant" is questionable. But one need not accept Sibley's epistemology in order to make sense of or accept his other two points.)

Sibley does not *argue* that the set of aesthetic terms is equivalent to the set of taste terms—he simply states that they are. And it does not follow from their being taste concepts that aesthetic concepts are not conditon-governed or that the properties to which they refer are or are not objectively real. One could, for example, claim that it is not taste that is required to see gracefulness, but rather some special training of the ordinary senses. Further, I do not think one must accept Sibley's lists. One might simply consider it and his analysis as an explanation of *some* aesthetic properties, terms, and concepts—that is, not buy the part of his view that states (not argues) that all of the terms anyone would ever want to call aesthetic act as he says they do.[13]

II. The main arguments in "Aesthetic Concepts" are aimed at proving that " . . . there are no non-aesthetic features which serve in *any* circumstances as logically *sufficient conditions* for applying aesthetic terms. Aesthetic or taste concepts are not in *this* respect conditon-governed at all" (Sibley's emphasis).[14] Sibley recognizes that the failure to find both necessary and sufficient conditions for aesthetic terms does not distinguish them from nonaesthetic terms. Several nonaesthetic terms, "noisy" or "clammy" or "curved", for example, defy such narrow delimitation. He does believe, however, that the absence of even sufficient conditions is an important feature of the aesthetic.

Nor can we find, for an aesthetic term, even a subset of conditions such that once they are fulfilled one can conclude that an object has the property in question. *Delicate* is thus distinguished from *intelligent* or *lazy*. Being able to play chess, solve Rubic's cube in a few minutes, read fourteen languages, compare and contrast Shakespeare and Proust, give the causes of the War of the Roses, and explain clearly the theory of continental drift is not equivalent to being intelligent; but if we believe that Mary can do all of them, then we can confidently conclude that she is intelligent. But there is no such list for "delicate." If told that Mary is blond, blue-eyed, has gentle curves, and weighs less than one hundred pounds, we may *expect* that she will be delicate, according to Sibley, but we shall not be able to *conclude* confidently that she must be.

Nor are aesthetic terms "defeasible." That is, no single property can preclude the correct application of an aesthetic predicate. One makes a contract if he or she knows how to read and signs the paper in the presence of a witness, *unless* someone is holding a gun at his or her head. ("Someone held a gun to his head" *defeats* the validity of a contract.) But being delicate or graceful lacks even this relation to a list of conditions. Even huge or dark or angular objects may be delicate. There may, Sibley allows, be descriptions that are *incompatible* with some aesthetic terms; for example, "has pale colors" negatively conditions "is garish." One can find features that count only for or against the presence of some property—for instance, being brightly colored always counts toward being garish. But no set of features logically clinches the presence of any aesthetic property.

Notice that none of these "arguments" (from our intuitions about how we use and apply terms) depends upon accepting Sibley's first point about the use of taste. Taste never appears (except in apposition) as he gives his reasons for believing in the non-condition-governed nature of aesthetic concepts. But if his second point is true, then we do have to explain how we learn to apply aesthetic terms to objects. That we "develop taste" is one obvious answer, but not the only possible one.

III. In "Objectivity and Aesthetics" Sibley raises the question of whether we can know that something is beautiful, delicate, and so forth. Sibley believes that aesthetic descriptions are *true* (or apt, correct, fitting) of the things they purportedly describe. His method for persuading his readers that aesthetic judgments are objective consists in comparing an aesthetic term like *graceful* to a color term like *red*, which, he says, is typically considered an objective property. Color terms are not objective in the sense of being primary or even provable, but simply in the sense that most people think that saying that an object is red is either true or false.

Aesthetic terms and color terms are alike in that their attribution does not follow from awareness of the presence of other properties, that is, they are not conditon-governed. What, then, is the basis for the belief that an object is or is not objectively red? For color terms the "ultimate proof" depends upon agreement, and Sibley believes that, in a more complex form, this is true of aesthetic terms as well.[15]

Physiologically, people tend to agree about the color of things in a world which, fortunately, has fairly uniform lighting conditions. Although perception is more complicated in the case of aesthetic terms—more than just adequate eyesight and lighting are involved—it is essentially the same, Sibley thinks. A *tendency* to agreement provides an objective foundation for the use of aesthetic and color terms. Disagreement can be explained by lack of attention, lack of interest, inadequate knowledge—or by a breakdown of machinery.

Aesthetic insensitivity is analogous to color-blindness, but harder to discover and test for. A proof that something has an aesthetic property "will consist in a convergence of judgments in that direction. But this may require time—to study the object, to acquire varied knowledge and experience, etc.: time also over generations, so that detailed agreement emerges from the temporary variations we call fashions, fads, etc."[16]

Thus, for Sibley, "objective" is not equivalent to "condition-governed." In spite of the impossibility of specifying even the sufficient conditions for something to be graceful, for instance, it is nonetheless the case that it is either true or false that any given object is graceful. Thus, meaningful disagreement about aesthetic matters is possible. Critics are not simply expressing idiosyncratic preferences when they discuss and debate over works of art.

This leads us back to the problem raised at the end of the discussion of point II: How do we learn to formulate aesthetic descriptions if aesthetic terms are not condition-governed? The answer, for Sibley, is that we do it by developing taste. But it is possible (even for Sibley) to answer this question without reference to taste by following the analogy with color terms. We learn to use *red* and *green* and all other color terms directly (some even learn to use *vermillion* and *azure*), without first learning a set of conditions governing their use. When we apply color terms we do not first believe that certain conditions are fulfilled and then conclude that a term applies; we simply perceive directly that an object is red or green or azure. Similarly, Sibley maintains that we perceive directly that a vase is graceful or that it is not. He posits the existence of a special faculty, taste, for this perception; but one could instead rely on ordinary sensation and cognition, perhaps developed or trained in special ways.

Sibley says that it is the job of critics to enable an audience to see (or otherwise perceive or conceive) aesthetic properties. For this they have a variety of tools and strategies. (Sibley describes these at length in "Aesthetic Concepts.") Essentially, critics point to the properties in more or less elaborate and more or less direct ways. Again, taste as an independently existing faculty need not be posited in order to explain the function and activity of critics.

Sibley does not get what he is after, namely a way of distinguishing aesthetic from nonaesthetic properties (or terms or concepts). It is not just aesthetic properties that are non-condition-governed. *Virus, chair, weed, comfortable, erotic, ponderous, cost-effective, unique, humorous,* for example are equally hard to define in the sense of providing a list of necessary and/or sufficient conditions. Clearly, these are not usually aesthetic terms. At most, Sibley has shown that their objectivity, despite noncondtionedness, is simply a feature that some aesthetic properties share with some nonaesthetic ones. This is an important point, but not the one Sibley was after.

Problems and New Directions

Several philosophers have criticized Sibley's theory, and their complaints point to several of the weaknesses that I hope my own view will avoid. Many have concentrated on problems with *taste*. Peter Kivy, for example, believes (as I do) that Sibley does not fully explain what he means by the term. Instead, Sibley's characterization, "an ability to *notice* or *see* or *tell* that things have certain qualities," makes it appear, according to Kivy, that aesthetic properties are "very much like the kinds of nonnatural qualities that have often been associated with ethical intuitionism."[17] Kivy also feels that Sibley's position is a throwback to eighteenth-century theories of taste—a throwback that unfortunately does little to clarify the term.

Kivy suggests that we try to relate the exercise of taste, as Sibley seems to envision it, with Ludwig Wittgenstein's discussion of aspect perception. In doing so Kivy has clear affinities with Hungerland, but he is less confident that this interpretation will do the job.

Kivy uses the widely-known example of the duck-rabbit figure, which one can "see-as" a duck or a rabbit, but not as both simultaneously. Or one may see the duck (aspect) but not be able to see the rabbit (aspect) or vice versa. Perhaps a person who does not agree with me that a green vase is delicate has seen the greenness but not the delicacy. Like missing a rabbit, one might just miss the delicacy. Viewed this way, the term "graceful" would refer not to a property, but to an aspect. Although Kivy believes that aspect perception provides a helpful comparison, he doubts that it will ultimately solve all of Sibley's problems.

One problem is that aesthetic blindness (inability to see the grace or delicacy, for example) is far more widespread and more difficult to correct than aspect-blindness (such as the inability to see the rabbit in the duck-rabbit figure). One who wishes to account for lack of sensitivity, then, is no better off relying on aspect perception than on taste.

A more serious problem is that "there are some cases where the analysis of what seems to be aesthetic-quality ascriptions into aesthetic-aspect ascriptions will not go through."[18] Kivy offers some musical examples to show this. We can say either

1. Haydn's symphony is unified in virtue of N (where N is some specifiable feature of the symphony, e.g. monothematic structure).

or

2. Mozart's symphony is unified, but I can't say exactly why.

Kivy believes that both are coherent, but that only the first can be construed on the aspect-perception model. Pointing to monothematic structure may constitute a strategy for getting someone to perceive the unity—the way pointing to the beak is a strategy for getting someone to see the duck. However, Kivy asserts, "*Figaro* is a 'number opera': that is, it consists of a succession of separate movements, musically unrelated as regards thematic material. Yet Mozart has apparently managed to embue this basically fragmented form with a unity that is as inescapable as it is ineffable."[19] Here there is nothing analogous to pointing to the beak in order to help someone to see the duck.

Kivy ends by suggesting that it is probably not possible to get all aesthetic descriptions to fit perfectly into any single logical model, and I agree. But his discussion centers on "ineffability," and I find this as disquieting as he find nonnatural intuitionistic qualities. If someone cannot point to *anything* in *Figaro* to account for its unity, then I believe we would be sceptical that he actually sees or hears something that we do not.

Ted Cohen shares Kivy's scepticism concerning the possibility of finding a single characteristic that will set aesthetic terms off from nonaesthetic terms. He is critical of what he takes to be the general approach or set of attitudes underlying Sibley's position. People who are sympathetic to such an approach insist that we (a) decide whether aesthetic claims have truth-value; (b) see whether aesthetic terms follow from nonaesthetic terms; and, if they do not, (c) see how aesthetic terms are related to nonaesthetic terms. Specifically, Cohen is critical of Sibley for what he takes to be a lack of argument for the claim that aesthetic concepts are not condition-governed, and for relying instead on a number of observations. Cohen has no counterexamples to Sibley's claim, but does want to show that the claim is vacuous.

Cohen agrees with my assertion that Sibley does not provide a characterization that separates the aesthetic from the nonaesthetic. Even if details of Sibley's "observations" were true, he says, they would not show what Sibley wants to show; they point to nothing that is special about the aesthetic. Cohen believes that Sibley's distinction should allow us to identify a judgment as aesthetic or nonaesthetic based on the presence or absence of aesthetic terms. Not every use of *graceful* requires taste. (Think of how readily children and untrained adults are able to tell whether the day is lovely or not, or whether a rock or glass vase is more graceful.) And there is no reason to talk about two senses of *graceful*. If all that is involved is the fact that more than normal competence is needed to handle a term, then we would have to say that there are two senses of an enormous number of non-aesthetic as well as aesthetic terms.

Cohen gives some examples ("noisy," "kafkaesque," "poetic," . . . the list is very long) that fly in the face of Sibley's claim that people can easily construct lists of aesthetic and nonaesthetic terms. This leads him to raise what I think is a very important question: What is it that we hope an aesthetic/nonaesthetic distinction, if found, will do for us? One way of seeing the mistake in approaches like Sibley's is this: Sibley attempts to provide a technical distinction (like those we have for squares and triangles) for a term that does not function in technical ways. "'Aesthetic' remains there in my language whatever the philosopher may do to mutilate its sense, and whatever I may do playing reformer. The strongest point to be made is that the argumentative use of the aesthetic/non-aesthetic distinction as a part of, or a prelude to, a 'theory,' cannot be justified solely on the grounds that 'aesthetic' is a certified non-theoretical term." [20]

I agree with Cohen. What I hope to do is not to turn a nontechnical term into a technical term, but to indicate what people are recommending when they urge us to look at something 'aesthetically'. It may be that there is ultimately no way of distinguishing this from all other urgings. But *something* is being urged nonetheless, and I hope at least to characterize it approximately.

Kivy and Cohen believe that Sibley makes what is characterized by Gary Stahl as an "ontological mistake," one that results from making unacceptable ontological assumptions. The view advocated by Sibley, according to Stahl, progresses from

1. Critics refer to *N*'s.

to

2. It is legitimate to ask for an explanation of *A*'s in terms of *N*'s.

to

3. Demand for *N*'s cannot be rejected.

to
  4. A's depend on N's.

Even Sibley's critics typically agree that the main problem centers on how we get from N's to A's or vice versa. And they assume, as Walton does, that aesthetic properties are not found in works in the straightforward way that colors or pitches or rhythms are. But Stahl wants to show that the fourth statement above "is plausible *only if* one implausibly assumes that the scientifically important is necessarily the ontologically real," a view that Sibley and his followers want to reject.[21]

If one believes the claim that A's depend on N's is true (that the balance depends on figure placement, for instance), then, according to Stahl, one sees something that itself requires taste (to use Sibley's terminology). Stahl maintains that this judgment itself must then be an A-ascription, not an N-ascription. Consider:

  a. The figures in the picture are all to the left of center.
  b. The picture is unbalanced.
  c. The picture's lack of balance depends upon the fact that all of the figures are to the left of center.

(a) is an N-ascription, based on Stahl's view; (b) and (c) are A-ascriptions. Therefore we never really are faced with a move from N's to A's or back again. The failure of Sibley and others to notice this rests on an ontological mistake, he believes.

Stahl thinks a mistake is apparent in the discussion of those (like Hungerland) who believe that the seems/is distinction that exists for N's does not exist for A's. Claiming that an object "really is N" is to grant ontological priority to N'ness. But as Quine and Strawson have shown, "On no plausible account are the physical categories ultimate. One cannot begin with an initial dualism in which self as self-conscious and the world as physical are neutral data (a logical and not a temporal point) and then proceed to work out the derivative ways of their interaction."[22] Since the physical (in terms of N's) is only *one* way of describing the world, why must it be taken as *the* way in which we must analyze the aesthetic (the A's)?

This mistake is, I think, comparable to claiming that the rabbit (in the duck-rabbit figure) must be describable in duck-terms or vice versa. That is, it would be to insist that the duck is primary, or that the rabbit figure must ultimately be reducible to description in duck-terms. My way of locating 'the aesthetic' does not depend on any argument that makes N's primary. For me, what is aesthetic (intrinsic and worth attending to) can as easily be referred to by a term from the scientific vocabulary as from the aesthetic; any *aspect* qualifies.

As I said above, I do not think Sibley gives us a way of separating the aesthetic from the nonaesthetic. I am doubtful that any single psychological, epistemological, or logical characteristic can be found that will accomplish this task. *There is no a priori way to determine whether a term or property or concept is aesthetic or nonaesthetic.* The context in which a claim is made will always have to be considered before we can tell if someone is making an aesthetic remark.

I do, nonetheless, find the search of Sibley and others illuminating. It points to an important feature of some aesthetic terms and to an important function of art critics. Sibley's starting point is the correct place to begin an investigation of the nature of the aesthetic. He asks us to consider the terms we use to describe works of art. When we do this (more systematically than Sibley did, by doing more than simply listing terms off the top of the head) I believe we will find that *some* of them *are* what we might call "sibley-terms," the application of which depends on something more than noticing that certain conditions are fulfilled. (The "something more" may, but need not, be something like taste. This issue I put aside for the time being.) More important, we shall then be able to subject these terms to a test that I wish to suggest does give us a way of marking off the aesthetic from the nonaesthetic. The test will consist of answering two questions:

1. Has the term been used traditonally to describe works of art?
2. Has the term been used to pick out an intrinsic property considered worth attending to or reflecting upon?

If an affirmative answer can be given to both of these questions, then the term is aesthetic—and the property it picks out is also aesthetic.

2
Locating the Aesthetic

In this chapter I will use an indirect method to prove that the aesthetic is marked by attending to and reflecting upon a thing's intrinsic properties and by the delight that accompanies this attention and reflection. That is, I will show that even in the face of changing aesthetic values, changing views of the nature and importance of the artistic process, and changing aesthetic language, the aesthetic is located *in* things that cause delight. In later chapters I shall discuss the meaning of 'intrinsic' and 'delight' in detail. For now, I shall use 'intrinsic' to refer to features that are located spatially or temporally *in* objects, people, or events. 'Delight' refers here to the rewards of sustained attention and reflection.

Changing Values

One of the characteristics of art that strikes both experts and nonexperts is not simply that tastes and preferences differ between individuals, but that works valued almost universally in one place or time lose their status when moved spatially or temporally. Everybody is familiar with stories of works that have not come to be appreciated until long after their creators could benefit from the adulation. The story of the artist who lives "ahead of" his or her time is common. There are also art forms that go in and out of fashion. Alan Tormey and Judith Farr Tormey have described the incredible popularity of intarsia—wood inlay—in fifteenth-century Florence, where masters were kept busy in no less than eighty-four workshops. Today we have very few of these, and such workers would more likely be called "craftspeople" than "artists."[1]

In our own period we are witnessing marked changes in what is valued—in what is considered suitable for aesthetic appreciation. It is not just that we value more and different things (quilts and other *women's art,* for example). Ideas about which properties matter aesthetically are changing as well. For much of the twentieth century, critics argued that formal properties such as shape or color or rhythmic or harmonic structures were the sole vehicles of aesthetic value. References to subject matter (love or autumn or a crucifixion) or to the artist's life, to a work's history or political repercussions, for example, were denigrated to such an extent that they achieved the status of "fallacy." The text or the canvas or the score was not merely thought to be central to aesthetic experience; attention to anything extrinsic was viewed as likely to pollute that experience.

> Ours has been a formalist century, interested more in [the analysis of light, fluid brushwork, pure hues, and so on] than in subject matter, content, and personal motivation.[2]

There are still plenty of critics who are dismayed by what they contemptuously call "literary" discussions of painting—remarks about content or subject matter. Some postmodernists have rejected any relation between art and the world. In a very interesting—and sometimes upsetting—article, "The Death of Character," Elinor Fuchs describes avant-garde theater as so self-conscious as to be self-contained.

> Writers and directors working at the edge of theatre seem to perceive that they are in a new kind of world in which there is no longer anything "out there" or anyone "in here" to imitate or to represent.[3]

And in explaining how photography achieved artistic status, Alan Trochtenburg asserts,

> The suppression of what is denoted . . . [signified] the coming-of-age of photography within an already existing system of discourse. Photography earned its place within that system by showing itself capable of a process similar to that implied by abstract and cubist composition. . . .[4]

But suppression of subject matter and refusal to talk about connections between art and what is "out there" or "in here" are no longer characteristic of all, or even most, critics. Even Impressionist works, which for many years were discussed primarily as studies of light, are studied as products of individuals who were interested in what was beautiful and in how the world should be interpreted. No longer are we told to concentrate only on color and light; it has become possible "to read Impressionist painting as we have read earlier painting, with an interest in subject matter and the personality of the artist, and in wider sociological, economic, and philosophical terms," asserts one author of a catalog for a recently successful exhibit.[5]

One of the leaders of the move away from purely formalistic discussion of art works is John Berger. Like formalists, Berger believes that the medium is aesthetically important, but for ideological or social reasons, not simply because of the way it reflects light. He insists, for example, that oil allowed painters to depict the lavishness of possessions, and this was what patrons often desired and enjoyed aesthetically during the seventeenth century.[6]

Berger has decried the repugnance that has been expressed in our century at talking about subject matter:

> The extraordinary fact is that nobody, faced with Lowry's pictures whose subject-matter is nearly always social, ever discusses the social or historical meaning of his art. Instead it is treated as though it deals with the view out of the window of a Pullman train on its non-stop journey to London, where everything is believed to be very different.[7]

Berger himself is extremely interested in subject matter, and writes about it in a way that has inspired others to take it seriously aesthetically.

> In 1645 Hals painted a portrait of a man in black looking over the back of a chair. Probably the sitter was a friend. His expression is another one that Hals was the first to record. It is the look of a man who does not believe in the life he witnesses, yet can see no other alternative. He has considered, quite impersonally, the possibility that life may be absurd. He is by no means desperate. He is interested. But his intelligence isolates him from the current purpose of men and the supposed purpose of God.[8]

After years of being urged to attend only to formal properties, it is often a great relief to be able to talk openly about subject matter and characters and artists' intentions and social context—to speak, that is, as if there were something out there and in here that art deals with. Even in the heyday of formalism these topics have always found their way into ordinary people's discussions of art and have been valued as partially responsible for aesthetic delight. Surely using such topics is the easiest way to engage students. Berger's descriptions are more interesting to most people than discussions limited exclusively to receding planes and patches of grey. Throughout history there has been much discussion of subject matter, which I believe is a truly aesthetic property. I offer it as an example of a feature that theorists have considered an aesthetic property in some periods but not in others. It is worth attention because we are witnessing for ourselves its return to favor. There are many other examples of such fluctuations.

Such changes might lead one to believe that 'aesthetic' cannot be defined because no necessary or sufficient conditions seem to exist that will serve to tie together what counts aesthetically or to distinguish the aesthetic from the nonaesthetic. This is what I want to deny. What is *aesthetic* remains constant even though specific features pointed to as aesthetically valuable may change. This becomes apparent, I think, when we look further at examples of changes in aesthetic values.

Among other places, these can be found in histories of art and culture.[9] Some scholars try to explain changes in taste or attitude. Raymond Williams, for instance, places heavy emphasis on the changes effected on our cultural history when masses of people learned to read.[10] Joseph Epstein has discussed the way acceptance of Freudian psychoanalytic theories altered the nature of literary biography.[11] Obviously, when such social changes occur there are corresponding changes in conceptions of art and the aesthetic. An outstanding study of the way in which culture affects art is Arnold Hauser's *The Social History of Art and Literature*. Speaking of the early Middle Ages he says,

> When the forms of property, the organizations of labour, the sources of education, and the methods of instruction remained practically unchanged, it would have been remarkable had any sudden change occurred in the current conception of art.[12]

Another historian who traces the history of art within the larger cultural and social context is William Fleming. Like Hauser's book, Fleming's *Art and Ideas* has many examples of ways in which cultures other than our own took interest in quite different properties of the objects they believed to carry artistic and aesthetic value. The Romans, wanting grandeur in their ceremonies, made musical instruments bigger. Quintillian wrote,

> And what else is the function of the horns and trumpets attached to our legion? The louder the concert of their notes, the greater is the glorious supremacy of our arms over all the nations of earth.[13]

Being *big* and *loud* were a source of delight; and they mattered for Quintillian and his contemporaries aesthetically as well as militarily.

But how can we know if the Romans actually experienced these instruments aesthetically? Do we have any reason for thinking that people in other times had experiences like those we identify as aesthetic? When they pick out quite different things for praise, can we say theirs was aesthetic appreciation? Our ability to do just that points us toward locating the aesthetic generally, I believe.

Consider this description of a wedding feast in Normandy at the beginning of the eleventh century.

> Everyone performed at his best and the noise of the instruments and the voices of the narrators made a considerable uproar in the hall.[14]

"Considerble uproar" might not, in isolation, be taken initially as naming an aesthetic property, but in this context, where best performance is also considered, it is clearly deserves to be described this way. The phrase "performed at his best" signals the presence of *delight taken in features in the performance*.

In the visual arts we also find unexpected features pointed out in periods removed from our own:

> Of all subjects, the most congenial to Veronese's art was festivity. Painted with the primary object of delighting the eye, his canvases nevertheless capture an important aspect of Venetian life—the conviviality of large social gatherings and the love of sumptuous surroundings embellished with fruits, flowers, animals, furniture, draperies, and jesters in bizare costumes.[15]

On the back of one painting is this note:

> If I ever have time . . . I want to represent a sumptuous banquet in a superb hall, at which will be present the Virgin, the Saviour, and St. Joseph. They will be served by the most brilliant retinue of angels which one can imagine, busied in offering them the daintiest viands and an abundance of splendid fruit in dishes of silver and gold. Other angels will hand them precious wines in transparent crystal glasses and gilded goblets, in order to show with what zeal blessed spirits serve the Lord.[16]

How surprising it would be to find such a note on the back of a twentieth-century canvas!

In seventeenth-century Holland, church services were simplified and churches were less and less decorated so that worshippers might not be distracted (aesthetically) from their (religious) purposes. Thus, art was found more and more in personal residences. Artists came to conceive their work differently. Patrons wanted to find in the paintings they owned indications of their worldly possessions. "The room shows my rug" would then have been part of a positive aesthetic description. Even religious paintings exemplify significant changes. The rather rebellious Protestant Rembrandt "was under no compulsion to conform to the usual iconographical tradition of Madonnas and Child, [or] Curcifixions. . . ."[17] Therefore pointing out a lack of standard icons would describe a feature in his paintings worth attending to.[18]

These few examples, which could be multiplied indefinitely, are sufficient for my purpose here—to suggest what is special about the aesthetic.[19]

What do these changes in the concept of art have to do with the aesthetic? My contention is this: The particular features pointed to—whether a thing is big or loud or shows Christ or a rug—may vary dramatically throughout space and time. However, what we *do* when our experience is aesthetic retains a common element. We attend to intrinsic features in the belief that this attention will be rewarded by delight. Thus, delight in what resides intrinsically in something is a mark of the aesthetic generally.

The Relevance of Artists

We certainly delight in the creative skills of artists. Those who cannot do what artists do—from lack of talent or training (and those who lack the skill never believe that mere training will provide it)—feel a special wonder. Aristotle asserted that human beings naturally delight in imitation, and although this does not imply that imitation is the only source of delight, we do appreciate others' ability to turn words and shapes almost magically into recognizable and coherent forms. According to Ernst Kris and Otto Kurz, respect has given artists even legendary and mythic status. In his preface to their book, *Legend, Myth, and Magic in the Image of the Artist,* E. H. Gombrich says, "To Ernst Kris, then, is due the profound intuition that the stories told about artists in all ages and climes reflect a universal human response to the mysterious magic of image-making." [20]

Kris and Kurz demonstrate that "the myth of the artist" reflects the fact that people value special creative talent. This is one reason that discussions about works of art are not limited to manifest or directly observable properties. We value not only *what* we see or hear but also *how* it came to be—aspects of cause as well as effect. Yet without the *what*, the value and importance of the *how* disappear. My claim is not that aesthetic experience demands attention to only intrinsic properties. A legitimate part of what we value often lies beyond the created object itself. An appreciation of artistry is often present. But when response is aesthetic, appreciation of the artist is directed *back* to features of the object. If we did not value intrinsic properties, we would not aesthetically care how they got there.

It is both interesting and instructive to note that sometimes conflicting claims are advanced to certify an artist's genius. One composition, we are told, was "done in a week." Of another we are assured that the artist "labored over a single word for months." Although at first these descriptions seem to imply inconsistent theories of aesthetic value, what they in fact do is draw attention to particular properties of particular objects. So they are not inconsistent. We value things done quickly *and* things done meticulously, although we rarely find both qualities in the same work.

Usually we are given such information when the work described seems otherwise—it looks as though it was done quickly (a Mondrian, for instance) or as though it required a great deal of time (a symphony, for instance)—and we are told that just the opposite is actually true. Told that a Mondrian was done in two hours, some observers might respond contemptuously that they could have guessed it. But told that he labored over lines and colors for months, viewers look more carefully—to see what about the painting could account for such prolonged care. Only this second look yields aesthetic appreciation of the work.

Kris and Kurz give examples of other claims made so typically about artists that they have become legendary or mythic. (Such tales function in heroic biographies generally; they are not unique to books about artists.) It is common to tell stories that show that an artist's abilities had become apparent in childhood, that he or she was marked for success from the beginning. But just as often it is said that fate made the difference—the artist was in the right place at the right time and the right person just happened to appear. Sometimes lucky accidents play a significant role in artistic achievement. Pliny told a story about Protogenes's attempt to depict a dog foaming at the mouth. When he couldn't get the foam right, he threw a sponge at the painting—and got just what he wanted.

The particular legend in ascendancy at any time reflects cultural interests and preoccupations. Such stories "work" only when they tell the audience something about an artist that it wants to hear and something that connects what the artist did with what is valued in the artwork and in the artworld. If we valued only what is put carefully, precisely, and intentionally on the canvas, then the sponge throwing incident would detract from the artist's contribution. But it does not. Kris and Kurz attribute this to the growing role of and emphasis upon imagination or "invention" in the history of art (an example of the sort of "changing value" that we looked at in the last section).[21]

This view is supported by David Summers in *Michelangelo and the Language of Art*.

> The Cinquecento no longer regarded the imitation of nature as the acme of artistic achievement, but rather viewed 'invention' as its foremost aim.[22]

Thus, what in a work of art was worth attending to and reflecting upon became what was considered a product of imagination. It was simply not enough that the object resulted from technique, dexterity, or intense labor. New appreciation of *il furore dell'arte* (artistic ecstasy) resulted in looking for and then, and only then, finding one set of worthwhile properties rather than another. As Aretino said,

> This point of view also decisively influenced the evaluation of the work of art itself. . . . Soon . . . the unfinished was highly appreciated in its own right; and the strange statement found in guidebooks to Florence, that Michelangelo's unfinished slaves in the grotto of the Boboli Gardens are in that state more beautiful and more impressive than if the master had completed them, is nothing but a reflection of the same aesthetic that has continued to exert its influence to this day. This is in complete contrast to what was valued in the Middle Ages which used as the aesthetic yardstick the degree to which a work was finished in the sense of craftsmanship.[23]

If imagination (in both artistic production and experience) is valued, then *unfinishedness* as an intrinsic property is worthy of attention and reflection; if craftsmanship is valued, then *finishedness* is what rewards our attention and reflection.

Both terms (*finished* and *unfinished*) become 'aesthetic' only within a context of a special sort—one that assumes valuing or taking delight as the goal. Both "done in two hours" and "took a lifetime" may be 'aesthetic' remarks if they invite attention to something with the promise of a satisfying perception. The appropriateness of *finished* and *unfinished* will depend upon particular aesthetic features that are being referred to.

The legends and myths about artists reflect the milieu of the viewer, and this will be made apparent in the sorts of things that he or she chooses to tell us about the object being discussed. Stories emphasizing long years of practice are not likely to emerge when the role of imagination and invention is foregrounded. In such contexts the more likely stories are those in which artists are born, not made.

The dichotomy between artist as faithful copier of nature and artist as surpasser of nature parallels the dichotomy between imagination and craftsmanship and the accompanying legends and divergence in properties to which attention is directed when first one and then the other is dominant. The latter provides the background for such famous stories as that told of Zeuxis, whose painting of grapes was so realistic that birds attempted to eat them. When this kind of artistic production is valued, viewers of the product will be expected to point to lifelike, naturalistic, deceptive, and illusionistic qualities. These will not support a positive assessment when an artist is supposed to go beyond the real to some ideal. This difference accounts for the following comment:

> Zeuxis is said to have raised the question why the birds pecked away at the picture of the grapes which a boy was carrying and why the picture of the boy did not frighten them away. Two different explanations were proposed. One, found in Pliny suggested that the boy was "not so well" painted as the grapes; the other, by Seneca, maintained that this very incident showed that as an idealized portrait the painting of the boy was superior to that of the grapes.[24]

Whether the boy or the birds is judged to be superior depends on what one supposes the artist was trying to do. And the *value* of what the artist was trying to do will differ from period to period. What remains constant is that the stories we choose to tell and be told are tied to the features in the works that we find delightful.

Changing Language

THE AESTHETIC HISTORY OF A TERM

Not only do people point to very different features when they describe aesthetic experience or justify aesthetic judgments, but the language of aesthetic discourse also varies tremendously from one place and time to another. There are cases in which language that seems clearly nonaesthetic in one context appears obviously aesthetic in another. These differences do not really show that there is not a common element in the aesthetic. Indeed, close scrutiny of linguistic practices provides a strategy for locating the 'aesthetic'. Edward Cahn, in a fascinating book called *Masterpieces*, gives a history of that term. He shows how its current use as a term of praise, functioning to point to an artwork of exceptional quality—the culmination of an artist's life work—developed from what was originally a narrowly legalistic meaning. It first implied competency, and pointed to an object that demonstrated that its maker was skilled enough to become fullfledged member of a guild.

As one examines the development of the use of 'masterpiece' one discovers support for the view that the aesthetic is marked by delight in intrinsic properties. Most people, I think, would agree that "x is a competent product" is a nonaesthetic *(N)* remark, and "x is an exceptionally good work of art" is an aesthetic *(A)* remark. If we answer these two questions,

1. What features (*F*'s) are pointed to in contexts where 'masterpiece' is used nonaesthetically (*N*-ly)?
2. What features (*F*'s) are pointed to in contexts where 'masterpiece' is used aesthetically (*A*-ly)?

we find that

1. If F_i tends to appear in contexts where 'masterpiece' is used *N*-ly, then F_i is *N*.
2. If F_j tends to appear in contexts where 'masterpiece' is used *A*-ly then F_j is *A*.

Once the *A*-features and the *N*-features have been identified, we can go on to characterize aesthetic properties—and what we find in the 'masterpiece' case is that aesthetic features are always intrinsic and delightful.

The word 'masterpiece' (or "chef d'oevre"—the English term did not appear until the seventeenth century) is of medieval origin. It is first encountered in the 1200s "in the context of regulatory legislation governing artisanal activity."[25] A masterpiece was produced as a necessary condition for any apprentice to become a master, whether blacksmith or sculptor or butcher or barber. Extant legal documents spell out the conditions of production, but not the standards used by the judges. These conditions included not only a description of the object to be manufactured or the task to be performed, but also such features of the productive activity as time or place of completion. Fulfillment was intended primarily to demonstrate *adequate* knowledge or skill. Thus, the main object of judgment was the maker, not what was made, although in order to complete the judgment the work produced would necessarily be scrutinized.

The conditions of completion differed, of course, for different guilds. Most seem to have had time constraints: a butcher may have been given a few hours, an embroiderer, several months. A customer's reasonable expectation naturally figured in setting these limits.

The *lofty* connotations we associate with an artist's masterpiece today seem to have been completely lacking in the contexts of the word's original use.[26] This is partly due to the relatively low status of manual labor in the Middle Ages—a fact that also explains the absence of signatures on these or other artisanal products. But it is also because these products were a test of competence or adequacy, not a mark of extraordinary skill or craftsmanship.

Of course, there would have been reference to standards by the team of judges. But this would not primarily have involved consideration of the aesthetic properties of the object produced. Consider the conditions one had to fulfill in fifteenth-century Reims in order to become a barber:

> (W)et well and shave in a competent manner, comb, trim and thin a beard; prepare lancets suitable for the bleeding of the ill, and be knowledgeable enough in this operation to be able to distinguish a vein and an artery . . . and know also the appropriate time to carry out a bleeding."[27]

The terms "suitable," "competent," and "knowledgeable enough" are not aesthetic evaluations here any more than they would be in a judgment by a team of professors at a Ph.D. oral examination. The master barbers who did the judging must have engaged in (something like) aesthetic activity when they determined that a beard had been made thin enough. But they did not have to do so when they determined whether the candidate had found a vein. Their task was not primarily an aesthetic one. One may call attention to succinct style or a well-turned phrase in a Ph.D. dissertation, but there, also, the examiners' main task is not an aesthetic one. The key words here are *primarily* and *main*. The things pointed to when 'masterpiece' was legalistic *tended* to be nonaesthetic properties.

From the initial intuitive assumption that 'masterpiece' was not originally an aesthetic term, one can proceed to discover what features were pointed to in the contexts of that use. Here we find such phrases as "done in three hours," "demonstrated adequate knowledge to distinguish veins from arteries," and "a tart made with jellied filling." I believe the properties referred to by these words do in fact fit my characterization: they are not intrinsic properties nor are they in themselves considered worthy of attention or reflection or as productive of delight.

Cahn argues that 'masterpiece' began to change as it became associated with another medieval term, 'marvel'. References to God as "divine master" and "skilled artisan" are found in the Scriptures. And as the status of manual labor improved, these metaphors became more and more prevalent in other writings. (In this context it is interesting to note that Aquinas's designer is more of a scientist, Hume's an engineer, and so on.) God's works are also described as "marvels"—predilection for identifying Seven Marvels in various categories advancing such talk. It is not surprising that when God came to be viewed as a master who creates marvels, 'masterpiece' came to be considered as extraordinary as marvels or miracles. Man, a *late* product of God's work, and woman, even later, were His greatest marvels. Hence, being created later in a career became more important in the use of 'masterpiece' because it indicated that skill had increased through much experience. It was something created not by a new master at the beginning of a career, but by an experienced expert—a "seasoned" master.

As 'masterpiece' became associated with the marvelous or miraculous, it also became used in what I have identified as the 'aesthetic sense'—to pick out those intrinsic features that delight by rewarding sustained attention and reflection. The first uses of 'masterpiece' in the aesthetic sense are in descriptions of churches. Sainte-Chapelle is described as a masterpiece in what is clearly an aesthetic judgment.

> . . . the boldest work on this side of the Alps . . . because it contains two perfect churches, an upper chapel and a lower one, in which there is not a single column or support, outside of those surrounding the edifice on the exterior. These are so high and straight, so slender and fine that it would seem that it could not resist the smallest injury from the elements.[28]

According to my hypothesis, one would expect that the things pointed to when 'masterpiece' began to be used aesthetically would be intrinsic properties considered worthy of attention and reflection. And that's exactly what is found in this passage. The church is bold, *so* straight, *so* slender, *so* high, *so* fine, admirable, large, and solid; it has supports that, in spite of *looking* incapable of it, bear great weight.

When Notre Dame is described using the aesthetic sense of 'masterpiece', it is also described in what we readily identify as aesthetic terms: 'beautiful' and 'magnificent'. Later, an English masterpiece/marvel is described as colossal, solid, capacious, and completed in a short time compared to the completion of St. Peter's (time of completion here has become something to appreciate in itself—not just a matter of reasonable expectation; thus, it has changed along with 'masterpiece').

Cahn says, "Excellence has variable esthetic and social dimensions, and the urge to single out its most conspicuous exponents is not everywhere and at all times the same."[29] What is considered worth attending to and reflecting upon differs from person to person and period to period. Saint-Michel was a masterpiece (in the second, *marvelous* sense) because of its

> extraordinary setting, the brilliant conception of the architecture, [and] the religious and political role which the monastery played.[30]

Today, this last feature would not typically be considered an intrinsic property worth attention. And it may not be. But I shall present evidence to show that it *could* be. Deciding whether or not it is (was) intrinsic and delightful and whether or not it is (was) an aesthetic property demands a fuller understanding of what the person who uses such a description is trying to get us to do.

Cahn says one other thing that is relevant to my purpose (he says it more or less in passing) and further supports my general claim about the way the vocabulary used and the kind of activity engaged in relate to and affect one another. Just as the conjunction of 'masterpiece' and 'marvel' altered the sense of the first and redirected attention, something similar happened with the recovery of the Classical past during the late Middle Ages and early Renaissance.

> The renewed or more sustained contact with Classical Antiquity fostered beyond the Alps not only brought about a renewal of art, but a new way of talking about it, itself largely derived from the esthetic and rhetorical vocabulary of the Ancients.[31]

Before a property can be considered pleasing, it has to be identified. The Classical vocabulary brought different ways of describing things; hence, it called attention to different things. Once that happened, it became *possible* to enjoy attending to and reflecting upon those things.

Determining whether a term points to intrinsic, delightful features can be used as a test of "aestheticity." I once asked a class of college honors students to do case studies, similar to the one done by Cahn, for aesthetic terms of their choosing. The results were fascinating. One student chose 'elegant' as a paradigm and found out that its origins matched her intuitions. It appeared that from its beginning it had been an aesthetic term. It came, evidently, from the Latin, meaning *to select*, and referred to things that were fastidious or dainty. It rather quickly came to mean *tasteful*. But as she looked for contemporary uses of it, she began to believe that it is no longer an aesthetic term (or at least has taken on non-aesthetic functions in certain contexts).

> I happened upon the magazine describing the 1981 Metropolitan Opera and quickly seized it, thinking that descriptions using 'elegant' would be within. There were no elegant operas; there were five elegant advertisements!

The word 'elegant' appeared, for example, in "descriptions" of restaurants. But the ads pointed not to intrinsic properties of the restaurants or the food served but to qualities of the restaurant frequenters: "Europeans love Chouette . . . but doesn't everyone?" "A menu to please any gourmet." 'Elegant' also appears with astonishing regularity in real-estate ads; and again it is used not with references to intrinsic properties of houses, but rather to something about the life style and economic status of the inhabitants. It is found in conjunction with such terms as *pretigious* and *upper bracket*.

It appears, then, that the strategy introduced at the beginning of this section can be applied to 'elegant' as well as to 'masterpiece'. Most would agree intuitively, I hope, that "*x* is tasteful" is an aesthetic sense of 'elegant' and that "*x* is upper bracket" is a nonaesthetic sense of 'elegant'. If we look at the features pointed to in *A*-contexts, and those pointed to in *N*-contexts, we can generate lists of features and terms that tend to be aesthetic and nonaesthetic.

WAYS OF PRAISING

Another use of aesthetic discourse is in evaluation. Here again we find that when the language is used aesthetically—even though the particular vocabulary items may change drastically—it is always used to point to features in things and events considered delightful.

Early responses to Raphael's portrait of Julius II (London, National Gallery) praised its naturalness and lifelikeness.[32] When it was first exhibited on the altar of Santa Maria del Popolo in 1513 (a few months after Julius's death), people went to *see* the Pope again, and they cared that they were seeing Julius, not simply a *generic* pope.

"Looks just like Julius" is aesthetic *praise*—it calls attention to a property *worthy* of attention only in certain circumstances. It would not have been important in the highly stylized, universalized statues of ancient Egyptian pharaohs; it is aesthetically relevant only if one *cares* about a lifelike image. An artist is more likely to strive for such an image in an environment where it is likely to be applauded.

Several art historians have maintained that portraiture as a genre goes hand in hand with the presence of individualism within a culture. Jacob Burckhardt, for example, says,

> Even if it did not "swarm with individuality," the culture of the Italian Renaissance was driven by complex sets of tension between tradition and innovation, patterns of integration and pressures for dispersion, conventions of thought and feeling and a fresh openness to experience. In such a culture the resources of the individual could surface to be thrust and measured against traditional expectations and collective restraints . . . [T]he concrete personality did become one persistent dimension of a search for bearings in Renaissance Italy. It is consistent

with this outlook that portraiture became a major genre of Italian Renaissance Art.[33]

The fact that a picture resembles a particular individual is only sometimes worthy of attention and hence of mention. As an aesthetically valuable feature, it is tied to other, nonaesthetic interests and values. We need to care that it resembles or reminds somebody of Julius II, not simply that it represents or reminds us of the papacy in general. Such caring will exist only in some cultures. Although Raphael's painting retains many of the stylistic conventions associated with earlier papal portraits, *Julius II* departs from them in significant ways. Julius is not shown kneeling, nor in profile; he is not in the presence of saints; he is shown fullface, not at an angle; he is not in formal dress; personal features, such as his beard, are rendered in great detail. Loren Partridge and Randolph Stern argue that these departures paralleled the growth of individualism. Thus, it was not accident or coincidence that "within a few months of Raphael's portrait Pope Julius convened the Fifth Lateran Council, where the doctrine of individual immortality was first officially established."[34]

The departures also paralleled a readiness on the part of Raphael's audience to view *inventiveness* positively. Raphael was praised not only for imitating the best models, but also for "contending with nature."[35] Models were to be altered to make them "live in the present."[36] Such praise signaled not only a developing view of painters as something more than manual laborers (and the parallel change in the meaning of 'masterpiece' discussed earlier); it also signaled a different way of thinking about artworks. Painters began to be encouraged to develop a personal style rather than be praised for strict duplication of a model. Obviously artists do not intend to produce only what will bring them praise; but neither is what brings them praise irrelevant to their intentions. "By the end of the Quattrocento it was not unusual for contracts to discriminate sharply between the individual master and his workshop and to demand works of his own design and execution."[37]

One of the fundamental tenets of my theory is that it is impossible to tell whether a property is aesthetic without knowing the context in which it is referred to. According to Frank Sibley (see chap. 1) we can scrutinize a list of properties, for example,

a. makes me think of the Virgin
b. makes my eye sweep rhythmically upward

c. is a proper house for the Virgin and her relics,

and tell which are aesthetic more or less immediately—for we can more or less immediately determine which require taste for their application. Using Sibley's method most people would probably identify only (b) as referring to an aesthetic property.

Part of the explanation for the appeal of Sibley's theory lies, I believe, in intuitive agreement that in the list, (b) does seem to be the only truly aesthetic predicate. The others seem more religious—that is, they seem to be of a sort that would be associated with religious, rather than aesthetic, discussions. But the appeal also comes from the way many in our culture and century think of aesthetic response as a direct or immediate response. Just as we see that an object is red without first having to carry out any reasoning process or comparison, or as we hear at once that something is shrill, so we seem to sense directly or immediately that something sweeps rhythmically upward.

Frank Sibley is so struck by the apparent direct, nonmediated nature of aesthetic experience that he believes aesthetic judgments are based on the exercise of a faculty (taste) in much the same way as visual judgments are based on the exercise of a faculty (vision).

I think it preferable, however, to account for this immediacy, and inclination to consider (b) as an aesthetic predicate, in terms not of taste but of training. People are trained to pick out upward sweeps, just as they have been trained to pick out redness or shrillness. And they are accustomed to references to upward sweeps in critical discussions of art in our culture. They know that rhythmic upward sweep is considered worthy of attention, and this is why they are invited to look for it.

In other times and cultures, it is possible—even likely—that (a) and (c) were aesthetic properties. Providing a subject does not necessarily allow us yet to determine whether one is speaking aesthetically. We must know what we are being invited to do. Consider the results of using Chartres Cathedral:

Ca) Chartres Cathedral makes me think of the Virgin.
Cb) Chartres Cathedral makes my eye sweep rhythmically upward.
Cc) Chartres Cathedral is a proper house for the Virgin and her relics.

and

Va) Those glorious vaults in Chartres make me think of the Virgin.
Vb) Those glorious vaults in Chartres make my eye sweep rhythmically upward.
Vc) Those glorious vaults in Chartres are a proper house for the Virgin and her relics.

It becomes clear now, I think, that (c), which might first have appeared to refer to a religious, not an aesthetic, property, can be every bit as aesthetic as (b) when it invites attention to the cathedral's vaults. In both (Ca) and (Va), (a) remains nonaesthetic when the primary reference is directed at the Virgin rather than at an intrinsic property of the cathedral. In (Vc), but not in (Cc), (c) is aesthetic for the same reason. (Vc) invites one to notice and reflect upon the vaults; (Cc) *may* issue the same invitation, but usually, I think, it will not; it is more likely to appear in a discussion of the Virgin's miracles or her role in medieval Catholicism. In a culture in which the Virgin is not worshipped one may be misled into thinking that even in (Vc) reference is not being made to an intrinsic property of Chartres Cathedral. This is one of the reasons it is important to remember that properties considered worthy of attention change from culture to culture and period to period. (Try substituting 'elegant' for 'glorious' and see how you react!)

In this century we are accustomed to the following kind of description—in the following case of the sculptures of the cathedral's transepts. The viewer is asked to reflect upon formal properties.

> The Apostles' foreheads are carved in straighter lines; the cheeks are sometimes framed by the beard in a peculiarly square way; and the brows really slant in tense lines. The lower lid of the eyes is often almost straight—something that is even more noticeable in the softer Parisian style of the early thirteenth century where drapery is also straighter.[38]

Today it is thought that noticing straight lines and square shapes and their relationships within a work is aesthetically relevant. Lack of shared religious outlook makes it more difficult to know what it is about Chartres per se (intrinsically) that made it a fitting place in which the Virgin could perform her miracles. But only unreasonable bias would dictate that *fittingness* of this sort could not possibly be, or be due to, intrinsic properties of the structure. Similarly, Sibley is wrong to dismiss a cataloging of treasure or reference to the quantity of wood used in the ceiling as a nonaesthetic consideration. Incidentally, when Sebastien Roulliard says that

> the roof is commonly called the 'forest' . . . because of the prodigious multitude and quantity of wood,[39]

inviting reflection upon intrinsic properties of the roof, my feeling that Sibley's "taste test" is inadequate is reinforced. Someone who notices and delights in the roof is surely engaged in aesthetic activity, and I see no reason to posit the existence of special sense or perceptiveness to account for either the noticing or the delight.

An early contrast between aesthetic and nonaesthetic discussions comes from a passage that totally lacks reference to intrinsic properties.

> Now, We, John, Archdeacon, And Arnulph, Canon, of Chartres, having diligently inquired into the truth about all afore-mentioned matters from persons worthy of credence, pronounce and ordain that the Reverend Father Matthew, by the grace of God Bishop of Chartres, and any bishop who will at any time be bishop of Chartres, shall henceforth pay and be bound to pay all expenses of food and drink, to all goldsmiths and silversmiths who at any time are working and have worked as well as those who shall in the future work on the chasse or holy reliquary of the Blessed Mary of Chartres, and on the frontal which is and will be before the main altar of the church of Chartres, and on the retable or tablets which are and will be upon the main altar of the church of Chartres at the back of the same altar.[40]

A second nonaesthetic passage is not lacking in reference to intrinsic properties, but lacks the necessary invitation to reflect upon them.

> We have seen the vault of the crossing: repairs are necessary there; and if they are not undertaken very shortly, there could be great danger.[41]

Here it is action, not reflection, that is called for. The action/reflection dichotomy is fundamental to understanding how the aesthetic and nonaesthetic differ (see chap. 7).

My position, then, comes to this:

> A discussion (or remark) is aesthetic if and only if:
>   a. it invites attention to an intrinsic property of the

object discussed, and
b. that intrinsic property is considered delightful, i.e., worthy of attention and refelction.

This principle provides a way of distinguishing aesthetic from nonaesthetic properties:

A property of an object is one of its aesthetic properties if and only if
a. it is intrinsic to that object, and
b. it is identified as a property worthy of attention and reflection.

Shifts in features pointed to and changes in the particular language of aesthetic discourse do not support the view that there is no core that sets off the aesthetic from the nonaesthetic.

3
A Necessary Feature of the Aesthetic

Strange Pain

Several years ago, I wrote an essay on a problem that I called "a strange kind of sadness."[1] Others have called it the problem of enjoying negative emotions, the paradox of tragedy, and aesthetic masochism. This chapter repeats much of what I said in that essay, but incorporates discussion that has taken place since. The problem and its solution, I believe, suggest something special and important about the nature of the aesthetic.

David Hume described the problem in this way: "It seems as unaccountable pleasure which the spectators of a well-written tragedy receive from sorrow, terror, anxiety, and other passions that are of themselves disagreeable and uneasy."[2] John Moreall more recently has put it this way: "How is it that nonmasochistic, nonsadistic people are able to enjoy watching or reading about fictional situations which are filled with suffering?"[3] I prefer to get at the problem by describing a personal experience; I suspect many people have had similar experiences.

There is a movie starring Steve McQueen, Jackie Gleason, and Tuesday Weld called *Soldier in the Rain* that I watch whenever it comes on TV. I have seen it at least half a dozen times. It is about the friendship of two noncommissioned soldiers and a young woman who lives in the town where they are based. One of the soldiers is overweight, canny, and intensely loyal; the other is spry, mentally slow, and intensely loyal. Through her involvement with the men, the young woman grows from ignorance and shallowness to intelligence and depth of feeling. Although often very funny (the movie is often described as a "comedy") the first man's physical and moral bulk brings about his tragic death. The first time I saw the film I cried at the end. The next time I saw it, I began crying just before the end. Now I choke up when it starts and cry more or less steadily through the whole thing. My husband and son find this exasperating. "Why watch it if it is just going to make you unhappy?" they ask. What they seem not to understand is that few things bring me greater pleasure than watching this movie. Or perhaps my son does understand when he disdainfully concludes, "You're crazy!"

If the sadness in such situations were *real*, one would not want it repeated; indeed, one would try to avoid it and prevent occasions that would evoke it. Certainly I do not go out of my way to bring about most occasions that make me sad, as I do when I rearrange my schedule to watch *Soldier in the Rain*. Sadness is not often thought of as enjoyable. People do not normally describe sad times as "fun" times. Yet I enjoy the movie and am tempted to say that watching it is "great fun." Moral people do not want others to feel sad, yet I recommend the film to my friends. When I do so am I being immoral?

I sit in front of the television set weeping. My family infers from my behavior that I must be sad. Yet other aspects of my behavior (rearranging my schedule, telling friends what a treat they are in for, and so on) imply that I do not find it painful. If someone at a concert smiles and claps and shouts "More! More!" we do not incorrectly infer that he or she is having a good time. But we seem to get into trouble when inferences are drawn from behavior in the painful cases—cases where terms referring to *negative* emotions are used to describe objects and experiences of them—*sad, pathetic, terrifying, horrible, agonizing, depressing*, and the like.

It is not merely sadness that causes trouble. We read terrifying ghost stories without doing the one sure thing that would bring the horror to an end (putting the book aside). We depress ourselves with fictional accounts of the pitfalls of human relationships (as if daily experience did not provide us with ample examples of them).

Could it be that aesthetic pleasure is real pleasure but that aesthetic pain is not real pain? Does pleasure-behavior exhibited in connection with certain aesthetic objects imply real pleasure, but pain-behavior exhibited in connection with objects not imply real pain? If so, why?

Can the "unreality" of pain in apparently painful experiences be explained by the way we deal with children who cry when *Bambi* is read to them or have nightmares after going to a horror movie? "Don't cry—it's just a book." "Don't worry—those things don't happen in real life." Since the incidents are not real, is there no call for real pity or fear?

This explanation is childishly simplistic. In the first place, such an explanation of the strangeness of sadness or fear would apply equally and undesirably to happy, buoyant, uplifting aesthetic experiences. To say, "Don't smile, it's just a book," is absurd.

Second, and more important, the "Don't cry, it's just a story" response simply is not appropriate to many adult aesthetic experiences. One would not say it to someone reading *Anna Karenina*, for example. And certainly it is a mistake or it is question-begging to claim that "these things do not happen in real life." It might reasonably be insisted that it is precisely because such things do happen that sadness results. Indeed, the more one thinks about it, the more thoughtless it appears even to say such things to children. As we shall see later, that *Anna Karenina*, like *Bambi*, is "just a story" is part of the solution, but a small part. The solution and the problem itself are far more complicated.

Philosophers have taken two sorts of positions with respect to this problem. Some claim that the sadness (and other negative emotions) we say we feel as part of an aesthetic experience is *not real*. Others say that it *is real* and then try to account for the puzzling questions it raises (why nonmasochists seek it, for example). We shall look at versions of both positions.

Probably the most influential member of the *not-real* school is the eighteenth-century philosopher Edmund Burke. He wanted to explain the foundation and nature of judgments concerning the sublime and the beautiful, and his account of the sublime provides an answer to what can, for abbreviation's sake, be called the "problem of sadness."

Burke believed that aesthetic judgments, like all judgments, are based in the senses. The fact that all human beings have similar senses provides him with grounds for believing in the objectivity of aesthetic value. He further relates aesthetic judgment to feelings of pleasure and pain. Pleasure and pain, he thinks, are the primary motivating forces in human actions. Both are real. Pain cannot be explained simply as an absence of pleasure, nor pleasure simply as an absence of pain. Concerts, finely shaped and brightly colored objects, fragrant flowers, delicate wine, and sweetmeats, Burke insists, are pleasant whether or not pain precedes the experience of them. Likewise, violent blows, bitter potions, and grating sounds are painful even when they have not been preceded by feelings of pleasure.

Nonetheless, one is forced to admit that the removal of pain is pleasurable, and the removal of pleasure is painful. Think of how pleased one feels when the dentist stops drilling, how disappointed, when the party is over. But the states accompanying the removal of positive pleasure and positive pain are not themselves positive, and must be distinguished from them. Thus, Burke calls the removal of pain "relative pleasure" and the removal of positive pleasure, "relative pain." Relative pleasure figures more prominently in Burke's aesthetic (for the obvious reason that aesthetic experiences are typically on the pleasant end of the continuum), and he gives it the special name, "delight".

Burke is fully and explicitly aware of what I have called the problem of sadness. He believes that experiences like the one I have watching *Soldier in the Rain* are quite common. Nonetheless, he admits that we must explain how woe can be pleasing—something in which we occasionally "indulge" ourselves.

> The person who grieves, suffers his passion to grow upon him; he indulges it, he loves it; but this never happens in the case of actual pain, which no man ever willingly endured for any considerable time.[4]

"Pleasing woe," he explains, is not a positive pleasure, for its existence depends upon the existence of something painful. However, it is not positively painful—why else "indulge" it? Relative pleasure or delight is produced when positive pain is removed, and in removal lies the explanation.

> When danger or pain press too nearly, they are incapable of giving any delight, and are simply terrible; but at certain distances, and with certain modifications, they may be, and they are delightful, as we everyday experience.[5]

One and the same object can be an object both of positive pain and of delight (relative pleasure). In painful cases we describe the object with adjectives like *dangerous* or *fearful*. In pleasant cases we say it is *sublime*. One of Burke's examples is a storm at sea. Here, actual physical removal is involved. We can take pleasure in the storm only if we are not actually endangered by it. Artistic treatment of fearful situations provides the appropriate modification or distancing as well.

> It is a common observation, that objects which in reality would shock, are in tragical and suchlike representations, the source of a very high species of pleasure.[6]

Burke thinks that imitation, which people find naturally pleasing, is one way of removing or distancing danger. But, he says, imitation should not be thought of as the primary cause of delight.

> Choose a day on which to represent the most sublime and affecting tragedy we have; appoint the most favourite actors; spare no cost upon the scenes and decorations; unite the greatest efforts of poetry, painting, and music; and when you have collected your audience, just at the moment when their minds are erect with expectation, let it be reported that a state criminal of high rank is on the point of being executed in the adjoining square; in a moment the emptiness of the theatre would demonstrate the comparative weakness of the imitative arts. . . .[7]

It is not the fact that an object is an imitation that accounts for sublimity (or beauty), but qualities in the object itself. Burke gives many examples of the qualities found in sublime objects. Typically they are infinite, powerful, vast, rugged, angular, obscure, dark, silent, solitary, gloomy, solid, massive, and difficult. Anything capable of producing fear can be sublime.

The heart of Burke's explanation is, then, as follows: When pain is removed, a kind of pleasure, delight, follows. It is different from positive pleasure, but is nonetheless pleasure. Upon contemplation one object can cause both terror and delight. The object remains the same; what differs is the context of contemplation. Remove the pain from the context and what is left is delightful.

In our own century, "distance" theories have also been offered to explain aesthetic sadness—theories that maintain that the emotions felt in aesthetic experience are not like those felt in ordinary, nonaesthetic situations. Indeed, many say that to the extent that one's experience is fearful or pitying, it is not aesthetic at all. If fear or pity or sadness is really aroused by film, for example, then the film is not being responded to as an aesthetic object. A central doctrine of these theories is that when people have aesthetic experiences they do not respond to objects or events as they ordinarily do. If one responds in ordinary or typical ways, this is taken as a sign that one is not responding aesthetically, but in some other (nonaesthetic) way. According to this view, a person's crying (because he or she is really sad) is evidence that his or her response is not genuinely aesthetic.

Examples provided by Edward Bullough and Ortega y Gasset illustrate this view. Bullough says that persons attending *Othello* who engage in practical activities are not viewing the play aesthetically.

> The expert and the professional critic make a bad audience, since their expertness and critical professionalism are *practical* activities, involv-

ing their concrete personality and constantly endangering their Distance.[8]

In this example, overdistancing makes genuine aesthetic response impossible. He also gives an example in which underdistancing makes it impossible—one that more closely resembles, he would probably claim, what happens to me as I watch *Soldier in the Rain*. He describes a jealous husband attending *Othello*.

> He will do anything but appreciate the play. In reality, the concordance will merely render him acutely conscious of his own jealousy; by a sudden reversal of perspective he will no longer see Othello apparently betrayed by Desdemona, but himself in an analogous situation with his own wife. This reversal of perspective is the consequence of the loss of Distance.[9]

For Bullough, actual arousal of jealousy interferes with aesthetic experience, and there is no reason to think that he would view the actual arousal of fear or pity any differently. My tears while I watch *Soldier in the Rain* would undoubtedly signal, for Bullough, a loss of distance, and, hence, a lack of aesthetic experience.

Likewise, Ortega believes that real feelings of emotion are unaesthetic. He asks us to consider a group of people gathered at the bedside of a dying man: the dying man's wife, a doctor, a newspaperman, and an artist. Only the artist has a truly aesthetic experience, he claims, for only the artist maintains exactly the right amount of distance and thus pays attention to what truly matters aesthetically (lights and shadows, for instance). The others are prevented from an aesthetic experience because their practical, everyday concerns interfere. The emotional involvement of the wife, especially, precludes her aesthetic involvement.[10]

The appeal of distance theories is related to the general appeal of theories that insist upon distinguishing form from content in works of art. There is always a danger that irrelevant and distracting elements—practical worries or emotional involvement—will interfere with aesthetic judgment. However, the *reductio ad absurdum* of this version of these theories is obvious in Bullough's remark about "concrete personality." The demand that our concrete personality be put aside is difficult to meet. Speaking of a fog at sea, he says,

> Distance is produced . . . by putting the phenomena, so to speak, out of gear with our practical, actual self; by allowing it to stand outside

the context of our personal needs and ends—in short, by looking at it 'objectively', as it has often been called, by permitting only such reactions on our part as emphasize the 'objective' features of our experience, and by interpreting even our 'subjective' affections not as modes of *our* being but rather as characteristics of the phenomena.[11]

Bullough's description makes aesthetic experience sound nearly schizophrenic. He is right to stress the objective features of the phenomenon (as I shall argue in a later chapter) but wrong to claim that they are necessarily blotted out by a feeling of real emotion. If in the end the test of genuine aesthetic experience is whether one is paying attention to the right things, then we can concentrate on what those things are and do without distance.

The main weakness with "nonreal" theories is that they fly in the face of what many people say about their aesthetic experiences. That is, many people report that they do actually feel sad, and that, in general, the feeling of emotion is often a significant part of aesthetic response. Let us look, then, at some "real" theories.

Gary Iseminger says that there are two versions of these theories: the coexistentialist and the integrationist views.[12] The first says that pain and pleasure are both present, but that the latter outweighs the former. By this view, I really feel sad when I watch *Soldier in the Rain,* but I also feel pleasure from watching such things as plot development, acting, and so on. I am willing to put up with sadness because in the end I feel more pleasure than pain. On the integrationist view, pain is seen as contributing to pleasure—although, of course, an integrationist must explain how this can happen for nonmasochists.

For the most influential of the "real" theorists we must go all the way back to Aristotle. In his early discussions of tragedy, he had to account for how we could feel pleasure when we felt pain. And in his writing we find both coexistentialist and integrationist elements.

For Aristotle, understanding the nature of tragedy (as of everything else) required understanding its function (as well as its maker, form, and material). The function of tragedy is to provide a unique kind of enjoyment. When one understands tragedy one will know what its proper or peculiar pleasure is, as well as how it manages to produce this pleasure—and why tragedy does it better than anything else.

The proper function of tragedy is "to arouse the emotions of pity and fear in such a way as to effect that special purging of and relief (catharsis) of pity and fear . . ."[13] Given the importance of the concept of catharsis and, in particular, the catharsis of pity and fear both in the *Poetics* itself and in the whole history of aesthetics, it is disappointing that Aristotle has so little to say about the natures of catharsis, pity, and fear. His definitions of *pity* and *fear* are simply (far too simply) put: "Pity is what we feel at a misfortune that is out of proportion to the faults of a man; and Fear is what we feel when misfortune comes upon one like ourselves."[14]

Aristotle concentrates instead on the way pity and fear are aroused and worked out. In the *Politics*, discussing the purgative nature of music, he suggests that different individuals feel these emotions to different degrees.

> For feelings such as pity and fear, or, again, enthusiasm, exist very strongly in some souls, and have more or less influence over all. Some persons fall into a religious frenzy, whom we see disenthralled by the use of mystic melodies, which bring healing and purification to the soul. Those who are influenced by pity or fear and every emotional nature have a like experience, others in their degree are stirred by something which specially affects them, and are again in a manner purified and their souls lightened and delighted. The melodies of purification likewise give an innocent pleasure to mankind.[15]

He adds that vulgar people are purged by vulgar music, more sophisticated people by more sophisticated music.

It must have occurred to Aristotle, although he did not present it explicitly as a problem, that the feeling of pity or fear is not in itself pleasant. If all tragedy did were to arouse these emotions, it would provide no pleasure at all. For him, of course, the pleasure depended upon the *relief* that the drama provides. But why seek out tragedies? Why intentionally arouse unpleasant emotions just to purge them? Clearly there should be more to viewing a tragedy than there is to banging one's head against a concrete wall—done just because it feels so good to stop.

The enjoyment comes in working out the pity and fear aroused by tragedies. Although self-mutilation, for example, is unreal when we see it on a stage, the emotions it arouses are not imitations. The relief and the purgation *depend* upon their being *real*. This, then, is the integrationist view of Aristotle: Pleasure results from pain. The consequences of pain are pleasant, and hence we seek it out.

Aristotle says so little about catharsis that emphasizing it raises more problems than it solves. Elizabeth Belfiore argues that this strain in Aristotle is overemphasized.[16] A more promising solution, she believes, is found in terms of the pleasures of imitation.

Aristotle believed that human beings by nature delight in imitation (this is fortunate, he said, because learning is based on imitation). All art is some kind of imitation; the various art forms are to be distinguished from one another in terms of the medium of imitation (shapes, sounds, words, etc.). People may or may not take pleasure in what is imitated—an ugly horse, for instance. But if the object is cleverly imitated they are pleased. Thus, there can be pleasing pictures of unpleasant things, enjoyable dramatizations of unpleasant events, and so forth.

This provides a coexistentialist answer to the puzzle: pain is derived from what is presented, but the pleasure from imitation outweighs the pain. People are sad about *what* is represented, but delighted by *how* it is represented—the sounds and shapes, the skillful acting, and so on.

There are other coexistentialist accounts of the problem of sadness. All maintain that people actually feel pleasure *while* they feel sadness; they think the integrationist view on which pleasure *follows* pain is incorrect. That is, if someone says, "Did you enjoy watching *Soldier in the Rain* last night?" I do not have to respond, "Yes, but not until it was over."

One version is the "roller coaster" theory. (I have used this phrase; the philosopher Don Crawford reports that it was used by one of his students in a doctoral dissertaton.[17]) According to this position, there is a sense in which it is quite reasonable, for instance, to say that one actually enjoys being afraid. The pleasant exhilaration one feels while riding a roller coaster could not exist without the accompanying sense of danger. If someone said, "Suppose you could ride a roller coaster and everything would be the same except that the fear would not be there—would not that be better?" how to respond, or even what to make of the question, would be puzzling. There are many experiences in which the risk involved makes the experience genuinely fearsome, but the removal of the fear would not only not improve the experience but would spoil the fun—for the more adventuresome, of race car driving or sky diving; for the less adventurous, of watching a horror movie. Crawford's student says that there are simply times when we like to feel our juices flowing, even if that entails actually feeling frightened or grief-stricken. When I watch *Soldier in the Rain* I am aware that the actors are able to make me feel sad; I admire their skill. Making me feel cheerful (which in any case may not require as much skill) would just not have the same exhilarating or intense effect.

Susan Feagin has suggested an answer along similar lines.[18] She believes that people do not enjoy being sad, but like being able to feel sad in appropriate circumstances. There are not only *responses* to art (feeling sad, for instance) but *meta-responses* (responses to responses: feeling glad at feeling sad). According to this view, as I watch *Soldier in the Rain* I am unhappy about what happens to the characters. At the same time, I am pleased with myself for being sensitive. We don't just enjoy feeling our juices flow—we enjoy that their flowing proves we are decent, caring human beings.

Yet another "real" theory—neither integrationist nor coexistentialist—is a more subtle articulation of the view expressed by my son's dismissal of my reaction to *Soldier in the Rain* as "crazy." His belief is shared, in a more sophisticated form, by Colin Radford. People, at least some of them, he says, feel concern for other people. Accounts of suffering can and do move us. But if later we find out that such an account was false, says Radford, we feel we have been duped. Why don't we feel this way, he asks, with respect to artistic accounts of the suffering of fictional people?

One answer is to say that readers do not really feel grief for Anna Karenina or Madame Bovary or Sue Ellen Ewing. After all, if one is really moved, one cannot also eat chocolates and say, "How marvelous!" But Radford believes that we really are moved by these characters—or least by accounts of them.

> What is worrying is that we are moved by the death of Mercutio and we weep while knowing that no one has really died, that no young man has been cut off in the flower of his youth.[19]

Radford discusses, and dismisses, several possible solutions. Do we forget that the people are not real? No—we are not unaware, for example, that we are watching a play. Are we moved by the knowledge that such happenings are possible or probable? If so, it is an actual phenomenon that moves us, and the unreality does not enter in the same way. Asserting that there are simply two kinds of being moved, real life and fictional, only begs the questions.

Radford feels he is forced to conclude that

> . . . our being moved in certain ways by works of art, though very

"natural" to us and in that way only too intelligible, involves us in an inconsistency and so incoherence.[20]

We are simply acting irrationally when we weep for fictional characters. It is like trying to hit a tennis ball over the net by gesturing from the back line. We sometimes do crazy things, Radford thinks. But it seems to me that we do not feel irrational or even sheepish about responding deeply to works of art, even fictional ones. Indeed, consistency and coherence demand that one respond to artistic tragedies in ways that resemble our responses to real life tragedies.

It is interesting to consider the solutions to the problem of sadness that we have considered in light of recent psychological studies of emotion. Peter J. Lang has studied emotions of mental patients, and has found that there is often inconsistency in reports of feeling, behavior, and physiology. Notice that it was an inconsistency (seeking pain) that created a problem for us: we report that we are enjoying ourselves but our behavior seems not to mesh with what we say. We cry, for example, or we leap in terror, but rearrange our schedules in order to watch the very things that seem to terrify us. Lang's patients sometimes said that they felt less anxious, but continued to ask for attention, or vice versa. And Lang believes that such findings are troubling

> . . . because they seem to question the existence of coherent emotion states, that are consistent within individuals and subsist across individuals and species.[21]

This seems to support Radford's belief that aesthetic behavior verges on the insane!

Lang maintains that emotional states always involve some "visceral and motor outflow."[22] This seems right. Claims of fright are almost always accompanied by motor or visceral states. These signs seem to be present when one watches a sad or scary movie: tears, screams, shudders, and starts. Lang argues that it is not necessary for the fear object to be real in order for

> . . . the prototype to be accessed and the motor programs run. The information is conceptual and does not refer to any specific pattern of sensory input. Films, slides, or models may contain enough stimulus propositions to activate the network. Even a verbal description may be sufficient, particularly if the subject is told to process the input as an image.[23]

Consider this last statement with regard to the experience of reading literature. Clearly there are some features of *real* emotional response present when we encounter some works of art. We cannot conclude, however, that feeling emotions in these instances is a sign of insanity.

Control

Let us review the theories we have looked at. What answers might I give to my family when they ask, "Do you really feel sad when you watch *Soldier in the Rain?*"

1. No, not really; what you see here is not real sadness.
2. Yes, but I know that pleasure will result, so I keep watching (integrationist).
3. Yes, but I also feel pleasure at the same time. The acting is so good. And it's just good to feel the old juices flowing and to know I can feel so deeply. The pleasure outweighs the pain (coexistentialist).
4. Yes, but I know it's crazy.

Gary Iseminger believes that these views are inconsistent.[24] And of course he is right if they are viewed as descriptions of what *always* goes on. That is, if what is sought is a *unique* explanation of the problem of sadness, then only one of the above can be true.

I believe, however, that all of the answers are appropriate in *some* circumstances. Sometimes people are not really terrified or sad. Sometimes they are, but believe that the suffering will rid them of pent-up emotions and make them feel better in the long run. Sometimes the acting is so good that the hideous human actions portrayed are bearable. Sometimes people simply delight in their own sensitivity. Sometimes people may actually irrationally confuse reality and fiction. The appeal of each theory we have looked at is due to the fact that each describes what *sometimes* goes on. None, I think, covers all cases.

What is interesting is not that one account is better than another, but that all point to an extremely important feature of aesthetic experiences. A horror story is fun to read only when readers are in *control* of the situation in which it is read. Why is there not the same pleasure when the same book is read alone in a creaky house late at night during a thunderstorm? An irrational fear of birds prevents me from watching or reading, let alone enjoying, *The Birds*. In both of these cases, failure to control the situation makes pleasure impossible. Often, recognition that what we are reading, watching, or hearing is *unreal* is enough to assure us that we are *in control*—although as the two examples above show, knowing that the object of attention is fictional is not always enough. Nor are we only able to feel in control if we believe the object of our attention is unreal. We do not enjoy a roller coaster that is *out of control*, but enjoy only one that we believe will stay on the track and stop at the appointed time and place.

Avid roller coaster fans or sky divers are never completely unafraid; indeed, as pointed out above, the sought-after feelings of exhilaration come only if some element of risk is involved. But it must be a risk that can be handled. People who refuse to ride roller coasters or jump out of planes wearing parachutes are precisely those who believe they are unable (mentally or physically) to handle the ride. Sky divers must feel a greater sense of control than I would in order for them to engage repeatedly in their sport. The reason that we feel duped (and not aesthetically pleased) in the situation described by Radford—when we learn that what has just made us very sad did not really happen—is that we believe we were not in control of something when we should have been. We may believe that learning what it is like to go through a divorce would be an enriching human experience, one that would make us grow as human beings. Since we fear that in the "real" case control might elude us very quickly, we go to see a film about it instead of actually initiating divorce proceedings.

In controlled surroundings, tragedy permits people to purge themselves of bottled-up feelings. Indeed, they seek out tragedies (and other moving art works) in the belief that a controlled experience will excite, enrich, purge, and/or sensitize them in certain ways, and they take genuine pleasure in this experience. Control is required for aesthetic experiences. When control is lost (as in my inability to watch *The Birds* although I know it is "just a movie") aesthetic experience becomes impossible.

When my aesthetic experience involves sadness or terror, a pattern consisting of sad or terrified behavior and reports of feelings and physiology (to use Lang's categories) is present. The things we do to avoid these negative emotions is missing—but it is still appropriate to use words like *sad* and *frightened* when in place of avoidance behavior we find control. There is genuine visceral and motor and linguistic *outflow* but not so much that other behavior (looking at colors, for example) becomes impossible.

It is a necessary feature of aesthetic experience that people maintain control sufficient to permit attention and reflection upon intrinsic features of objects and events. The enjoyment that accompanies this attention and reflection makes any negative aspects worthwhile. (If the movie is rotten, people will not put up with the pain.)

Fortunately it is not absolutely necessary that we be exact about providing a complete explication of the term 'control', for it is difficult to state precisely what the important and relevant features of control are. 'Control' is admittedly just as nontechnical a term as 'distance'. In the rather loose formulaton, "x controls y," several different sorts of things are candidates for x and y. I control *myself*, Hitchcock controls the *buildup of suspense*. Although they involve quite different kinds of action, both are meaningful and involved in aesthetic experiences. They may even be related; for example, Hitchcock creates a situation in which I am (or am not) able to control myself. Responsibility for control (or the lack of it) may be to Hitchcock's credit or to my discredit. An artist's self-control or lack of it may even be criticized. Monet is reported to have disparaged himself for carrying his analysis of *seeing* to his wife's funeral.

> (Seeing) haunts my days: it is their joy, their torment. To the point that once by the bier of a woman who had been and still was very dear to me, I caught myself, my eyes fixed on her forehead, in the act of mechanically looking for the sequence of tones, seeking to make my own the gradations of color which death had just settled upon the immobile face. Tones of blue, or yellow or gray. . . . See to what a pass things had come. The desire was natural enough to reproduce the last likeness of her who was going to leave us forever. But even before the idea occurred to me of fixing the features to which I was so deeply attached, my organism automatically reacted to the stimulus of color. My reflexes led me in spite of myself into an unconscious operation which repeated the daily course of my life. So the beast in his treadmill. Pity me, mon ami.[25]

In this case we seem to have an exercise of control that is itself out of control.

In the absence of an exact analysis of 'control' it is still possible to notice what we can do when we have control that we cannot do when we do not. When we have control we are excused from certain demands generally placed upon us, and we are able to react in appropriate aesthetic ways. This frees us to formulate and consider descriptions of objects and actions and events that we do not find ourselves able to formulate or consider when we lack control. Once I have articulated, "This is a fire that will burn me," or "This is a truck that will strike my son," I am not likely to go on to articulate, let alone dwell upon, color descriptions of the flames or design components of the vehicle. We do not always (perhaps not even typically) have the time, inclination, or freedom to articulate a wide range of predicates that may be satisfied by things or events. Even if we do articulate them, we do not dwell on them. That is, once we become aware of properties like the closeness of the fire or the dangerous speed of the truck, our attention becomes fixed upon them. But when action is not called for, we can dwell upon a whole range of other features.

Objections and Support

There are two possible objections that must be considered. The first arises from the fact that people say they have aesthetic experiences while they dream. Since dreams are not something we control, how can control be a necessary feature of the aesthetic?

I do not quite know how to respond to this. Dreams are hard enough to understand without raising the question of whether or not we have genuine aesthetic experiences during them. Perhaps one can only have an aesthetic experience while dreaming if one is in a controlled situation in the dream. Or perhaps dreams provide a mode of distancing. In any case, since dreams are private, perhaps they need not be considered by a general theory that seeks to explain what common aesthetic experiences entail.

The second objection is more important. It is common to hear people describe aesthetic experiences in such terms as "carried away" or "completely transported." Do not such descriptions run counter to what I have said about the necessity of control?

My response here involves emphasis on the possibility of *knowing* when we or someone else is having an aesthetic experience. If one is totally "carried away" or "taken completely outside oneself," how could we know whether to say that experience is aesthetic? If he or she cannot tell us anything, what grounds would we have for inferring anything about his or her experience? How would we even know that it was *that person's* experience. We might just take note of their behavior. But now, I think, we are brought back to control. People must at least demonstrate *controlled attention and reflection* to an object or event.

The same is true of ourselves. If I am really completely carried away, how can I identify my own experience as aesthetic? Knowing that I am viewing something aesthetically requires enough control to realize that *I* am paying attention to certain features of things or events.

What I have proposed about the necessity of control is suggested in other contexts—in the writings of people who study our responses to the environment. (In chapter 4 I shall discuss several of these in detail.) Several writers in this area have identified control as a necessary feature of appreciation of nature. John Stilgoe, among others, argues that enjoyment of wilderness is very recent in human history—it has waited upon our abilities to control it.[26]

In *Conflict, Arousal, and Curiosity,* D. E. Berlyne argues that "ludic behavior"—behavior engaged in for for its own sake—is marked by a seeking of external stimulation.[27] We enjoy things that arouse us (note the similarity to the roller coaster theory of Crawford's student). But we must be careful not to be too stimulated, too aroused:

> Departing too far from an intermediate degree of potential, upsetting the balance between the factors that raise arousal and factors that allay arousal, results in discomfort. Since the pursuit of aesthetic enjoyment means deliberately seeking out stimulation and excitement, we must suspect that a mechanism of the arousal-jag type is in operation. This means that there must be some way of ensuring that arousal is kept within bounds and that it is speedily brought down again, a requirement fulfilled by the order of organization element.[28]

The tigers cannot get too close to the van, nor the boat too close to the waterfall! The same point is made by Kevin Lynch.

> There is some value in mystification, labyrinth, or surprise in the environment. Many of us enjoy the House of Mirrors, and there is a certain charm in the crooked streets of Boston. This is so, however, only under two conditions. First, there must be no danger of losing basic form or orientation, of never coming out. The surprise must occur in an over-all framework; the confusion must be small regions in a visible whole. Furthermore, the labyrinth or mystery must in itself have some form that can be explored and in time be apprehended. Complete chaos without hint of connection is never pleasurable.[29]

Control (like Bullough's and Ortega's distance) accounts for our ability to take pleasure in mystification.

Jay Appleton bases an entire theory of appreciation of landscape on its capacity to present us with refuge—for only when we are provided with safe vantage points are we able to enjoy the thick vegetation or rushing water, he believes.[30] A closer look at his theory comes in chapter 5.

Note that all of these theorists believe that when nature is experienced aesthetically there is controlled attention to certain properties. In aesthetic experiences of works of art the same thing is true. We select properties for attention and are free to linger on them because practical action is not demanded.

However, control is only a necessary condition of aesthetic experience. It is not by itself sufficient, for controlled attention also characterizes observations of many other kinds. Feeling *in control* distinguishes heroes and heroines in life-threatening situations. And controlled experimentation is, of course, an earmark of scientific and social scientific study. When Erving Goffman researched mental hospitals, he did it from a controlled viewpoint, not from the stance of an inmate. Consider the following passage from his famous work:

> In mental hospitals in general, there seemed to be one interesting variety of buddy relation: the "helper" pattern. A patient, often himself considered by others to be quite sick, would take on the task of regularly helping a certain other patient who, by staff standards, was even sicker than his helper. The helper would dress his buddy, roll and light his cigarettes, occasionally protect him from fights, guide him to the cafeteria, help him eat, and so forth. . . . The interesting point is that to the occasional observer the relationship was one way: the person helped did not make a visibile return.[31]

What distinguishes Goffman's remarks from aesthetic remarks is not control. Rather it is what he finds "interesting." In order to explain fully what the aesthetic is, one must discover *which* of a variety of interesting features are attended to in controlled situations.

Thus, it can be said that control permits attention to properties that provide aesthetic delight. But there must be a way of distinguishing aesthetic delight from delight in general. The delight felt riding a roller coaster is not (usually) aesthetic delight. Nor is the delight that Goffman clearly took in the observations required for his study aesthetic delight. A necessary condition for aesthetic delight, as for delight in general, is that it must result from attention to certain features of a situation, features to which attention would be impossible or inappropriate if we (or others) were genuinely endangered or otherwise thoroughly engaged or practically committed. Nor is it enough to limit ourselves to intrinsic properties. To understand aesthetic delight one must restrict these features in some way. That is the task of the remainder of this book.

4
Applied Aesthetics

When people are asked to "take the aesthetic point of view" ("Forget about how much it costs or how morally offensive it might be—just consider it aesthetically"), they seem to know intuitively what they are expected and permitted to do—but only very roughly. And since we aren't often free to make our decisions based exclusively on our aesthetic inclinations, knowing roughly what this means is usually enough.

However, intuitive notions are having to be refined in legal areas. Laws are now on the books, and being added every year, that *require* taking the aesthetic point of view; and I believe that by looking at what happens when people are forced to take 'aesthetic' seriously, we can gain a better understanding of what that term denotes and connotes. One way to get a more precise notion of what taking the aesthetic point of view entails is to ask ourselves how philosophers might respond to the legal requirement that forces people to take seriously society's aesthetic concerns.

One particular environmental study is worth detailed description. This case study will provide a context for material presented later in this book, especially to those readers who are unfamiliar, as I was, with this kind of work. There are some general questions and problems that confront people when they try to locate aesthetic responses to the environment and try to determine what gives rise to them. I want to show that purely empirical studies of environmental aesthetic resources (that is, studies that attempt to describe aesthetic preferences without reference to or inclusion of value judgments) fail to deal adequately with these issues.

Although it might seem to some readers that the use of 'aesthetic' in discussions of the natural environment and of art works is so divergent that it becomes two different words, I hope to show that 'aesthetic' functions much the same way in both contexts. The discussion of applied aesthetics in this part of the book will be drawn together with the theoretical and historical discussions in the first part when I present my theory of the aesthetic in the final part.

Problems With Assessing the Upper Susitna

In 1975 a Seattle consulting firm, Jones & Jones, was asked by the Army Corps of Engineers to determine how the recreational and aesthetic resources of the Upper Susitna River in Alaska would be affected by the construction of four hydroelectric dams and their reservoirs. The result was a 320-page report with many tables and drawings that demonstrates in a fascinating way how the assignment was carried out. (The report also contains a substantial bibliography, but the section on aesthetic assessment does not include a single work written by a philosopher.)

Jones & Jones began by dividing the river corridor into segments.

> This classification was generated from a nested set of patterns defined by physiography and geology as well as characteristics of the river, notably channel type and major tributaries. Existing natural, cultural, and aesthetic resources were quantitatively inventoried in each segment; however, river segments could not be directly compared on the basis of resource magnitude because fundamentally different landscape types were represented. Building on previous work by the consultants and others, comparability was achieved without reliance on paradigm landscapes by devising component measures of resources' importance. In combination, these measures quantified the extent to which natural processes characteristic of each landscape type were operative (Natural Value) and visually expressed (Aesthetic Value), both before and after the dams. Together, these two measures were taken to indicate relative Environmental Quality, considered in terms of landscape health and integrity.[1]

The authors declined to make proposals concerning recreational use because, they said, they lacked a "conceptual recreational plan." The existence of aesthetic proposals thus implies that they believed themselves in possession of a conceptual aesthetic plan.

Chapter 1 presents a summary of findings with regard to the four sites: Devil Canyon, Watana, Vee, and Denali. A dam at Devil Canyon would, they reported, have very high effects on the value of aesthetic resources. These resources are primarily identified as the steep-sided gorge and its spectacular white water, unique in the region, and perhaps in the nation.

In proportion to the effect of a dam and reservoir at Devil Canyon, construction at Watana or Vee would be less destructive, they found. In the regional context, the section of the river at Watana was considered very attractive, but not unique. Construction at Vee, which appeared moderately unique, would have greater effects, again due to a canyon and abundant white water. Notice here the presumption in favor of white water. Although I am certain we would all agree intuitively, some theoretical foundation is demanded if we are to be certain that the preference for white water is genuinely aesthetic.

After assessing the effects of dam construction at other sites, the first chapter ends with the investigators' principle recommendations, the first of which relates most directly to aesthetic concerns.

> If the dams are built at the proposed locations . . . the following measures are recommended: *flow regulation for fisheries below Devil Canyon (salmon) and Denali (grayling): annual monitoring of the Nelchina herd's calving migration; siting studies of roads, transmission lines and other ancillary facilities to mitigate potentially very severe aesthetic and environmental impacts.* (Emphasis in original.)[2]

Chapter 2 is a description of the Susitna basin: its geology (past and present), climate, hydrology, vegetation, fauna, history (Indian habitation, Russian settlers, gold miners, railroad, Mt. McKinley Park, recreational use), current land uses, and status (hunting, fishing, seasonal).

Chapter 3 describes the consultants' methodology, with a summary diagram (see table).

Many readers, I expect, will not find this table very helpful. I include it here because it shows the authors' eagerness for a *scientific* appearance of their report. As we shall see later in this chapter, applied aestheticians often feel the urge to make their work appear as scientific as possible.

A map of both the watershed (lands draining into the Susitna) and viewshed (visual domain of the river) classifies the river into segments. This takes into account the river's characteristics and the landscapes it drains and passes through. The map characterizes the river by categories of fixed channel, braided channel, looped meander channel, and branched channel zones. Twenty-eight "runs" are identified, each with a distinctly different "sense of place." These segments are then "inventoried" in terms of 112 natural and cultural variables, 27 of which are said to be relevant

Applied Aesthetics

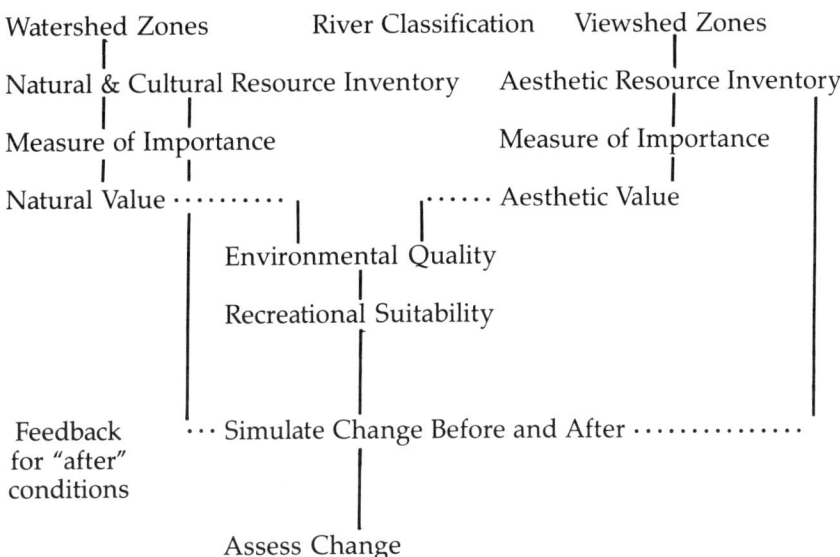

to an aesthetic inventory.[3] Physical factors include, for example, bedrock, patterned ground, and glacial scars; biological factors include the presence of tundra, brush, or mammals; landform factors include spatial definition, surface patterns, and viewshed; and cultural factors include the incidence of campsites or archaeological sites, and the accessibility and ownership of land.

The authors realize that because of the distinctive characteristics of the zones, one cannot always be directly compared with another. They are also worried that the presence of qualitative evaluations may give their report the appearance of being based upon subjective preferences of the investigators. They believe, on the contrary, that basing their assessments on what they call an area's "inherent capacity to evoke perceptual response" results in an objective report because this avoids cultural and historical conditioning. One of their fundamental presuppositions is this:

> Preference testing is highly appropriate when used to prioritize the results of a resource-based landscape assessment. The resource-based assessment itself can attain a high degree of objectivity by breaking into an overall measure of character or value. A considerable degree of consistency in qualitative judgments between groups with markedly different preferences has been achieved with this method, which may be interpreted as an empirical demonstration of success.[4]

The authors proceed to articulate a formulaic model for aesthetic assessment, which they believe captures the capacity to evoke perceptual response, that will allow for comparisons and objectivity, and that will avoid reference to "idealized landscape types."[5]

The authors do not explain what they mean by "the capacity to evoke perceptual response." Nor do they defend the claim that it is independent of the influence of individual preferences. I believe one cannot and does not want to avoid cultural and historical conditioning. Ultimately, the assessment is based, or at least depends in significant part, upon landscape ideals.

According to Jones & Jones, aesthetic value *(AV)* is determined by vividness *(V)*, visual intactness *(VI)*, unity *(U)*, and visual uniqueness *(VU)* in this way:

$$AV = \frac{V + VI + U}{3} \div VU$$

Since scales can be arbitrarily chosen, the one Jones & Jones use is not important. (They rate V, VI and U on a scale of one to seven, with seven, the low.) They use averages (hence division by three); others might have chosen to go with a straight sum. They make *AV* inversely proportional to *VU*; other investigators might have constructed a formula in which proportions were direct. Applied aestheticians can use a great variety of formulas to capture what they are after.

What is crucial are the variables themselves. These investigators leave unanswered several questions that must be addressed in order to explain and justify the four factors being weighed. Why is equal weight given to V, VI, and U? Is unity really of equal importance with vividness, for example? And why use these four qualities? The authors mention in passing that they have been used in other studies. But this is not sufficient justification; and, in fact, other studies use several other qualities as well.

Vividness is defined as "the strength of the visual impression, or the 'memorability' of the visual experience."[6] Jones & Jones assert, without explanation, that thirteen factors contribute to vividness. Some are features of the terrain: landform spatial definition (enclosure), landform surface pattern and edge definition, relief, landmarks, and landform sequence. Other features relate to what is called "cover": skyform, waterform of the run and its tributaries, watershed features, vegetation, wildlife, and non-natural structures.

We see above that Jones & Jones want to explain aesthetic value purely in terms of perceptual response. Vividness does seem related intuitively to aesthetic value. But notice that the vividness score is achieved not by considering how viewers respond but by assessing features in the landscape. Thus we have gone from viewer response to something in the landscape outside the viewer as the basis of judgment. In the absence of evidence that definite edges, for instance, always or typically make for a more memorable experience, there is no justification for making vividness depend on it.

Visual intactness is "the relative degree of apparent natural condition of the landscape or its elements."[7] Visual encroachment is the "presence or absence of visually disturbing foreign landscape elements such as junk yards or distracting billboards," or simply evidence of human alteration.[8]

"Disturbing" does not simply describe a *level* of perceptual response. It is *evaluative* as well. Someone who likes junkyards will not be disturbed by them. How can disturbance be determined without reference to some preexistent ideal? Either it reduces to vividness or depends upon preferences—something the investigators had hoped to avoid. To some extent the same is true of level of development, although we could probably get a purely quantitative assessment that would not necessarily depend on a preexistent ideal.

Jones & Jones believe that uniqueness is a quantitative measure. But again there are problems in interpreting it purely perceptually. What would it mean to say that a perceptual response is unique, apart from saying that it occurs rarely? This would mean that all landscapes off the beaten track are unique—and ugly ones would weigh as heavily and positively as beautiful ones.

Following a section on recreation, the investigators provide an assessment of existing conditions in each of twenty-eight areas. Here are two examples, along with some questions that point to a consistent lack of rationale for the assessments made.

> Stephen Lake. Because of its almost oppressive linearity, absence of views and monotonous side-slopes, this run received the lowest vividness rating of any existing Susitnan landscape.

Why, we must ask ourselves, isn't oppressiveness memorable, and hence vivid?

> Dogsled. . . . The moraine landscape is quite monotonous, consisting

largely of small potholes and expanses of black spruce, with no major tributaries. Existing aesthetic value is moderately high, primarily due to the untouched character of the run.[9]

Doesn't the fact that this site is monotonous though untouched show that there is something wrong with weighting intactness so heavily?

In chapter 5, a description of future conditions, the investigators predict there would be no increase in aesthetic value from the dam-reservoir construction; for the most part, areas would go from very high to high or moderately high using the suggested scoring system. The major effect would be a decrease in intactness and unity.[10] For example, at Lower Devil

> . . . the construction of Devil Canyon Dam would have a very high effect on the aesthetic value . . . since the resources on which that value is based would be largely inundated: the gorge and its white water. The dam structure and its attendant facilities would also affect the visual intactness of the run adversely . . .[11]

Presumably the lakes would have less memorability. But how about the dams? Aren't they vivid? Without fuller explanation of the concepts of memorability and vividness, the predictions as well as the current assessments seem arbitrary.

This report is fascinating reading. It was obviously undertaken in good faith by careful, serious, intelligent individuals. Although I have indicated problems that I think prevent their study from clarifying the aesthetic, I do think it reveals aesthetic concerns. And the study was carried out not in isolation, but within a social, ideological, and cultural context that makes it meaningful. When we better understand this context, we will, I believe, better understand the *aesthetic*.

The Legal Requirements

Since the late 1960s in the United States (as in other parts of the world) there has been a great deal of legislation requiring attention to aesthetic value in the environment. Indeed, Jones & Jones's study is one example of response to this legislation. As early as 1954 (Berman v. Parker) the Supreme Court found that "it is within the power of the legislature to determine that the community should be beautiful as well as healthy."[12] What this seemed to signal was that buildings could be condemned for not fitting in aesthetically, as well as for being rat-infested. Citizens could urge state and federal representatives to act in ways that would protect what they considered the beautiful aspects of their surroundings.

Urge they did; and act they did. The National Environmental Policy Act (NEPA) of 1969 states as one of its six goals the assurance "for all Americans [of] safe, healthful, productive, and esthetically and culturally pleasing surroundings." It also requires that each member of the Council on Environmental Quality "be conscious or responsive to the scientific, economic, social, esthetic, and cultural needs and interests of the Nation." Recognizing that environmental "amenities and values" are "presently unquantified," the NEPA also requires development and "utilization of a systematic interdisciplinary approach, which will ensure the integrated use of . . . environmental design arts in planning and decision-making."

The National Wild and Scenic Rivers Act and National Trails Act had already been enacted in 1968. Other legislation quickly followed. In 1972 the Coastal Zone Management Act found that "important ecological, cultural, historic, and aesthetic values in the coastal zone which are essential to the well-being of all citizens are being irretrievably damaged or lost; special natural and scenic characteristics are being damaged by ill-planned development . . ." (sec. 302, e.f.); and it encouraged states to give "full consideration to these values in coastal management programs" (sec 302. b). The Endangered Species Act mentions the *visual* values of animals. Other agencies—the Federal Land Policy and Management Act (1974, 1976), National Forest Management Action (1976), Surface Mining Control and Reclamation Act (1977), and the Clean Air Act (1977)—stipulate that planners must attend to aesthetic values when formulating policy. Similar legislation was passed in other countries; an example is the Scottish Countryside Act of 1967. The Sierra Club is the best known of the many citizens groups that have brought about suits based on this legislation.

An excellent history of aesthetic legislation has been written by Richard C. Smardon. A summary of one of his articles will help us get an overview. Smardon believes that the story begins in common-law nuisance doctrine. Courts were not comfortable ruling against a storage tank in a neighbor's backyard, for example, simply because it didn't look good. "Courts feel uncomfortable administering a subjective standard relating to taste especially if it affects private property rights. . . . However, courts have recognized personal smell and hearing nuisances."[13] (It is worth noting that smell is not one of the senses usually considered important aesthetically.)

There were some exceptions. In 1912 (Gus Blass Dry Goods Co v. Reinman & Wolfort, Arkansas) a court found that a particular land use or activity could be disallowed if it would constitute a nuisance to the "normal man, the man of ordinary habits and ordinary sensibilities."[14] So much for Sibley! But when nuisance factors were ruled relevant, courts tended to base them on incongruity—for example, auto wrecking in a residential neighborhood—rather than "mere unsightliness."

Suing on the basis of aesthetic interest alone was not successful until *legislation* protected aesthetic interests specifically. Only then did individuals and groups gain some power. Also, courts are more likely to attend to injury of a specific individual or group than to the general public interest. Objects themselves (oceans, dunes, etc.) do not have standing, so injury to them provides no basis for a claim. Rather it must be shown that someone with standing is being injured. (C. D. Stone has urged in his paper, "Should Trees Have Standing?" that a guardian for the environment should be appointed.[15] Appointing a guardian may be right and helpful for ecological reasons, but it doesn't do much for aesthetic purposes.)

Some recent cases have referred to general welfare, but they are rare. "Despite the apparent trend toward a quality environment for visual purposes, the absence of a clear standard or authority for legislation and other regulations grounded on aesthetics remains problematic for the use of aesthetic police power in most jurisdictions."[16] Sometimes eminent domain has been used. In Kamroski v. State of Wisconsin, 1966, legislation prohibiting residential or commercial development of an area along the Mississippi River was challenged on the basis that "public enjoyment of the scenic beauty of certain land is not a public use of such land."[17] The court, making use of the concept of "visual occupancy," took the opposite view.

Both qualitative and quantitative methods of assessing scenic values have been used in courts. An example of the qualitative method appears in Scenic Hudson v. F.P.C. (1965). One expert testified to the value of Storm King Mountain:

> It rises like a brown bear out of the river, a dome of living granite, swelling with animal power. It is not picturesque in the softer sense of

the word but awesome, a primitive embodiment of the energies of the earth. It makes the character of wild nature physically visible in monumental form. As such it strongly reminds me of some of the natural formations which marked sacred sites in Greece and signal the presence of the Gods; it recalls Lerna in Argolis, for example, where Herakles fought the Hydra, and various sites of Artemis and Aphrodite where the mother of the beasts rises savagely out of the water. White Breakneck Ridge across the river resembles the winged hill of tilted strata that looms into the gulf of Corinth near Calydon.[18]

(It is fun to imagine a jury trying to decide if this witness was telling the truth. It certainly sounds like a guidebook description of a local landmark or an art-historical description of a work of art. We can perhaps be sympathetic with jurors who would not find such testimony very helpful—who would prefer, "I give it a six on a one to seven scale.")

There is some scepticism about the value of "aesthetic legislation." For example, Michael McCloskey, a former executive director of the Sierra Club, believes that attempts to quantify quality do little more than "belabor the obvious."[19] He believes that environmental regulations will serve better than aesthetic regulations. For instance, requiring reclamation of strip mines will automatically, he thinks, have aesthetically pleasing consequences.

> By requiring that high walls be eliminated, that the original contour in hilly country be restored and by planting native vegetation, all sorts of environmental problems will be dealt with. . . . In the process esthetic problems will also be incidentally minimized. But there will be no need to argue with an industry or agency about the esthetics of high walls. They will just be eliminated. . . . Moreover, a debate over the esthetics of tailing pile landscaping can divert attention from less viable but more insidious problems.[20]

Of course it can. But it need not. Regulations against high walls in areas deemed scenically valuable would have precluded the Great Wall of China or Christo's *Running Fence*. McCloskey's scepticism, what he fears is endless debate about what people like, is difficult to combat in the absence of a theoretical foundation for aesthetic legislation.

The lack of theoretical underpinnings is constantly exemplified in the diverse reactions to the requirements articulated in the variety of legislation. Court orders, as one would expect, have produced a flurry of aesthetic inquiry in areas where it was not typically found before. In particular, a great many people have begun to express "the presently unquantified values" in ways that would enable diverse public and private agencies to prove that they have given due attention to "aesthetic and cultural amenities." For example, the Bureau of Land Management has announced that

> ... now [1979] with nearly fifty landscape architects in the various thirteen western states, including state and district offices, the Denver Service Center, and Washington, D.C., there is an extensive and intensive ongoing training program in visual resource management and the key support field of computer graphics. In addition, there has already been one major manual updating and the program has received considerable strength and support from a cadre of young energetic professionals who are constantly questioning, criticizing, and making suggestions for improvement, as well as providing for proper visibility and communication of the program.[21]

But the cadre of young professionals and manual writers—urban planners, landscape designers, economists, psychologists, computer scientists, biologists, ecologists, foresters, etcetera—does not include philosophic aestheticians. Perhaps their absence is initially striking only to a philosopher with a speciality in that area. But on reflection, it is not surprising that people who must make decisions with some dispatch should fail to turn to philosophy for help. Philosophy has a history of asking, and not answering, questions. Furthermore, there has been a trend in twentieth-century Anglo-American aesthetics to deny specifically the inclusion of *evaluation*.[22]

I hope to show that philosophic aesthetics does have something helpful to say to policy and decision makers. Along the way I think we shall learn something crucial about the nature of the aesthetic. We shall begin by looking critically at the sorts of responses the *professional* cadre has made to the request for a model that enables due consideration of aesthetic amenities. Although I find many weaknesses in them, several are intuitively quite appealing. And in fairness to individuals who have introduced strategies for evaluating various aesthetic resources, it must be remembered that they were often acting under time pressures—and were always expected to provide a basis for definitive action. Philosophers rarely work under such conditions. Nonetheless, philosophers can at least suggest something important about how realistic nonphilosophers' expectations can be, and may even contribute to more successful outcomes.

Problems with Describing Aesthetic Amenities

The problems that arise in studies done to aid those who must assess aesthetic amenities can be roughly divided into several categories. The first I call "descriptive" because the primary aim is describing or naming the features that seem to contribute to the value of a scene. In some cases the investigators look at landscapes or cityscapes that are known to be valued (perhaps visited by hundreds of people) and give an *inventory* of the features found there. Comparing inventories of different spots will then ideally provide a list of good and bad features. Robert Ross is among many who believe that a correct list is in fact obtained. "What had been considered extremely subjective (aesthetic judgment, particularly in the landscape) was found to have identifiable consistent qualities which can be described and measured, and about which people with diverse opinions will tend to agree."[23] Ross believes that visual quality is based on form, line, color, and texture. The stronger the influence exerted by these properties on a given landscape, the more interesting it will be found. Add variety to these—if it is variety harmonized—and the view will be even more aesthetically pleasing.

Similarly, the Bureau of Land Management reports it has found that what was considered subjective aesthetic judgment contains "identifiable, consistent qualities that can be described and measured."[24] The bureau has developed a program for landscape management training based on this. It also uses form, line, color, texture, and variety with harmony, and has a scoring system based upon their presence or absence in a scene.

These people have relied more or less on textbook principles of art and design—and, as I shall show later, I believe that it is appropriate to do exactly this sort of thing. But we may wonder if in fact the author has *discovered* that two types of vegetation are less valuable than three types, or that rich color is in every case better than muted color. Ultimately there is little basis for believing that what the BLM asserts is more than an expression of personal preference.

Kenneth Craik is another who believes that descriptive analyses will be successful. He likes them because they lack what he feels is the subjective bias of evaluative appraisals and reports of preferences. Having questioned people during automobile drives through the countryside, he believes he has discovered that, "an extent of view greater than three miles is *positively* related to aesthetic appeal," and that "a sense of vertical enclosure which blocks off the line of vision directly ahead of the observer is *negatively* related to aesthetic appeal."[25]

Another descriptivist, R. Burton Litton, provides a much more detailed model for inventorying the landscape. Assuming that aesthetic value is equivalent to visual value (as I do in part) he chooses four criteria for evaluation: vividness (memorability), intactness (the apparent naturalness of a scene), encroachment (the presence of degradation of the natural environment), and uniqueness (the relative scarcity of a particular configuration).[26] He suggests, "Design policy concepts—expressive of compatible relationships—may be suggested by *combinations* of the following illustrative list: proportional similarity, pattern emulation, color contrast limitation, dominant line attitudes, scale replication/compatibility/subordinance, shape/edge types and linkages, location/dispersion pattern, recovery/temporal phases, form and shape complements."[27] The problem is not that the items on the list are vague; Litton explains what he means by them. But with Litton, as with Craik and the BLM program developers, it is hard to know whether most people would identify the same features as the ones responsible for making the scene valuable. This is largely due to the investigators' failure to provide a theory supporting reasons for picking out one set of features rather than another.

This failure typifies many other descriptive strategists. In a variety of contexts a more or less a priori list of features is presented that seems to be based upon the authors' own experience or introspection. Familiarity is believed important by one;[28] another likes diversity.[29] A group of highway management course developers pick out vividness, intactness, and unity.[30] A river assessor thinks that variety, general beauty, uniqueness, remoteness, trash, and detrimental structures affect a riverview's scenic value.[31]

Evaluators of recreational areas have tried to judge what is called "visual carrying capacity." Carrying capacity is generally understood in physical terms—the extent to which an area can be used for recreation, for example, without being damaged or losing its value. Since visual experience, they believe, is an important part of overall recreational enjoyment, it is important to know "whether various levels of intrusion adversely affect a visitor's visual experience; and, if so, to attempt to determine which elements appear to be most visually disturbing."[32] So they test for the effect of perceived crowdedness, the presence of human-made elements, and the influence of human activity—all features that they, apparently intuitively, found important. A purview of abstracts provided by Peter J. Dooling and Stephen Shephard shows that many authors recommend that cutting and reseeding of forests should be carried out with attention to maintaining diversity, retaining a canopy, creating sharp and undulating brush edges—all of which result from general attention to form, line, color, texture, and lighting.[33] Again, although some fundamentally Western art principles are implicit in these studies, no theoretical foundation for attending to these particulars is offered.

An elaborate list of features to be inventoried if one wants to evaluate a given scene is provided by Sarah Haskett, and it is useful to present it here in order to show how complex such studies often become. Haskett believes that the visual component of visual quality perception can be analyzed in terms of the physical scene and the viewer's perspective. (She is, incidentally, one of the few writers in this area who recognizes that there is a nonvisual component—a component that I believe is central to the aesthetic.) Here is her list (partial, she acknowledges) of physical settings that influence visual quality.[34]

I. Landscape elements
- Landforms
- Vegetation
- Waterforms
- Shoreline forms
- Structures
- Groups of structures
- Paved surfaces
- Open spaces

III. Landscape dimensions
- Complexity, variety, diversity, incongruity, surprisingness, mystery, ambiguity
- Contrast, deviation
- Vividness, uniqueness
- Unity, harmony, congruity
- Rhythm, balance, scale

III. Landscape properties
- Breadth
- Height
- Width
- Texture, grain
- Color
- Degree of naturalness

Degree of urbanization
Edge definition

What is at work in Haskett is even more pronounced in other descriptivists—a desire to present a scientific, objective model that will ultimately generate a factual landscape assessment. The desire and inclination to come up with a *formula* for describing what we value is very strong. Thus we often find definitions like this:

$$\text{topographic texture} = \frac{\text{number of crenulations}}{\text{area of view}}^{35}$$

(A crenulation is an even, rounded, notched depression caused by the erosion of water.) Or, as we saw in Jones & Jones' report,

$$\text{Visual quality} = \frac{\text{Vividness} + \text{Intactness} + \text{Unity}}{3} \div \text{Uniqueness}.$$

But we have not been told *why* we should count the paved surfaces or uniqueness or edge definition, or why vividness and unity should be equally weighted. What makes these things 'aesthetically' relevant? In most cases there is even a noticeable lack of ad hominem arguments for the lists provided—that is, the authors neglect to support what they are doing by referring to theories of experts in other fields such as design. Most of these "young professionals," as they were referred to earlier (landscape architects, city planners, foresters, etc.), have at some time studied design, and their intuitions about what is visually important seem to come from that experience. This accounts, I believe, for the recurrence in their writings of things like form, light, texture, or unity in variety. But this is my speculation, not their explanation.

Repeatedly in their urge to objectify, the investigators that I have studied commit what I think is the *fallacy of confusing objectivity with quantifiability*. The drive is to produce an assessment with a numeric score or ranking. The fallacy is not that numbers or ratios are used in a way that gives an appearance of mathematical certainty when none is really there (although this is a weakness of many studies); the fallacy consists in assuming that objectivity can be achieved only quantitatively; that is, that qualitative objectivity is impossible. Objectivity is not a matter of reducing things to numeric formulas; it is a matter of grounding one's claims in evidence in such a way that interpersonal agreement or disagreement is meaningful. Neither claims nor evidence need be reduced to numbers in order for objectivity to be achieved. One can objectively claim that an area has a canyon and white water on the basis of what one sees. Objectivity does not demand that either the claim or its basis be quantitatively stated or statable.

Problems with Using Photographic Studies

Determining what people's environmental preferences are involves a number of procedural problems. It is very expensive to take people in sufficient numbers to actual sites under study. Thus investigators often use photographs; and this brings up several interesting issues.

My own favorite use of photography for this purpose is that in which individuals are given cameras (usually Instamatics) and instructed to take pictures themselves. This is called "visitor employed photography," and the assumptions are clear. Suppose you want to know which spots along a ten-mile trail or river stretch are beautiful. Ask people who walk or canoe along it on a given day to taken ten pictures of beautiful spots. Then see what kind of agreement you get. In a study of the St. Croix river in Wisconsin, the investigators believe that a consensus emerged— one that cuts across diverse backgrounds and different seasons. The results, they believe, enable them to identify "perceptually exciting nodes" (identifiable areas).[36] "The more sensory and landscape diversity there was at any one spot, the more likely it was to be photographed. For example, an area that contained a bed of yellow wildflowers, a dead snag, and an abundance of birdlife was more likely to be photographed than an area with a dead snag alone."[37]

I find this sort of study appealing. I like the idea of asking ordinary people to take pictures of things they like as they travel through a given area. But the problems are legion. How representative is the sample? How much can photos from the same spot differ from one another? When do we know that a given photographer has taken the instructions seriously? What if a shot was taken accidentally? In the study along the St. Croix, most people considered human structures not beautiful. But think about photos taken by tourists on a boat trip along the Rhine. They are filled with structures—mostly castles. Are these results in some way contradictory? Would a castle along the St. Croix add or detract from the scenery? Bridges on the St. Croix were considered positive features by some, negative by others. What, if anything, does this tell us about bridges—or rivers—or people?

More questions arise when studies involve more passive subjects—when they are given photos and asked a variety of questions. The simplest of these is "Which do you prefer?" In one "urban vs. nature" study, for example, it was found that the latter was consistently preferred. "In fact, the only slide in the urban subset that was liked as much as any of the nature scenes was one showing a few trees against a backdrop of tall buildings in a downtown park."[38]

Even if we put aside questions raised in connection with visitor-employed photography, a serious question remains: are responses to photographs enough like responses to the scenes they show to serve as a basis for aesthetic decision making? This problem has itself been the topic of several studies—with quite varying results. Rachel Kaplan has found an inconsistency between responses to photos and to verbal descriptions of the same thing.[39]

Nonetheless, and with varying degrees of explicitly expressed awareness of the photography/reality problems, photos continue to be widely used in the hope that when we have discovered what pictures people like we can discover what accounts for their approbation. That is we can identify what variables in photographs of landscapes are significantly related to public preferences for those landscapes. Using factor and multiple-regression analysis, one group developed an equation "that used six variables and accounted for 66 percent of the variation in preference scores for photographs of landscapes. It can be concluded that it seems possible to quantify aesthetics through the methods described."[40]

In interviews with Adirondack campers, the authors of the above study identified the following as having positive effects: the perimeter of immediate vegetation, the perimeter of nonimmediate nonvegetation, the perimeter of distant vegetation multiplied by the area of water, the area of intermediate vegetation multiplied by the area of distant nonvegetation, and the area of intermediate vegetation multiplied by the area of water. On the negative side are the perimeter of vegetation squared, the area of water squared, the perimeter of vegetation multiplied by the area of intermediate vegetation, and the perimeter of intermediate vegetation multiplied by the area of distant nonvegetation. "The 33 percent of the variation in preference scores not explained by the model may have been caused by the respondents' personal preference and past experience," the authors suggest.[41]

I suggest that it may be caused by any number of other factors. Who is to say that personal preference and past experience are not 'aesthetically' of primary importance—in which case the model misses almost everything. With this photographic study we encounter with a vengeance an expression of the urge to quantify.

Problems with Quantitative Studies

With respect to quantitative studies, I believe the main criticism (and the one crucial to characterizing 'the aesthetic') is this: Even if we are able to establish quantitatively a basis for predicting agreement, we are not assured of having hit upon an *explanation* for agreement, and consequently may not have given due regard to 'aesthetic' amenities.

The simplest quantitative studies are done with respect to preferences for specific sites, and involve questionnaires or surveys. For example, in 1977 the Gallup organization tried to identify the proportion of the national population that takes an interest in the California Desert Recreation Area. 1,506 people over the age of eighteen were questioned about frequency of visits, and what they would and would not like to see done there. Question 6 was this:

> This card lists a number of things which might have a negative effect on the scenic quality of the desert. For each item listed, please tell me if it has a negative effect on your enjoyment of the scenery or not:
>
> Grazing activities
> Electrical transmission lines
> Power generating plants
> Mining activities
> Off-road vehicular activities
> Mountain-top communication sites
> Surface scars due to underground pipelines

Most were not bothered by grazing, but they objected to the remaining items.[42] People agreed about what would make the area ugly. Indeed, Robert Kates suggests that the vast agreement about what is *ugly* should be the basis of public policy on beautification and protection, and that attempts to find a consensus about what is beautiful should be abandoned.[43]

A more complex methodology is "cognitive mapping," a "coded neurological network that consists of abstract representations of the external world."[44] Using numerical questionnaires (usually quite carefully carried out, with due attention to both users and nonusers), maps can be drawn showing an area's most beautiful spots, according to people who practice this methodology.[45] But such studies are only as strong as the weakest links in basic survey studies—that is, the ways in which rankings of individual points are obtained.

Numerical evaluation of semantic-pair testing is another popular way of trying to get at preferences. In this example, used in assessing timbering practices, the following pairs were matched:

Evaluative	*Potency*	*Activity*
Good-Bad	Rugged-Delicate	Varied-Repetitive
Beautiful-Ugly	Smooth-Rough	Active-Passive
Clean-Dirty	Humorous-Serious	Vibrant-Still
Pleasant-Unpleasant	Gentle-Violent	Hot-Cold
Sacred-Profane	Unique-Commonplace	
Valuable-Worthless		

Based on percentage of responses, it was found that "patch clearcuts with top-lopping yielded more favorable impressions than patch clearcuts without top-lopping or any kind of strip clearcutting within each location."[46] Without a firmer theoretical foundation, however, it is doubtful that the study gives more reason to believe this statement than normal reflective experience would have provided.

Most quantitative studies involve more sophisticated techniques than the mere reporting of percentages of the responses to specific questions or tasks. Some take into account that people with different attitudes prefer different things. For example, one study of preferences for more or for less natural maintenance of roadsides found that some people believe that billboards make trips more interesting, others, that they are eyesores. People in the first group also prefer more cutting of grass than the second.[47] And surely people distinguish between billboards that they consider intrusive and those that make a trip less boring—Burmashave ads, for instance.

Such problems lead people to choose a variety of statistical approaches (although I am convinced that many *experts* use whatever statistical tests they remember from basic college courses). One obvious problem is the extent to which the people participating in a survey represent a broader population. Often university students constitute a majority of the sample. Other times it is a group of canoeists or hikers. It may be quite all right to use hikers if a project proposes to improve land for hiking; but usually the aim is much broader—to find out what people in general like in the landscape.

Whose preferences should one take into account? This problem is only occasionally addressed in preference studies. Should *experts* have a greater voice than laypeople? Although some writers believe that there is fairly close agreement between the two groups, Stephen Kaplan believes that experts actually perceive things differently. He believes that experts have networks of thought that make retrieval of and access to information easier and that they have a greater capacity for manipulating elements.[48] He recommends that nonexperts be consulted in environmental planning if the purpose is to achieve surroundings that will please most citizens.

In addition to the expert/nonexpert problem, wilderness planners also encounter a purist/nonpurist conflict. There is a fair number of people who want areas left untouched. Studies report that some individuals would rather see three canoes in an hour than one motorboat.[49] How are we to compare preferences of individuals who want isolated campsites with those who place a high premium on ready access to flush toilets and electrical hookups?

In Dennis, Mssachusetts, a citizens group developed its own way of assessing visual resources. One group was asked to categorize landscape photos as beach, marshland, or suburban development. Another group was asked to Q-sort (divide the photos into piles whose sizes resemble a normal curve) for preference. The assumption was that judgments could then be compared to determine which categories were most highly valued.[50] But unless the groups are homogeneous, how can we be certain that comparison is apt?

One pair of writers is aware of the problem, but they dismiss it rather quickly.

> The participants in the test were all affiliates of RSRI; however, they do not constitute a rigidly homogeneous group. They have been

raised in areas ranging from rural to urban, their educational levels vary from high school diploma to post-doctoral work; they range in age from early twenties to about fifty. Some own houses, others rent apartments. Some live in the city, others in the suburbs. Some are natives of the Eastern United States, others come from various parts of the United States, as well as other countries.[51]

And in one test, the authors admit, they used two judges; the most they ever used was ten!

The trouble with many studies is that they give only a deceptive appearance of objectivity because of their numerical veil. Gray, Ady, and Jones asserted that they trained people to rank landscapes on a 1–100 scale according to vividness, intactness, and unity; they also said that they had thus diminished the intrusion of personal bias.[52] But *has* personal bias been circumvented? Vividness ratings, for example, may vary tremendously from one person to the next.

Numerical rankings have appeared from time to time in the history of art criticism. Early in the eighteenth century, for instance, Roger de Piles undertook an analysis of the great masters by ranking them on a scale of 1–20 with respect to four components: composition, drawing, color, and expression. Raphael won with a combined score of 65.[53]

	Composition	*Drawing*	*Color*	*Expression*	*Total*
Raphael:	17	18	12	18	65
Michelangelo:	8	17	4	8	37
Titian:	12	15	18	6	51
Carravagio:	6	6	16	0	28

And Carravagio, one of my favorite artists, received a total of only 28. The zero in Carravagio's score shows exactly what I mean by the "quantitative/objective fallacy." If our rankings differ from even those of so great an expert as Roger de Piles, does this or does it not suggest that his numerical scores are every bit as personal or subjective as ours would be? When masters are being compared, the question, "Which has the better composition?" does not automatically become factual or scientific simply because a number is assigned. Nor does a *vividness score* necessarily eliminate personal bias.

This is not to say that there is no objectivity in artistic or aesthetic criticism. One may believe it is an objective fact that Michelangelo's statues are compositionally superior to a child's sandcastles. But one has to do more than assign numbers to prove the fact. One danger of the quantitative/objective fallacy is that it leads to the belief that a judgment is objective only if it is based on a number. I believe that aesthetic judgments have a genuinely cognitive, objective basis; but this does not mean that I will show how to give a numerical score to the Grand Canyon.

David W. Lime has pointed out other problems with preferential studies. Typically, no follow-up investigation is done. Too little attention is given to seasonal effects. Only one, often atypical, area is involved in most studies.[54] But such shortcomings have done little to diminish the overall confidence of the people carrying out the projects I have been describing.

By far the most mathematically sound studies appear to be those using linear regression techniques in what are called "policy capturing models."[55] These are designed to "represent the manner in which an individual or group weights separate bits of information to arrive at an overall decision."[56]

Suppose, for example, that someone is asked to rank potentional employees based on scores for personal appearance, high-school rank, and experience in similar jobs. Based on the final rankings, using a linear regression model, we can see which factors matter most. Similarly, given a descriptive inventory of overall preferences for a particular area, we can determine which features people seem to weight most heavily. One forestry study, for instance, concludes that the following features matter aesthetically: number of trees per acre, diameter and height of trees, amount and distribution of slashed areas, and percentage of ponderosa pine as opposed to variety of trees. All of these have the advantage of being numerically expressible.

A primary objection to linear regression techniques is that although they are mathematically sound, they are sometimes interpreted as giving more information than they actually contain. It may be that an individual or group is pleased by an area where trees are more than twenty feet high, more than thirteen inches in diameter, and distributed so as to give each tree twenty square feet. It does not follow that the *cause* of their pleasure is trees of such height, diameter, and density. Explanations can be suggested and predictions can be made by manipulating factors—by multiplying lake area by tree area or by squaring the perimeter of vegetation, for example. But if we are to be certain that *aesthetic* amenities are being given due consideration, we have to know *why* trees and lakes are important. Otherwise we can be certain of little beyond the abilities of the investigators to manipulate figures cleverly.

Dennis Propst explicitly recognizes this problem. He believes that he has provided a theoretical foundation for using linear regression formulas, but beyond accounting for weighting, he does little to connect scores to the aesthetic. One of his papers on applications of the policy-capturing model begins with a fable in which several of a king's advisors trying to choose a harem for him are guided by a few initial choices of women made by the king himself.[57] This fable points out several of the problems I am posing. The advisors assume that the king's choices were based on the visual appearances of the women. Although this is probably not an incorrect assumption, no reason is given for it. And chances for confusing the aesthetic with the nonaesthetic are increased when the advisors select particular visual features as the values of the variables in their formulas. Suppose they decide that eye color is important. If eye color is contingently associated with hair style, and the latter is what the king likes, then clearly it would be a mistake to explain that the king's aesthetic is based upon eye color (and the advisors run the risk of eventually coming up with an inappropriate harem!).

Propst says that the purpose of "using a linear model is to make the judge's policy explicit."[58] It is true that his test comes closer than that of the king's advisors, for unlike the latter he does not produce a list of factors by observing choices. Instead he presents a list (of foreground vegetation, visible distant landform, green colors, etc.) to subjects and observes the results. But even this does not ensure that he has discovered their *policy.* An individual might not be able to say what matters. We often hear, "I don't know why, I just like it." We can watch and make guesses. But unless we have some independent way of connecting the guesses to what we believe to be an aesthetic evaluation we have no way of knowing that we have discovered an 'aesthetic policy.' We could, of course, *ask* the individual if foreground vegetation matters aesthetically to him or her. This will help. But we may still miss other features that are crucial, and that provide a deeper foundation for the relevance of the features that we correctly hit upon.

Propst himself is careful to avoid applications of the policy-capturing model that are beyond it. It can be used, he says, for assessing individual preferences, but not for identifying in general the dimensions that determine them. For one thing, "Preferences may not depend so much on the physical elements themselves but on configurations of these elements."[59]

The trouble with most preference studies is that they are done, in an important sense, out of context—even when questionnaires are passed out at the end of a trail or on a mountain top. In order to determine what is valuable, or what is worth saving, preferences have to fit into an overall system of valuation (see chap. 5).

Some of the projects that must be carried out by aesthetic impact studiers can perhaps be done without attention to these problems—whether most citizens in a given area are willing to sacrifice some trees in order to have a dam, or whether they prefer one dam to another, or one site to another. But if we are to *predict* what will aesthetically please people, we have to ground the work more securely in adequate theories.

Problems with Economic Theories

"(I)f scenic quality could be assessed in the same quantitative fashion as the more tangible resources, there would be a common basis for the comparison of scenic beauty benefits with the more traditional timber, water, and forage products."[60] This statement not only expresses the urge to quantify, but also implies a connection between the tangible and economic, for that is "traditionally" how timber, water, and forage products have been measured. Thus it has been said that "scenic value has become equated with economic value. . . . The effectiveness of roadside appearance along a parkway may contribute to the marketability of that roadway as a scenic site."[61]

Ease of measurement and numerical clarity of result are, of course, seen as advantages of economically based aesthetic assessments. One can easily ask, for example, "How much office space would you be willing to trade for the view of a tree outside the window?"[62] Or questionnaires can determine how much one is willing to pay to use a campsite, or how far one is willing to drive to see a mountain range or cranberry bog. As with other methods, some people are overly confident about this one's possibilities. "The state-of-the-knowledge regarding measurement of recreational user benefits is such that it is now possible to measure them with confidence. The total willingness-to-pay measure of value . . . is the relevant measure given maximization of net social benefits as the decision criterion," asserts one author.[63] Thus, willingness-to-pay measures are often recommended.[64]

Certainly economic arguments carry weight with financially strapped governments. For example, a member of the county school administration of Gwinnett County, Georgia, garnered support for beautification in precisely this way. He argued that

" . . . the improved appearance of the school grounds enhanced the county's bargaining power in recruiting teachers. He also mentioned the increased real-estate value of adjoining properties, and the increased pride of the children in the appearance of the school grounds. It may be pure happenstance, but the football team of this school advanced to the state finals the first year after its football field was renovated."[65] The beautification seemed to *pay off* in enhanced student endeavor (of primary importance in many areas) but surely it is not necessarily a measure of the aesthetic!

"Returns may be assumed to be *at least equal* to the levels of total expenditures."[66] But *what* returns? The valued consequences of a visit may or may not include, let alone be identical with, aesthetic returns. We cannot know what is valued; a given spot may just be a good place to make love!

Problems with Psychological Studies

In describing the several approaches above, I have repeatedly criticized them because they appear to be carried out with little or no attention to theoretical underpinnings. Choices of environmental features contributing to aesthetic value often seem the arbitrary and subjective choices of the experimental designers. This weakness is explicitly noted, and attempts are made to remedy it, by what might be called psychological environmentalists. By proposing a psychological model for aesthetic valuation, by fitting preferences into a larger picture of human response and behavior, several people have tried to explain why and how certain features are connected to our environmental aesthetic norms. These approaches are primarily perceptual or motivational.

Not surprisingly, perceptual studies take the form of visual investigation. Some of these are essentially physiological—for example, attempts to identify neurological configurations accompanying positive emotional responses associated with certain visual experiences.[67] Or they attempt to relate eye movement to aesthetic judgment.[68] But these studies are at the earliest stages of development, and conclusions are extremely tentative.

Quantitative studies of the sort discussed above are also found among psychological studies of aesthetic preferences. One such study is that of Maitland Graves, who believes that the visual arts (and aesthetically judged scenes generally) "are subject to natural

forces that are as potent as gravity," namely, reactions to line, shape, and color.[69] He has constructed a visual design test in which people are asked which of two alternatives is better, in this case, *YZ* or *LO*.

According to Graves,

> YZ is the correct choice. The contrast between the circle and rectangle is greater than the contrast between the rectangle and the triangle, and therefore produces a subdominant shape contrast. The dominant contrast is between the triangle and the circle. These three unequal shape differences create a variety of contrasts that make it more interesting than LO. This design is also more unified because it more clearly approaches a dominant shape. In YZ the spaces or distances between the shapes are unequal and therefore produce interest.[70]

Such principles, although not rigid, can be used as guiding rules in design decisions, he believes. But like most of these studies, the tentative results make their application difficult at best.

Another perceptual psychologist is Gyorgy Kepes. Kepes has developed a theory of design based on vision. Noting common preferences—nobody ever seems to tire of watching flames and waves, for example—he suggests that

> the significant aspect of such experiences is that they mobilize wide responses, thoughts, and feelings not directly connected with the seen image. . . . (T)he rhythmical order of flames or waves can induce larger and larger, wider and wider, dimensions of experience. From the perception of sensory patterns, one moves to corresponding structures in emotional and intellectual realms.[71]

Kepes believes that we organize what we perceive into patterns based on contiguity, repetition, rhythm, etc., but that these qualities connect with other human needs—the need for light, for example. But, again, more work is required to use such theories in very practical or productive ways.

The view that aesthetic preferences are tied to basic human needs is also at the heart of motivational psychological studies of those preferences. D. E. Berlyne uses a stimulus-response model to explain historically important concepts like unity in diversity or uniformity in variety, as based on high arousal conditions such as complexity, novelty, heterogeneity, numerosity, ambiguity, and surprise. Organization "represents the conditions that make for clear-cut cortical responses that allow arousal to be moderated" in order for tension to diminish to the point where enjoyment becomes possible.[72]

Many ecologists favor a motivational explanation associated with theories of evolution. Some explanations are biological—based on the belief that we tend to prefer conditions that favor biological survival. But most explanations are what is termed *informational*. Good environments are *legible* environments and are valued for "the ease with which [the parts] can be recognized and can be organized into a coherent pattern."[73] They are also valued for the readiness with which they "give the individual . . . a starting point for the acquisition of further information."[74]

Using Gibson's affordances theory, Stephen Kaplan believes that aesthetic rankings are based on what objects or scenes have to offer. Species evolutionarily prefer what suits them, and if this is true, preferences are not arbitrary. As human beings we have two basic purposes: making sense and being involved (the characterization of these is deeply confused). When we look at a landscape we want to make sense of it—for example, make a map of it (compelling us to look for features that simplify the task), but we also want to find features that challenge our capacities. Obvious landscapes, like simple-minded poems, fail to afford us involvement. We like *mystery*—the sort of challenge provided by a bend in the road. Thus, a balance of legibility and mystery, not simply a balance of form, line, color, and texture, make for a desirable scene.[75]

William Hammett believes that his own studies of people's reactions to bogs support Kaplan's views. When questioned, visitors report that they like ease of entry, the possibility of getting closer, help with identifying plants, provision of overview scenes (all of which contribute to legibility) and novelty, complexity, and rare species (which fall on the mystery side). "An environment whose informational components 'make sense' to the viewer and at the same time offer opportunity to become cognitively involved in terms of processing additional information, will be an environment that is appreciated and preferred."[76] A practical application of this is the recommendation that information centers should provide material that is involving rather than passive.[77] The problem, of course, is how to produce it.

Although the studies cited in this brief survey are praiseworthy for their attempts to explain the *source* of aesthetic pleasures taken in the environment, they leave many unresolved issues. For example, how much complexity or novelty is good? "The right balance between legibility and mystery," really tells us very little more than "uniformity in variety" does. Without more information it will not be possible to decide whether or not a dam should be built at a particular site.[78]

There are some preferences that seem to have the status of *natural laws*. We like trees and water—particular white water. Add a running stream to an area or plant a few trees and you almost certainly improve it. The famous story about Frank Lloyd Wright's being asked to improve the appearance of Stanford University's architecture is relevant. He is supposed to have said, "Plant vines—lots of them!" But I think we must look further for an explanation that clarifies whether these are truly 'aesthetic' preferences.

I have repeatedly criticized authors who commit what I have called the quantitative/objective fallacy. Like Lord Kelvin they seem to believe that "when you can measure what you are speaking about, and express it in numbers, you know something about it." With Lewis Thomas, I think it is dangerous to be too quick in assigning numbers. As Thomas writes,

> The task of converting observations into numbers is the hardest of all, the last task rather than the first thing to be done, and it can be done only when you have learned, beforehand, a great deal about the observations themselves. You can, to be sure, achieve a very deep understanding of nature by quantitative measurement, but you must know what you are talking about before you can begin applying the numbers for making predictions.[79]

I believe a discussion of the "first thing" is important here—so that we can better learn what we are talking about when we study the aesthetic.

5
Measuring What Matters

Understanding human experience—aesthetic or otherwise—demands understanding its context. The methods of humanists, who study the traditions that shape that experience, will help us to determine whether we have measured what matters, that is, whether we have gotten at the aesthetic. I believe that historians, philosophers, and people who study literature and the other arts have a great deal to contribute to the understanding of aesthetic preferences in such areas as landscape assessment.

To identify a preference as aesthetic, one must know whether it reflects values of a certain sort. Values are systems or networks of desires and preferences and purposes; they cannot be uncovered or understood merely from people's responses to individual questions. Due consideration can be given to aesthetic amenities in environmental planning only by ensuring that values in general, not just particular preferences ("90% of the people interviewed prefer site A to site B"), receive due attention. I believe that appreciating the role of values leads to a clearer understanding of what 'the aesthetic' is.

My basic argument is this: The history of art and aesthetics cannot be separated from the history of society. Explanations of 'art' and 'aesthetic' must reflect this social involvement.

Individuals have values that figure in their decisions and evaluations. But individual values develop within familial and societal contexts, and in large measure are shaped by them. And the values of the society in which individual values are shaped do not just suddenly come into being. They, too, develop gradually and are always rooted in the past. In particular, understanding scenic valuations demands understanding where such valuations come from. In turn, this will lead to a fuller understanding of the aesthetic in general.

The Language of Aesthetic Assessment

Ludwig Wittgenstein claimed that languages develop within communities that share what he called "forms of life." What communities do and what they say cannot be understood in isolation or apart from one another. Meaning reflects use and vice versa. We do not just learn syntactical and semantical rules when we learn to speak a language; we also must learn the interests and intentions of the speakers.

Building on this general view of Wittgenstein, William G. Lycan and Peter K. Machamer explain that the language of aesthetic judgments often combines descriptive and evaluative functions.[1] Words like *unified, harmonious, expressive,* or *vivid* do not just point to objective features of a landscape (or poem or symphony); they point to features that our (Western) language community values. It is conceivable that communities—groups with different forms of life—might use the same words neutrally.

What we value is intricately enmeshed in the language that we speak. We learn *what* words point to, but at the same time we learn *what is worth* pointing to. What we point to is thus tied to our interests or values. If two people speak different languages, it is quite possible that they will pick out different things to point to, or point to the same thing with different interests or purposes.

No one ever speaks a completely new language. Like art and the aesthetic, language is rooted in the past. Values are transmitted via language; language is rooted in traditions—understood here as existing and preexisting values and practices. Thus, understanding current values depends upon understanding those traditions. We cannot know or understand what is valued unless we have access to a language whose meanings are determined by traditions.

Obviously traditions differ among various cultures, among different language communities, and within language communities to the extent that differences exist between subgroups within a larger community. Thus, in the West there are differences between eighteenth-century Parisians and nineteenth-century Plains Indians, or between twentieth-century American blacks and American whites. Traditions are not static. New interests develop; old ones die. The history of art is only one indication of this. As we shall see, landscape values also have a varied history. Nonetheless, traditions do not change all at once. Getting a foothold demands that there be some ground that does not shift.

Suppose someone says, "That is loud music." Before we can know whether it is meant as an aesthetic remark, we must understand the meaning of the sentence and know something about the traditions that form part (a crucial part) of the context in which it is uttered. The fact that a language enables someone to point to loudness implies that the language community is interested in loudness. But we must know a great deal more before we can know if that interest—even if it is music that is being described—is an aesthetic interest.

Since expression of values is transmitted via languages, we can use language as a means of getting at values. The feelings and interests that people have are not determinable unless we have access to their language. I do not intend to prove that people cannot or do not have aesthetic experiences unless they speak a language that can be understood. I do intend to show that we cannot *know* whether people have aesthetic experiences unless we understand their language. In chapter 2 we saw how vocabulary changes accompany conceptual changes. Here we shall look at developments in landscape values as they affect the concept of the aesthetic and our understanding of it.

History of Landscape Values

People have suggested that enjoyment of trees and water is so pervasive in our society that it almost assumes the status of a natural law. But even if such a *law* describes twentieth-century culture (or some significant subset of it) it has not always held. "People . . . are apt to assume that the appreciation of natural beauty and the painting of landscape is a normal and enduring part of our spiritual activity. But the truth is that in times when the human spirit seems to have burned most brightly the painting of landscape for its own sake did not exist and was unthinkable."[2] Not only does the history of painting show a change of attitude toward landscape painting; history in general shows a change of attitude toward landscape itself—and toward that history. Confronted as we are by environmental destruction and pollution, it is hard to believe that not so many years ago, in optimism and good faith, the philosopher John Dewey wrote,

> In the interests of the maintenance of life there is transformation of some elements in the surrounding medium. The higher the form of life, the more important is the active reconstruction of the medium. This increased control may be illustrated by the contrast of savage with civilized man. Suppose the two are living in a wilderness. With the savage there is the maximum of accommodation to given conditions; the minimum of what we may call hitting back. The savage takes things "as they are," and by using caves and roots and occasional

pools leads a meagre and precarious existence. The civilized man goes to distant mountains and dams streams. He builds reservoirs, digs channels and conducts the waters to what had been a desert. He searches the world to find plants and animals that will thrive. He takes native plants and by selection and cross-fertilization improves them. He introduces machinery to till the soil and care for the harvest. By such a means he may succeed in making the wilderness blossom like a rose.[3]

It is precisely the belief that what occurred is the opposite of "blossom" that led to the aesthetic legislation we reviewed above.

Before looking at the history of landscape values generally, it is worth noting some examples of changed attitudes toward specific features. Until fairly recently, Americans disliked deserts. In 1835 Thomas Eakins said that landscapes are defective without water. But in 1960 Harold Brueler said, "I don't like New England. I don't like green mountains. . . . I like desert, and I like the sense of the West. . . . There are things you've got to go to the edge of— an abyss—and look in, and the thing opens up. What I try to get in paintings is a quality of discovery."[4] These two attitudes demonstrate more than mere differences in personal preferences; they exemplify corresponding changes in the culture as a whole.

The same sort of difference marks views of muddy areas. "Long considered useless, unattractive, and even dangerous, swamp and tidal marshes are now widely appreciated for their fascinating ecosystems and for the significant contribution to the productivity of lakes and oceans."[5] Concomitantly, they have come to be considered visually attractive.

The particular forms of water that people prefer differ considerably even among those people who agree that water is aesthetically pleasing. In addition to motion, sound, and play of light, people have also valued water because of its deeper implications— its "evanescent joys, cleansing of the spirit, the transcience of perfection, the insubstantiality of dreams, the flowing continuity of life, and a consummate fleeting beauty."[6] It is not just that some like it hot and some like it cold, some like it still and some like it rough. In the eastern hemisphere people seem to prefer it quieter.

> The beauty they sought was gentle and placid. The effects they created were artfully natural and heavy with symbolism in carefully constructed garden ponds and lakes in China and Japan; quietly evocative in the flat, reflecting sheets of mogul palaces and tombs; and solemnly impressive in the great temple tanks of India. . . .[7]

Eastern ways were brought by the Moors to Spain. We appreciate such ways. Consider the pleasure contemporary tourists take in the reflecting pools of the Alhambra. But, if there is validity in some of the reports discussed in the last chapter, Western culture is biased in favor of white, or at least running, water. Technical advances have made possible elaborate fountains, including light and sound; in our public and private spaces these combinations are becoming more and more popular.

Technology has also played a central (and some would say devastating) role in the way we view the countryside. How different it is to walk through it and to speed through it. Describing the experience from horse and buggy, Edgar Anderson writes,

> There was often grass in the roadway outside the actual wheel-tracks; shrubs like sumac and elderberry pressed so close to the road that you could smell them as you drove by, and children snatched at the flowers. Accommodating drivers of the local stageline learned to snip off small twigs with a snap of the buggy whip and present them to lady passengers.[8]

It is hard to hear cassettes played in a car going fast with windows open. No wonder delicate smells or the calls of birds are not associated with rides through the countryside. This is not to say that such are experiences are less pleasant. They are simply different. As J. B. Jackson suggests,

> The new landscape, seen at a rapid, sometimes even terrifying pace, is composed of rushing air, shifting lights, clouds, waves, a constantly moving, changing horizon, a constantly changing surface beneath the ski, the rudder, the wheel, the wing. The view is no longer static, it is a revolving, uninterrupted panorama of 360 degrees.[9]

Scenic planners must surely take into account that today's travelers more typically take a sportscar than a stage coach.

And if "Plant vines—lots of them!" is an aesthetic law today, it has not always been one. It was not until the eighteenth century that planting in urban settings began. Philadelphia, as planned by William Penn, had trees, but only in five squares. Insurance companies before 1784 would not insure houses with trees in front of them.

Gradually trees took on more importance within cities; they began to appear as part of city planners' proposals. A commission appointed to find a site for the capital of Mississippi in 1821 said in its report, "And even in a small town they would be a comfort, convenience, and greater security against fire, as well as a fairer promise of health, all combined, by having every other square unoccupied by anything except the native trees of the forest, or artificial groves."[10] But notice that there is no reference to 'beauty' as a desirable consequence; trees provided safety and health in the early nineteenth century.

Finally, by the end of that century, as more and more suburbs appeared, a natural, treed setting began to be equated with the good life, as is evidenced in their names: Lake Forest, Forest Hills, Woodland, and so on. A recent Louis Harris poll reported that 95 percent of respondents favor an environment with green grass and trees. In the mid 1800s *desolate,* to an American, referred to land not yet cleared. A century later it would describe what a hurricane had done![11]

The causes of all of these changes of attitude are incredibly complex. There is probably a fair amount of rather crude conditioning involved. Postcards from touring friends help determine what people will enjoy when they tour the same regions. But to attribute their pleasure totally to this sort of thing would be gross oversimplification. As the examples above show, aesthetic evaluations are part of larger value sets.

In the 1800s the word 'sublimity' was widely used to describe the landscape.[12] But that term is no longer familiar. When I introduce Edmund Burke's writings on the sublime to students, they are unable to define it. They do not use it anymore, except occasionally in the expression "going from the sublime to the ridiculous." They generally feel it means something like 'beautiful' or 'elevated'. Their misunderstanding has been magnified by the growing use of 'awesome' which Burke, but not today's teenagers, would have thought synonymous with 'sublime'.

It is a mistake to think that people from time immemorial have stood on hilltops and admired the landscape. To say, as we do, that they "enjoyed the landscape" involves assuming the existence of certain responses we can be fairly certain did not take place. Saying this entails believing that what they enjoyed, at least in part, was a certain arrangement of lights, shadows, shapes, and textures. Perception of such arrangements *followed* the appearance of seventeenth- and eighteenth-century landscape paintings. The term *landscape* referred originally not to nature but to representations of nature. Thus, to say that someone "enjoyed the landscape" is quite different from saying that "someone enjoyed nature."

Appreciation of nature has been expressed in artifacts from

primitive, mother-earth statuettes to sonnets. But appreciation of nature and appreciation of the landscape are by no means the same thing. The ancients looked favorably at nature when it offered a friendly place in which to live, unfavorably when it did not. Landscape painting as we know it was rare, although there were clear depictions of individual species of animals or plants.

Remarking that early painters ignored landscape painting, John Ruskin pointed out that " . . . as for lakes, they merely showed they knew the difference between salt and fresh water by the fish they put in each."[13] This lack of interest continued into the Middle Ages. Ruskin continues: "Mountains! I remember none. Some careless and jagged arrangements of blue spires or spikes on the horizon, and, here and there, an attempt at representing an overhanging rock with a hole through it; but mainly in order to divide the light behind some human figure."[14] Kenneth Clark asserts that "[medieval] laymen would not have thought it wrong to enjoy nature; he would simply have said that nature was not enjoyable. The fields meant nothing but hard work (today agricultural workers are almost the only class of the community who are not enthusiastic about natural beauty), the seacoast meant danger of storm and piracy. . . . No wonder that the few references to nature in the early epics, the sagas and Anglo-Saxon poetry, are brief and hostile or dwell on its horrors. . . ."[15]

But lack of aesthetic enjoyment does not imply lack of other kinds of value. In the Middle Ages, and for centuries after, nature was viewed as a divine symbol of the workmanship of an omnipotent being. Three main ideas dominated Western thought until the end of the eighteenth century, according to Clarence Glacken. "Man . . . lives on a divinely created earth harmoniously devised for his needs; his physical qualities such as skin and hair, his physical activity and mental stimulation are determined by climate; and he fulfills his God-given mission of finishing the creation, bringing order into nature, which God, in giving him mind, the eye, and the hand, had intended that he do."[16] Exactly three hundred years before the Environmental Policy Act, the French passed a forest ordinance. Based on law, custom, and miscellaneous regulations, this ordinance controlled cutting, piling, posturing of animals, use of kilns and furnaces, removal of acorns, and so on.[17] But the object of this was to conserve the forest as an economic, not as a visual, resource.

The presence of gardens may seem to counter the assertion that nature was not looked at as something to enjoy. But the derivation of the word *garden*, as well as practices it points to, dispel this doubt. Like the word *paradise*, which comes from a Persian word meaning "a walled enclosure", the Indo-European root of *garden* is *gher*, meaning "enclosure". Gardens at once close a house in and shut inhospitable visitors and elements out.[18] Social and aesthetic features were and continue to be closely related. The garden, unlike the outside world, could be controlled to some extent. And the history of gardens in many ways parallels the attitude toward landscapes.

Medieval gardens were symbolic; like unmanipulated nature they revealed God's signature. The humanism of the Renaissance produced an attitude toward gardens that put greater emphasis on the visual. Like many paintings from the sixteenth and seventeenth centuries, Poussin's and Claude's for example, gardens became geometrically composed. (The same attention to geometry is found in cities as grids replaced clumps or pods in the arranging of buildings.) But nature outside the enclosure was still largely a realm in which survival was the paramount concern. In town, houses were built facing in toward the center (often around a market or square or plain) with their backs to the outside, less hospitable world. Early landscape paintings are *agricultural*—rural scenes with cows and harvests. They celebrate controlled, inhabited nature, not wilderness.

The term *landscape* derives from *landschaft*, which originally referred to a small group of dwellings in a cleared pasture or meadow that included inhabitants and was surrounded by an unimproved area. *Landscape* entered English at the end of the sixteenth century, when England began importing Dutch *landschape*—a term then used exclusively to refer to paintings. By 1630 *landscape* referred to paintings of large rural vistas done predominantly in greens and browns, and sometimes including ornamental gardens.[19]

Painting was historically thought to be inferior to poetry and music, and landscape painting, when it appeared in England in the seventeenth century, was considered an inferior form of painting. Reynolds raised portraiture to the level of poetry by "drawing unabashedly on the sublime language of the great masters," according to Andrew Wilton.[20] But there were no great masters for landscape painters to draw on. One strategy was to use titles that borrowed from poetic themes or preoccupations: *Cicero at his Villa*, or *The Destruction of the Children at Niobe*, for example. Even in the nineteenth century, Turner included people engaged in activities that would contribute elements of virtuousness to what, without this, might have been interpreted as merely titillating. This "gave literary interpretations to many pictures which seem to us to stand perfectly satisfactorily without them."[21] But we do not view the wilderness as Turner's audience did.

Wylder ness was the Anglo-Saxon term meaning "lair of a beast". The first settlers in North America thought of the new land both literally and figuratively in just that way. Folktales are filled with horrors of the wild. Wilderness was "the spatial correlative of unreason, or madness, of the unhuman anarchy that informs so many folktales emphasizing the ephemeral stability of Christianity, society, and agriculture."[22] It is in comparing contemporary views to this picture—as recent in white American history as the Mayflower—that profound changes become obvious.

The first settlers, of course, brought with them attitudes from the Old World. They include two quite different expectations for the New World: a paradise providing refuge from worldly corruption and a frightening, unruly wilderness that God intended to have subdued.[23] John Smith praised the new land as a place that would produce "any grain, fruit, or seeds you will sow or plant."[24] But there were also serious doubts. Sermons were preached against the wilderness, "for beneath the florid plenty of the New World, the Puritan settlers saw the Devil lurking in the wilderness."[25] In the Christian/Satanic dichotomy wilderness was clearly identified with the devil. Although this was frightening, it provided added incentive to do God's work by fighting the devil and saving the Indians. Towns continued to be built facing the ocean—back toward the Christian world—or on squares turned in on themselves. Eighty percent of the *witches* lived beyond Salem's boundaries. Bad people were compared to weeds, unruly trees, vines, brambles, or other botanic specimens found outside the garden, or unwanted in it. Among the most respected early writers, Hawthorne depicts the forest as, at best amoral. Journeys into the countryside were rarely undertaken alone.[26]

But undertaken they were, for in that way only could the wilderness be tamed. "By viewing themselves as the children of Israel, the Puritans saw the hazards of settlement as part of a divine plan to purge the colonists of their iniquities before they could enter the Promised Land. . . . Only by defeating the forces of evil concealed in the wilderness could the settlers of New England hope for salvation among the elect."[27] "A place of tryall," Thomas Shepard called it (and those who like to *rough it* still enjoy viewing it this way occasionally). Their view of themselves as a chosen people gave them confidence that they would withstand the test and eventually conquer Satan.

In southern settlements with a somewhat easier physical environment, tobacco and livestock farming made settlers more venturesome. Tobacco depleted soil quickly and scraggy fields were soon abandoned; livestock had to be rounded up. Thus these people more rapidly became familiar with the wilderness.[28] Eventually in all parts of the new country, industrialized urbanism drove many citizens beyond familiar township areas.

In the seventeenth century, a Dutch engineer, Simon Stevin of the Hague, produced an urban grid design with different focuses—markets, cathedrals, palaces. This grid, of course, was transported to the United States, and eventually territory was divided into thirty-six sections of 640 acres per township. As roads and canals were built, this geometrization succeeded in creating a less terrifying realm. The wilderness was regularized, if not wholly dominated.

The romantic movement emphasized the paradisical elements of the view toward the New World. The call to nature brought with it increased feelings for natural beauty. Intense attitudes toward forests, mountains, lakes, and torrents in their original state developed. These "derived in part from the belief that the landscape untouched by man revealed most clearly the spirit of its Creator, and that the solitary spectator could merge his identity with nature, and be inspired by the experience of greater self understanding."[29] Untampered nature of the sort found in the Hudson Valley attracted writers and painters who shared these new attitudes.

The nineteenth-century view of *picturesque* nature contributed to the increasing tendency to identify beauty with the natural landscape. The 'sublime', explained by Edmund Burke as a source of delight, became increasingly popular. Natural resources characterized by vastness, jaggedness, dramatic light contrasts, and so on, best exemplified Burke's theory.

In the nineteenth century, the "spikes" that John Ruskin found so unremarkable in medieval paintings became a central interest of artists; human figures became secondary. In this century the popularity of landscape painting grew phenomenally fast, as did our capacity to control it; the two must be connected. "A beautiful scene, with water in the foreground reflecting a luminous sky and set off by dark trees, was something which everyone agreed was beautiful, just as, in previous ages, they had agreed about a naked athlete or a saint with hands crossed on her bosom."[30]

This scene is still thought of as beautiful, although there are certainly differences between the 1980 and the 1880 experiences of the landscape. For many moderns, the religious attitude toward nature has faded. Kenneth Clark, however, thinks landscape remains "part of that complex of memories and instincts which are awakened in the average man by the word 'beauty'. Almost every Englishman, if asked what he means by 'beauty' would begin to describe a landscape—perhaps a wood with bluebells and silver birches, perhaps a little harbour with red sails and whitewashed cottages; but at all events a landscape."[31]

Clark goes on to say that although contemporary society continues to be pleased by landscapes, nature does not lend itself to the delight in geometric forms that accounts for our fascination with motor cars.[32] But he forgets that he himself argued that the ideal landscape of Poussin in the seventeenth century was geometric.[33] Today's appreciation may well combine the picturesque and the geometric. What is unquestionably true is that the automobile has influenced our perception of nature, as well as the features valued in it. "What makes one landscape appear harmonious, another incongruous, is the entire experience of the viewer."[34] Speeding through a national forest yields a markedly different response than strolling through.

Everybody experiences changing values as he or she grows older. One summer, after having spent about a year reading and thinking about aesthetic values in the environment, I went by automobile from the Quad Cities to Galesburg, Illinois. It was a trip that I had made many times. And although as a child and as a teenager I always enjoyed "taking a ride," I had always thought this stretch of land quite a bore. But suddenly I was looking at textures, planes, rhythms, places of *mystery*; and the ride became subtle and beautiful.

As I have said, today's cultural point of view has shifted as well. Philip Wagner makes this point strongly. "I submit that the astonishing changes recently manifested in the cultural geography of the United States have come about because *all, or nearly all, of these basic man-land relationships* [location, perception, territoriality, emotion] *have undergone a drastic transformation within our culture in recent years.*" (Emphasis in original.)[35] We are urban dwellers who often live far from where we work or travel for recreation. "A map of the United States in 1930, accurately showing recreational, agricultural, extractive, industrial, residential, institutional, and commercial land use in color, would have had to be enormous to be useful."[36] This is no longer the case; we work and play in ways that can be depicted in clumps of color on a map.

John Kenneth Galbraith, among others, has emphasized the

economic explanation of changing attitudes. As economic needs are satisfied, he claims, people become more concerned with beauty. "Society has advanced from a point when getting goods was the only concern to one in which value is placed on surroundings that can be enjoyed."[37] Regulations are based not only on whether land use will affect the value of adjoining land, but whether it will be its "best" use.[38] Land is no longer seen purely as private property, but often as a community resource. Limits are put on what people can do with their own land.[39]

But as Wagner points out, land—how it is used and the speed at which it is usually viewed—is changing its appearance. J. B. Jackson has described the incredible effect of just one change—methods of farming. New farm technology requires larger, more artificial, and more uniform topography. For example, efficient harvesting requires that lemon trees grow to a prescribed height.

> The ultimate in soil manipulation is probably the procedure followed in the Monrovia Nursery in California. All topsoil has been removed from the 250 acre tract, deposited in piles and chemically treated, then put in cans. Completely terraced and scraped, the land is merely a platform on which to set the plants and operate the nursery. To many commercial farmers the soil has become one item in the production process—as much subject to improvement as is the machine or crop itself.[40]

Similarly, rural architecture is changing. How long is it since you have seen a *new* red barn? Thus Jackson says: "It is dangerous to assume that the American countryside can continue to play its traditional role. . . ."[41]

Like Wagner, Jackson sees radical shifts in our relationahip to nature. Picket fences are no longer *in*. The FHA even forbids them in housing developments it finances. " . . . (T)hey disturb the uniformity of a street vista; [and] they introduce a dangerous note of individualistic non-conformity. . . . They still have something of their old meaning as symbols of self-sufficiency and independence. No qualities in twentieth-century America are more suspect than these."[42]

Senses are often dulled by living in noisy, ugly, urban environments. The occupants do not *know* what their forebears did in or about nature; and they know different things. "The *strength of oak, the ferocity of the tiger, the swiftness of the eagle*, are expressions which are out of place in the new world of form revealed to us by modern science."[43] Telescopes, computers, stop-action cameras, microscopes—all have made us expect more; we need more and more drama to excite us in nature and in visual images of it.

We have unquestionably come a long way from the time when nature was considered best if safely enclosed within a garden wall, or when it was studied because it revealed the workings of one or many deities. But we must not exaggerate the changes. They are after all modifications rooted in the past. People asked to give examples of natural beauty still offer, as they did in 1886, cottage gardens, sunsets, mountain peaks, and little harbors. And there is no lack of awe at the rim of the Grand Canyon or even speeding along the freeway coming down from the mountains into Salt Lake City—even if we don't call the scene 'sublime'.

The theoretical foundation for aesthetic assessment of the environment (and for everything else) rests in awareness of the *history* of values. Aesthetic delight is determined largely by traditions. Scientific studies of preference or viewer psychology will be truly objective only if they are placed within a humanistic context. I believe that this context leads us to see that 'the aesthetic' is delight taken in intrinsic qualities identified through historic and cultural traditions as worth attention and contemplation. It relates to problems in applied aesthetics of the sort that were surveyed in the previous chapter.

Humanistic Applied Aesthetics

The history of landscape values shows that aesthetic choices operate within a larger context of attitudes and conditions—that the grid to use one of J. B. Jackson's examples, is not just a logical, geometrical arrangement, but "the symbol of an agrarian Utopia composed of a democratic society of small landowners."[44] Such *symbols* appear and reappear, and understanding them requires attending to human history and experience.

Another way of contextualizing (and hence conceptualizing) aesthetic preferences is to use what has been called "humanistic psychology." This is the kind of study that Jackson calls for, one that looks not merely to see how landscapes "conform to an aesthetic ideal, but how they satisfy elementary needs: the needs for sharing some of those sensory experiences in a familiar place: popular songs, popular dishes, a special kind of weather supposedly found nowhere else, a special kind of sport or game played only here in this spot."[45] It was common during World War II for people in the most unlikely spots (remote swamps or deserts, for instance) to *complain* that their area was high on the list of places to be bombed by the enemy. This shows that people develop a sense of place—often based upon what people from other areas would consider insignificant at best. Humanistic psychological approaches to scenic values, unlike what can be called social scientific psychological studies, attempt to tie these values to other human needs and interests; indeed, they see people's interests as complexes that cannot be separated from one another.

John W. Sinton and Geraldine Gender interviewed people about their reactions to the New Jersey Pine Barrens.

> Almost every person interviewed expressed concern and had concrete perceptions about the use of the landscape, whether for cordwood, sawboards, hunting and fishing, berry picking, wildflowers, or picnicking. The complexity of residents' visions of their landscapes in fact presented a problem because they neither could nor would separate what they saw from how they lived in and worked with their environment.[46]

This integration of values and interests was poignantly described by the philosopher William James after a trip through the mountains of North Carolina. He saw repeatedly what he considered denuded squalor. But after talking with mountaineers who saw it as cleared civilization, he wrote,

> I instantly felt that I had been losing the whole inward significance of the situation. Because to me the clearings spoke of naught but denudation; I thought that to those whose sturdy arms and obedient axes had made them they could tell no other story. But, when *they* looked on the hideous stumps, what they thought of was personal victory. . . . In short, the clearing, which to me was a mere ugly picture on the retina, was to them a symbol redolent with moral memories and sang a very paean of duty, struggle, and success.[47]

James, as well as Sinton and Gender, are referring to likes and dislikes as they grow out of individual human interests—those special to a person or group. But humanistic psychologists seek to relate human preferences to *general* human needs—those found in us all.

In an intriguing book, *The Experience of Landscape,* Jay Appleton sets out to answer two questions: What is it we like about landscapes? and why? He believes that both art and science are needed if answers are to be adequate. Landscape involves both human and physical geography; so both human and physical processes must be studied. The grid system, to use an example referred to above, was an economic/social development that has affected the North American landscape as much as have physical processes.

This interconnectedness means that aestheticians should not ask, "What makes landscapes beautiful," because, Appleton fears, doing so begs important questions (for example, do beautiful trees and ponds share a common *property*?). It is better to ask, "What is the source of that pleasure which we derive from the contemplation of landscapes?"[48] Appleton thinks that the source of one's pleasure or displeasure is a belief that a physical environment does or does not meet one's needs. Appleton's theory is a form of "habitat theory," or, as he calls it, "prospect-refuge theory." According to the latter, we like environments that let us know where we are and that make us feel safe. We like places where we can see without being seen.

Specific variables operate in our experience of the landscape, according to Appleton.[49] These include the objects employed to symbolize prospects and refuges, the manner and intensity of the symbolization, the spatial arrangement of symbols, the equilibrium of prospect and refuge, and the physical media by which the arrangement is communicated to the observer. These variables provide a framework with which he hopes to refer to actual features of the environment and thereby provide "an explanatory link between aesthetic concepts and actual landscapes."[50]

A landscape can be described in terms of prospect and refuge, and, according to the theory, we like things that potentially provide refuge: trees, caves, rocks with clefts, vines, even mists. But too much of any of these presents a hazard that may restrict the advantage of prospect. Other things symbolically assume the advantages or disadvantages of refuges and hazards.

> . . . A tall bright cloud may be unattainable except by the imagination, and yet may suggest symbolically an extension of the field of vision, so apertures of all kinds which invite penetration only by the imagination can be to that extent effective. It is, after all, the imagination which is principally involved in experiencing the environment aesthetically. A woodland surrounded by a wall or fence is less satisfying than one which is open to the adjacent sward, because the impediment hazard frustrates the concept of the refuge. Even a straight boundary of a wood or forest suggests a 'margin' which is more forbidding than an irregular or 'frayed' edge with the occasional outlying tree or bush suggesting the protection of sporadic cover as gradual access or egress is achieved.[51]

Appleton believes that most positively and negatively evaluated landscape features can thus be explained in terms of vision and protection. Carpet vegetation offers prospect, as usually does water. Arboreal surfaces offer refuge. Sunsets and sunrises are popular because they are sources of prospect. At high noon the light is too blinding to allow scrutiny.

Obviously we can desire prospect and refuge only if we feel the presence of some hazard. The ideal landscape therefore must balance the two. A bending road, for instance, at once titillates and assures. The history of changing tastes, Appleton believes, can be read as "an acquired preference for particular methods of satisfying inborn desires."[52] People discover and develop new and different ways of seeing and hiding.

I doubt that Appleton's categories can be used to explain all scenic values, let alone all aesthetic preferences. I find the sunrise/sunset examples particularly farfetched. But I am indebted to him for the title of this chapter, and I most admire his realization that aesthetic involvement and appreciation are not segregated from the rest of our lives, and his own recognition of the limitations of the system. Like me, he is worried that the urge toward quantification displaces some genuine issues.

> The temptation to press ahead with attempts at quantification is obvious. It is also highly commendable academically as well as politically, to do so as soon as we possibly can; but we simply cannot go ahead with propriety until we understand much more about the mechanisms which induce us to experience satisfaction in one environmental situation and dissatisfaction in another. Only then can we be sure that we are measuring what matters. I make bold, therefore, to suggest that we are as likely at this stage to make progress toward the aesthetic evaluation of landscape by looking at places subjectively in terms of the hypotheses we have been considering, as by attaching numerical values to environmental objects whose function in the aesthetic process we do not properly understand.[53]

This attitude is shared by the leading humanistic geographer, Yi-Fu Tuan.[54] Like Appleton, Tuan interprets scenic values by relating them to other human needs, by associating perceiving with purposeful activity. Different purposes and attitudes assure different aesthetic valuations, he argues. Visitors and residents, for example, will perceive things differently, as will people with different cultural foundations. Tuan believes the Navaho and Zuni exemplify cultural differences.

> Both cultures admit the supremacy of the sun, share a common color symbolism, and embrace the sacred number four; but unlike the Zuni the Navaho people have no calendrical sequence that regulates ceremonial life and ensures the steady flow of blessings. The two people interpret the categories 'pretty' and 'ugly' differently. 'Pretty' to the Zuni is a picture of abundance and well-being that is the fruits of labor. For the Navaho it is a vision of green, a summery landscape that supports life. 'Ugly' to the Zuni means the difficulties inherent in livelihood and the maliciousness of human nature. The Navaho, on the other hand, tend to see 'ugly' as the description of the natural order: it stirs memories of hardship, parched land, illness, accident, and aliens.[55]

Although the two views are not totally inconsistent, they are different. Asking members of the two groups to assign numerical scores to a particular scene would reveal little.

Kenneth Clark has suggested that pure aesthetic response is very short-lived. "I fancy that one cannot enjoy a pure aesthetic sensation (so-called) for longer than one can enjoy the smell of an orange, which in my case is less than two minutes; but one must look attentively at a great work of art for longer than that, and the value of historical criticism is that it keeps the attention fixed on the work while the senses have time to get a second wind."[56] Tuan believes that this is also true of our appreciative attention span with respect to the environment. It is short and needs rejuvenating. "However intense, [it] is fleeting unless one's eyes are kept to it for some other reason, either the recall of historical events that hallowed the scene or the recall of its underlying reality in geology and structure."[57] My belief is that segregating pure aesthetic response is at most very rare. There is undoubtedly a difference between the pleasures of playing badminton and playing bridge; but to separate and consider *only* the pleasure parts of these two phenomena, if possible at all, is difficult. To talk of separating the pleasure of seeing the Grand Canyon from consideration of its geological aspects strikes me as equally ill-conceived. Tuan seems to agree. 'Topophilia', the word he has used as the title of one of his books, refers to the complex of "delectable sensations" and "physical intimacy" associated with the experience of the landscape. One aspect of topophilia is aesthetic appreciation; another, for example, is patriotism.[58]

Conceding changes in taste, Tuan is more interested in pointing out a congruence of feelings across time and cultures. For example, serene countryside life—sitting under a tree by a spring—

seems to have had universal appeal. The following quotation from Theocritus, he thinks, could have been written at almost any time:

> Many of poplar and elm murmured above our heads, and I heard at hand the sacred water from the cave of the Nymphs fall plashing. On the shady boughs the dusky cicadas were busy with their chatter, and the tree-frog far off cried in the dense thornbakes. Larks and finches sang, the dove made moan, and bees flitted humming above the springs. All things were fragrant of rich harvest and of fruit time. Pears at our feet and apples at our side were rolling plentifully, and the branches hung down to the ground with their burden of sloes.[59]

This passage lacks any purely evaluative terms (of the sort Sibley would identify as aesthetic) but it clearly expresses delight—and the delight is undoubtedly partly aesthetic. Some environments have had a persistent appeal: seashores, valleys, and islands.[60] Attention to changing tastes should not blind us to this, Tuan argues.

The main theme of Tuan's work is urging readers to recognize that landscape values are part of attitude networks.

> Topophilia takes many forms and varies greatly in emotional range and intensity. It is a start to describe what they are: fleeting visual pleasure; the sensual delight of physical contact; the fondness for place because it is familiar, because it is home and incarnates the past, because it evokes pride of ownership or creation; joy in things because of animal health and vitality.[61]

Most people would pick only some of these values as aesthetic. But I believe, with Tuan, that they are connected. All are delights that have their locus and focus in intrinsic features of what is perceived.

The Particularity of Individual Aesthetic Response

Thus far in this chapter we have been looking at the writings of persons whom I have identified as humanists because they relate aesthetic preferences to a range of human needs and interests. To the extent that they are human, they are general or universal. But human experience is neither of these: it is particular. This might appear to create a problem.

Several aestheticians have argued that all aesthetic responses relate to particular objects or events, and that generalizations in the form of laws relating properties to judgments are not discoverable.[62] Putting that special argument aside for now, let us look instead at how *particularity* is seen as crucial by a number of writers who want to relate scenic values to overall human experience.

Some of them are dubious about the value of the sort of inventory study described in chapter 4 because they are sceptical about the uniform applicability of such lists.[63] Many of the sources of delight named by Tuan are described by others as accompanying a "sense of place," which entails a sense of a *particular place*. For example, John Ruskin describes a mountain scene at a particular time, "when the night mists first rise from off the plains," and he recalls the

> lake-like fields, as they float in level bays and winding gulfs about the islanded summits of the lower hills, untouched yet by more than dawn, colder and more quiet than a windless sea under the moon of midnight. . . . Wait a little longer, and you shall see those scattered mists rallying in the ravines, and floating toward you, along the winding valleys, till they couch in quiet masses, irridescent with the morning light, upon the broad breasts of the higher hills, whose leagues of massy undulation will melt back and back into that robe of material light, until they fade away, lost in its lustre, to appear again above, in the serene heaven, like a wild, bright, impossible dream, foundationless and inaccessible, their very bases vanishing in the insubstantial and mocking blue of the deep lakes below.[64]

Ruskin's prose may be too purple for some tastes, but it describes a specific experience that he had, and it is this that quantitative studies lack. He sees not merely mountains, but mountains at a particular time and place, and he responds to them as a particular person: this is at the heart of what matters. The sense of *a* place, *an* experience of *a* particular object or event always characterizes an aesthetic experience. It is what Andrew Wilton praises as Turner's "overiding object . . . to impress us first with the grandeur of nature, and second with the reality of that grandeur as experienced by human beings like ourselves, who live out their lives in the conditions he presents."[65] It is what makes the uniqueness of a scenic resource important, and what Fred Bosselman urges legislation to take account of.

> People who become aware of the special qualities of a particular place tend to broaden their consciousness of the special qualities of land in

general. Those who have recognized that their neighborhood has an individual character tend to see special qualities in other neighborhoods that they might not have perceived before.[66]

Valuing special, individual places is nowhere better expressed than in some rather less familiar *Lyrical Ballads* of William Wordsworth, "Poems on the Naming of Places." In a brief introduction he says that "where little incidences [have occurred], private and peculiar interest" is taken in places. Thus in a series of poems he assigns friends' names to spots. At once the sense of place is enhanced, and the spot takes on greater value. There is Emma's dell—a "wild place," and lovely Joanna's rock, and beloved Mary's beech. Assigning individuals' names contributes to a location's particularity. The shortest of the lyrics (no. 3) deserves quoting here.

> There is an Eminence,—of these our hills
> The last that parleys with the setting sun.
> We can behold it from our Orchard-seat,
> And, when at evening we pursue our walk
> Along the public way, this Cliff, so high
> Above us, and so distant in its height,
> Is visible, and often seems to send
> Its own deep quiet to restore our hearts.
> The meteors make of it a favorite haunt:
> The star of Jove, so beautiful and large
> In the mid heav'ns, is never half so fair
> As when he shines above it. 'Tis in truth
> The loneliest place we have among the clouds.
> And She who dwells with me, whom I have lov'd
> With such communion, that no place on earth
> Can ever be a solitude to me,
> Hath said, this lonesome Peak shall bear my Name.

Above I discussed the connection between traditions and language. Interests are reflected in the language of communities that share forms of life. As those interests change, so does the language. What is *common* to or shared by members of communities is generally reflected in and by what they say. However, languages also provide for particular experiences. Wordsworth's imaginative use of assigning proper names to places is one device for expressing his own, individual response. Another author, Henry James, applies a similar strategy when he criticizes misnaming—an activity that he thought concealed aesthetic value precisely because it suppressed crucial features. After twenty years' absence from the United States, Henry James returned and traveled around the country. His experiences are described in *The American Scene* (1905).

> You learn, after a little, not to insist on names—that it is not wise to inquire of them. And are happiest perchance when the answer is made you as it was made me by a neighbour, in a railway train, on the occasion of my greatly admiring, right and left of us, a tortuous brawling river. I had supposed it for a moment in my innocence, the Connecticut—which it decidedly was not. It was only, as appeared, a stream, *quelconque*, a stream without an identify. Better, somehow, than the adventure of a little later—my learning, too definitely, that another stream, ample, admirable, in every way distinguished, a stream worthy of Ruysdael or Salvator Rosa, was known but as the Farmington River. This I could in no manner put up with—this taking by the greater of the comparatively common little names of the less.[67]

Misnaming is only one way in which aesthetically important features are sometimes made inaccessible. These features may also remain concealed if an individual does not feel engaged by a scene. For example, Arnold Berleant proposes a special kind of environmental aesthetics in some ways reminiscent of Appleton's. But he uses *invitational* in place of *prospect/refuge*. One can find, he argues, numerous instances of invitational qualities in the visual arts; various features are used whose purpose is eliciting a participatory response on the part of the viewer. For example, in Cimabue and Giotto, the steps leading to the dais on which the Virgin, Child, and Angels sit are left empty—thus allowing the viewer to mount them imaginatively. We find unplayed musical instruments with their necks facing out invitingly toward viewers. We are forced to peer over the shoulders of crowds in order to see what is beyond. "Paintings of landscapes offer a particularly effective illustration of environmental action, for they continue the same kind of features the environmental designers must fashion and thus become instructive models."[68] Roads, for instance, provoke the imagined movement of our bodies into the space of the painting. Literature as well as painting is full of paths that invite loitering and provide a place to stop and look at the surroundings. Like Appleton, Berleant believes that preferred spaces are inviting, that they have "characteristics to which perceptual consciousness is receptive and to which it responds."[69] In the environment, "what is important is not physical traits but perceptual ones, not how things are but how they are experienced."[70]

Figure 1. Crystal Court, IDS Center, Minneapolis, Minnesota.

Presence or absence of "invitation" can, I think, be used to explain some successes and failures. In the downtown area in Minneapolis there are two courts—the Crystal Court in the highly praised IDS Center, and one in the new, highly criticized City Center (see figs. 1 and 2). The first invites participation, the other demands that you get through it as quickly as possible. Escalators in the first invite taking a look around; in the second they are obviously located to demand maximum exposure to shop entrances. The first provides a sense of place; the second a sense of noplace or anyplace. The designers of the City Center show no awareness of the special urban location, so visitors have none either.

Figure 2. Court, City Center, Minneapolis, Minnesota.

So far I have looked at the importance of paying attention to the role of language, human needs, and individuality in determining the nature of the aesthetic. Throughout I have referred to the role of *traditions* and it is now time to examine this more closely.

Traditions

How we perceive and experience our surroundings depends upon our history and our humanity—the things we value. Paul Shepherd claims that efforts to save the Green River in Dinosaur Park were successful largely because it

> was publicized by pictures showing whole families—children, old ladies, ordinary persons—as they emerged from rubber boats onto the green, gardenlike fringe at the mouth of the canyon. Their triumph over the perilous mountain valley had been possible because of strong young men, who, like Tannhauser, had forsaken the humdrum world.[71]

J. B. Jackson would say that such pictures work because they "remind us that we belong," and "foster experiences and relations." Hence, they are valued and valuable.[72]

Henry James argues, in the travelogue from which I quoted above, that failure to consider traditions results in ugliness. Environmental planners would benefit from reading James's thoughts about what accounts for the sordidness of many areas. Immigrants, uprooted from their old values, had not yet had time to develop replacement values, he thought. This he found evident not just from slums encountered, but from huge, expensive residences as well. Both "have nothing to do with continuity, responsibility, transmission."[73] He has this to say about skyscrapers:

> They never begin to speak to you, in the manner of the builded majesties of the world as we have heretofore known such—towers or fortresses or palaces—with the authority of things of permanence or even of things of long duration. One story is good only till another is told, and skyscrapers are the last word of economic ingenuity only till another word be written. . . . Such a structure as the comparatively windowless belltower of Giotto, in Florence, looks supremely serene in its beauty. You don't feel it to have risen by the breath of an interested passion that, restless beyond all passions, is for ever seeking more pliable forms. Beauty has been the object of its creator's idea,

and, having found beauty, it has found the form in which it splendidly rests.[74]

The foundation in tradition required for beauty is lacking in much modern urban space, and a preeminent economic concern has failed to provide sufficient basis for delightful human experience.

> The reflecting surfaces, of the ironic, of the epic order, suspended in the New York atmosphere, have yet to show symptoms of shining out, and the monstrous phenomena themselves, meanwhile, strike me as having, with their immense momentum, got the start, got ahead of, in proper parlance, any possibility of poetic or dramatic capture. That conviction came to me most perhaps while I gazed across at the special skyscraper that overhangs poor old Trinity [church] to the north—a south face as high and wide as the mountainwall that drops the Alpine avalanche, from time to time, upon the village, and the village spire, at its foot; the interest of this case being above all, as I learned, to my stupefaction, in the fact that the very creators of the extinguisher are the churchwardens themselves, or at least the trustees of the church property.[75]

Distance from traditions here resulted in loss of contact with that which is supposed to give meaning to the lives of the churchwardens. In the final chapter I will explain how I think the concept of the meaning of life integrates people's aesthetic interests with other concerns.

Christopher Lunnard insists that painters have a special ability that allows them to provide what James feels is lacking in so much of the American scene, for " . . . the painter may yet see deeper into the needs and obligations of society in maintaining a cultural fabric for the future than we are apt to acknowledge."[76] Reading Charles Dickens or Upton Sinclair is at least as valuable as inventory assessments or semantic pair-tests if we want to know what is wrong with our urban surroundings. "[S]ystems of visual notation, view 'envelopes', pressure points, and other analytical aids, provide rudimentary guides for government functionaries. Nothing takes the place of the *insight* of truly humanistic observers who are moved by the forces of nature and who can invest even a humble forest trail with mythic and classical imagery."[77]

By now it is apparent that I believe that the weaknesses of environmental assessment and planning rest on failure to ground the values on traditions. It is not an accident that Berleant uses Cimabue and Giotto as examples of what he thinks scenic planners should attend to, or that Shephard refers to Tannhauser, or that Aldous Huxley at one time decried the mistreatment of nature because it would eliminate the basis of half of English poetry.[78] Assessment of scenic values, as Appleton, Tuan, and others have shown, can be theoretically grounded in humanistic traditions. Indeed, there is a sense in which humanistic foundations are implicitly present in most of the theorists at whom we have looked—often in spite of themselves.

It is not an accident, for instance, that the items in the inventory lists in chapter 4 are what they are. All of them come directly or indirectly from historic aesthetic traditions. David Pitt, describing landscape assessment techniques, says that "historically, these terms, dimensions, and procedures have been intuitively defined by designers and managers. . . . The dimensions remain subjective and unsubstantiated."[79] He is wrong. These intuitions are not innate, nor merely *intuitive*. Almost all come from people who have had design courses in which they learned a traditional vocabulary. Their responses may be individual and personal, but to say that they are thus unsubstantiated (merely subjective) is to commit the quantitative objective fallacy.

Lack of quantifiability does not imply lack of objectivity. A better test of objectivity is one suggested by Anthony Savile. "A report will remain objective if it is sensitive to argument, if it holds out a hope of our coming to an agreement about the appropriate description to apply, and if it is responsive to the evidence that counts for and against it when the evidence arrives."[80] The fact that we *decide* what features matter in no way by itself proves that agreement is not possible. Indeed, we must always *decide* what counts as evidence. Savile continues:

> When we are concerned with cases of natural beauty it is the beholder who selects the parameters of judgement. . . . In the case of the work of art they are laid down in the shape of problem and style chosen by the artist, and here the beholder has to follow, not give the lead. So in this sense natural beauty *is* in the eye of the beholder and we have nothing to say about the choice he makes. But it would be wrong to think that it follows from this that judgements of natural beauty are not true or false. This they remain, but relative to the choices that are made.[81]

My claim is that the necessary choices are made based upon traditions and thus are not arbitrary, as has often been maintained. That some features are relevant is determined traditionally. And they provide a base for real argument and for the possibility of coming to agreement. Speaking the same languages assures that there will be a basis for agreement. As William Lycan and Peter Machamer argue, the words we use to describe aesthetic objects are learned in the context of language per se, not as a special, isolated vocabulary. People learn words and what they are used for simultaneously.[82] We learn that landscapes are to be described as "beautiful" when they can also be described as "abounding with white water" or "lush with trees."

Consider 'unity', for example. It appears on several inventory lists, although in most cases with little, if any, justification for putting it there. Justification exists, however. 'Unity' is one of the terms that appears frequently, from Aristotle on, in the history of Western aesthetics and art criticism. It is not always obvious what the traditional writers mean; like all terms with a long history this one is ambiguous and vague. But generally it refers to the existence of an organizing structure or pattern that connects the parts of an object or event.

John Burke says of successful biographies that they develop from a selection of "those details that matter. . . . The biographer must keep an eye out, not for trivia, but for the significances of trivia."[83] Such activity—organization of a welter of detail into satisfying patterns—is at the heart of aesthetic activity as our culture knows it. "The less an artifact interests our eye as imitation, the more it must delight our eye as pattern."[84] 'Unity' is entrenched in our traditions. Assessors of the environment could make profitable use of this principle in the development and justification of their programs—particularly in law courts where precedent is so important. For by pointing to entrenchment within traditions, they show that considerations are genuinely aesthetic.

One important conclusion is this: *Experience is probably aesthetic if it is described using terms that appear within the traditions of art criticism* (no more than probability can be expected here, as is always the case with empirical judgments).

R. J. Tetlow and S. R. J. Sheppard made an inventory for assessing spatial dimension and character in a study of a northeastern coal area that includes, among other items, cross-section complexity, cross-section contrast, skyline, and floor.[85] These things are part of the mass of detail that may form patterns that delight the viewer. But items on any inventory must be justified. The enormously complex charts that inventory producers present must be tied to humanistic traditions of valuing and valuation if we are to see their aesthetic relevance.

A laudable step in this direction has been taken by a group in a study of the role of water in the landscape.[86] Here the authors relate a lengthy inventory of water features (boundary definition, prominence, edge features, etc.) to Monroe Beardsley's analysis of the aesthetic in terms of unity and regional vividness. They acknowledge the necessity of combining features in such a way that the individual's experience is unified and intensified.[87]

A similar attempt is made by Ian C. Laurie, who tries to tie assessment to the existing practices of designers, artists, and critics.[88] He suggests the use of unity, composition, variety, contrast, balance, form, mass, shape, and so on. If landscape produces aesthetic response as art does, he argues, these are the things that must be considered; for these are the things we find in discussions of art.

In general, one knows whether someone is assessing an object or event aesthetically by seeing if he or she talks the right way—by listening to the words used to describe and evaluate the experience and its objects. 'Unity' is one good clue. There are, of course, others. Herbert E. Echelberger reports in a study he carried out, that when people were given an opportunity to comment—in addition to completing a semantic pair-testing assessment—many mentioned unusual light and shadow contrasts as contributing positively to their experience. This strongly indicates that theirs was aesthetic pleasure. On the other hand, people who pointed to the "quality of forest management" were probably pleased in other ways. Others referred to "high and low slash and obstructions to walking on trails" as "detracting from their experience."[89] This would be an indication of aesthetic detraction only if the assessors went on to explain how slashing destroys or interrupts the perception of patterns rather than, for example, ease of getting to the restrooms.

The scepticism often felt and expressed with regard to rationalizing aesthetic values is unfounded. Colin Stillman, for example, worries that "there can be no objective, interpersonal, intergroup value in a landscape. Nor can there be any objective, interpersonal, intergroup determination of what is natural beauty. Achievement of a consensus on natural beauty is an indication of dominance within the community concerned."[90] But we have seen that there is some agreement objectively based in cultural traditions.[91]

If I am right that we can tell an experience is aesthetic by seeing whether art historical and critical terminology is used to describe it, then there is an important sense in which the aesthetic depends upon art and not vice versa. This is not to say that the artistic experience always comes (and came historically) before aesthetic experience. But identification of an aesthetic experience demands the availability of an artistic vocabulary and this depends upon prior experience of art.

It is a commonplace that works of art influence the way later artists see things and the way individuals see and interpret things. " . . . Cezanne's vision of Provence influenced landscape painters all over the world. I have even see Japan rendered in the Cezanne manner, with Fujiyama turned into Mont-Stainte-Bictoire."[92] As has already been pointed out the very term *landscape* initially referred not to nature but to paintings. We want to see in real life what we have already seen in pictures. " . . . The visual arts paved the way for the enjoyment of reality which came later, and gradually educated people into lingering among the majesties of nature."[93] This is only one example of the way in which new kinds of art and newly acquired aesthetic values develop.

I have argued that we must look to artists to help us to see what is valuable in nature. But there is a stronger claim here—one put succinctly in a Scottish landscape report:

> It is axiomatic that unless [the raw materials of our environment—landforms, plants, animals, atmosperhic effects] are first analysed and then synthesized into a new unity, they cannot be regarded as works of art, and hence cannot enter the area of formal aesthetic criticism.[94]

We have seen some claims that what people value in scenery is that they have been conditioned to like by paintings, travel brochures, postcards, and so on. The assertion is often made in such a way that it implies there is something wrong about this, that people should value something else. What else *could* they value? Aesthetic value makes sense only within such practices.

Suppose you could send someone *innocent*—someone who has never seen paintings or postcards—out into the landscape. Ask him or her to indicate preferences. How could we know that the preferences are aesthetic except by relying on concepts taken from art history and criticism? How do the people who derogate "postcard conditioning" develop their aesthetic preferences? Even if there is a psychological basis for human response to the landscape, we can only discover that such a response has occurred in a particular case if the individual can use the appropriate language to describe it.

There are problems with listening to what people say. Some are more articulate than others; some will be likely to say only the sort of things I heard one gentle woman say of Saint-Chapelle's windows: "Aren't they lovely!" *Lovely* may strike many as insipid or trite; it is a good clue nonetheless that the speaker's experience was aesthetic.

What I've said is in no way intended to deny that people stood on mountain tops and enjoyed sunsets before there were works of art. But one cannot know that theirs was 'aesthetic' pleasure unless they use aesthetic terms, and aesthetic terms come largely from the history of art.

There are, perhaps, purely perceptual pleasures—backrubs or sweet smells. But the sensuous part of aesthetic delight (a topic in the next chapter) should not be misconstrued. Sunsets do not soothe our eyes the way a damp cloth does. Aesthetic pleasures are more reflective or cognitive. They involve comparing, contrasting, fitting things into patterns, and figuring out meanings and connections. Perceptual pleasures become aesthetic when they are, in a sense, conceptualized; and the conceptualization in our culture has been provided primarily by art and discussions of it. It has not happened, for the most part, with touch, taste, and odor. There are no art forms for these, and this is why they are usually not considered the locus of aesthetic pleasure. As E. H. Gombrich has written, "Do we not tend to judge human bodies by their resemblance to those Greek statues that have become traditionally identified with the canons of beauty?"[95] The canons of art have usually provided the standards of aesthetic excellence.

In some art forms, (music and the visual arts, for instance), perception per se retains a key position. In others, the kind of conceptualization that turns physical pleasure into aesthetic pleasure is dominant. Indeed, in some forms of literature perceptual aspects seem almost to have disappeared.

I believe that all of this has practical implications. We can ask whether a highway constructed in a given area will destroy views that have traditionally delighted viewers. It will do this if it covers up a creek, destroys trees, or scars cliffs. It will not if it runs along a creek, or among trees, or allows the view of gently sloping, tree-covered hills. A fountain in Minneapolis's City Center would induce pleasure because people like water. We can devise a test for quality that would replace asking, "On a scale of one to ten, how good do you think this scene is?" with "Does it have intrinsic properties identified traditionally as sources of delight?" The latter is an objective question that admits an objective answer. It is a question that courts might find helpful.

When something worthy of attention—the sunset seen from a mountain top, for instance—is considered within and described in terms that come from traditions of artistic discussion and treatment, it is aesthetic. And this is what is measured when we measure what matters aesthetically.

Some readers may object that my heavy use of *tradition* results in a characterization of the aesthetic that is conservative, elitist, and fascist. But seeing traditions as necessarily involving elitist domination is a distortion. In the West, the history of art can arguably be described as the materialistic production of one group of powerful upper- or middle-class white males after another. Transmission of culture has largely consisted in arbitrary, dilettantish, and faddish attention given to "great art"—"masterpieces" identified by a more or less educated power elite.

There is, unfortunately, some truth to this description. However, the theory I lay out in the next part of this book can be interpreted to avoid elitism. *Tradition,* as I use the term, embraces love of a Michelangelo as well as a grandmother's quilt, enjoyment of Scott Joplin as well as Chopin, cherishing of nursery rhymes and limericks as well as Shakespeare. Our culture's traditions include both the *high* and the *low,* and if measuring what matters demands attention to traditions it does not necessarily follow that only the history of white, powerful males will be taken seriously. An unintended but happy feature of my consideration of landscape values in this connection is, I think, the extent to which aesthetic enjoyment of nature seems to escape class, race, or gender specificity.

At the same time, my theory will not preclude the existence of standards. I insist that aesthetic judgment cannot take place without reference to ideals traditionally rooted and transmitted. Reference to tradition serves to connect objects and events and places to the values of an audience, and thus increases the chances that a meaningful aesthetic experience will occur. A couple of examples may explain the sort of thing I have in mind.

About five years ago a piece of public art (see fig. 3) appeared in a public space across the street from a Minneapolis beach. It is a colorful, playful work, and people I have observed seem to enjoy it—particularly the rings that sway in the wind. But they are confused. They wonder what it is supposed to be. Most conclude that it is a dog or a dinosaur. Supporters of the latter argue the rings represent the ridge along a dinosaur's back and suggest the sluggish movement of those prehistoric beasts.

Quite by accident I learned (from the friend of a friend of the

Figure 3. Bruce Stillman, Untitled. *(Courtesy of Ackerberg and Associates, Minneapolis, Minnesota.)*

artist) that the statue is in fact a Viking ship. Invariably when I tell this to passersby, they say, "Oh yes, now I see. That's much better!"

Why is it much better to view the work as a Viking ship than as a dog or dinosaur? I believe it is because the experience is fuller when the work is connected to traditions. Not only does it make more sense to have a boat near a beach, but this particular sort of boat is related to the general history of the European discovery of North America and the particular Scandinavian heritage of Minnesota. Viking ships *mean* something to viewers in Minneapolis because of their traditions. These are not elitist references; this symbol, once connected for viewers, is readily and generally accessible.

When the sculpture appeared, it did so with no explanation of who had done it or who had decided to put it there. Certainly people in the neighborhood were not consulted. I think the private group responsible for its placement made a serious mistake not to have involved the citizenry by at least informing them of their rationale. A small sign identifying the artist and giving the work's title would have invited viewers to connect the work with their traditions. This is not to *force* viewers to see the object as a Viking ship; people who want to are certainly free to view it as a dinosaur. *Invitations* are not demands; they can be issued without restricting freedom.

A program at the Minneapolis Institute of Arts in August 1986 provided an excellent example of the integration of the aesthetic with other traditions. A Thorvaldsen statue (see fig. 4), a film series, and a lecture series centered on the subject of raptors (birds of prey). These birds have figured in cultural traditions from ancient Egypt to the present. A prominent Raptor Research and Rehabilitation Program at the University of Minnesota has made these birds locally significant. The symbolic role of the birds in American Indian as well as Christian, Buddhist, and Judaic legends provides nonelitist but traditional grounding for peoples

Figure 4. Bertil Thorvaldsen, *Ganymede and the Eagle*, (Courtesy of the Minneapolis Institute of Arts, Minneapolis, Minnesota)

Figure 5. Viking Souvenir.

with various cultural backgrounds. The museum's program was focused on "the lure of flight"—"compelling myths about birds, the psychological significance of the human yen to fly as well as the real ecological predicaments of birds, especially raptors."[96]

Aesthetic planners would do well to use such a program as a model to prove that they have taken due account of "aesthetic and cultural amenities" in their studies. If intrinsic properties of areas can be tied to traditional *lures*—and thus to reasons we value attending to and reflecting upon them—objective evidence exists for claiming the existence of aesthetic value in a nonelitist fashion.

Connection to traditions is not sufficient to ensure that something will have aesthetic value. Standards with respect to the intrinsic properties of objects will also matter. Traditions alone will not support the "schlocky" viking in figure 5. It may be cute, but it does not merit serious and sustained aesthetic attention or reflection.

I began chapter 4 with a summary and criticism of a particular study. It is only fair to ask myself if I could do better. In this chapter I have indicated what I believe is required if we are truly to measure what matters. In the next chapter I shall explain what I think 'aesthetic' means. Then I shall go back to the problem that Jones & Jones were asked to solve and see whether I can improve upon their work.

6
A Characterization of 'the Aesthetic'

Chapter 5 emphasizes the importance of considering scenic assessment and evaluation as part of the larger context of human experience. But I insisted that aesthetic experiences are particular. They are individual reactions to specific rivers or forest, symphonies or statues, cathedrals or rural cottages. My insistence that a particular or individual response be present in every aesthetic experience, and thus my characterization of the aesthetic, as such, is connected to a main stream in modern aesthetics.

The term 'aesthetica' was coined in 1750 by A. G. Baumgarten for a study on "inferior cognition."[1] He hoped to do for sense perception (the Greek *aistheikos*) what he thought logicians had done for reasoning. Instead, he concentrated on *feeling* as the core of aesthetic experience, and it is this sense that was initially, and has remained, at the core of the word's use. Throughout the history of aesthetics, philosophers have pointed to the subjectivity of aesthetic experience. Many have argued that before any aesthetic attribute can be ascribed to an object, a *subject* must respond to it. Immanuel Kant actually equated the subjective with the aesthetic.[2] More recently, Ruby Meager has emphasized the subjective aspect of aesthetic experience, and she believes that it precludes any general or public aesthetic ranking.[3]

Although I think both Kant and Meager go too far, it is evident that the aesthetic involves a personal response. Roy R. Behrens makes this point cleverly by drawing attention to the opposition between 'aesthetic' and 'anaesthetic'; an anaesthetic works precisely because it dulls or blocks out an individual response.[4]

I have called the individual response in aesthetic experience 'delight'. This is not a wholly felicitous term. In the first place, it is a positive term, and there are negative aesthetic responses—"aesthetic pains," as I have called them elsewhere.[5] I believe we are responding aesthetically (albeit negatively) when we dislike hearing orchestras play out of key, or are irritated at reading trite doggerel. I think, however, that a positive account of the aesthetic—in terms of a favorable, positive delight—will rather easily explain negative reactions.

In the second place, 'delight' is not a term without a history, nor will it stand for the same thing for everyone. I use it simply to refer to an individual subject's response that is interested and positive. People enjoy and want to have aesthetic experiences.

Delight always has an object—a thing or event or person, or something abstract like an idea. Both the discussions of control (chapter 3) and of measuring what matters (chapter 5) suggest that *in aesthetic experience certain features of the object are attended to and appreciated*. Control allows us to pay attention to some things rather than others, and the ones that count as aesthetic are identifiable within our cultural traditions. What counts, I argue (as many others have done—supporting, I believe, my dependence upon traditions), are always *intrinsic* features.[6]

Perception and Aesthetic Experience

Reliance upon intrinsic features by people engaged in practical aesthetic assessment shows how much they share with art critics. For the larger part of this century, the things in an object—text, painting, song, and so on—have played a prominent role in art theories generally. This has been especially true for formalist theories. All the many versions of formalism have in common the insistence that perceivable qualities, not extrinsic information about works, are the only features truly relevant to aesthetic interpretation and evaluation.

> Now I venture to say that no one who has a real understanding of the art of painting attaches any importance to what we call the subject of a picture—what is represented. To one who feels the language of pictorial form all depends upon *how* it is presented, nothing on what.[7]

Murray Krieger believes that formalism has its roots in Kant's emphasis on the subjective, noncognitive character of aesthetic response. In formalism, content is minimized and interest in a thing on its own terms (unrelated to either scientific or ethical interests) is maximized.[8] For many writers in the twentieth century, form has counted for everything, content for nothing. Thus, attention has been exclusively directed, or urged toward, features like color, shape, repetition, symmetry, contrast, balance, rhythm—things right there in front of us.

In the most extreme versions of formalism, there is a drive to quantification as pronounced as any that we came across among the social scientific aesthetic assessors discussed in chapter 4. In 1933, George Birkhoff published *Aesthetic Measure*, in which a formula for the aesthetic value of polygons was proposed:

$$M = \frac{O}{C} = \frac{V + E + R - HV - F}{C}$$

where

M = aesthetic measure
O = order
C = complexity (number of indefinitely extended lines which contain all the sides of the polygon, e.g., quadrilateral = 4, Greek cross = 8)
V = vertical symmetry
E = equilibrium
R = rotational symmetry
HV = relation to horizontal-vertical network (preference is given to the square over the diamond)
F = unsatisfactory form (e.g., too small distance from vertices to other vertices or to sides, lack of symmetry, etc.)

And on his system

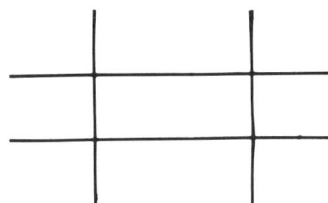

gets a score of 1.5 and

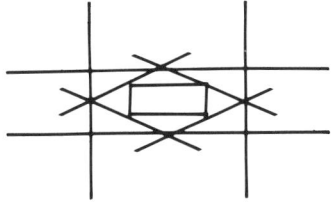

gets a score of only 0.17.[9] Birkhoff reported that he got a consensus with respect to these scores in his classes; but for the most part his arguments are ad hominem and one expects as much intimidation—even if unintentional—as unbiased observation.

What Birkhoff emphasized in his study was the extent to which aesthetic experience involves perceptual response. The role of perception has been highlighted by aestheticians in other ways. Arnold Isenberg, for example, argues that criticism is directed at perceptual activity. The way that critics communicate, according to Isenberg, should not be confused with the way scientists communicate, nor with the way in which we communicate in everyday conversation, when the intent of discourse is to bring about a belief on the part of a reader or hearer. Critics do not attempt to *convince* hearers of anything in the sense of getting them to believe something; hence, they do not give, or should not be construed as giving, an *argument*. What they try to induce is perception, not belief.

Suppose I say to my husband, "The Smiths must still be out of town. I haven't heard the children screaming and their mailbox is overflowing." Here my purpose is to convince him by means of a lawlike generalization: usually when you don't hear the children and the mail hasn't been picked up, the Smiths are out of town. More sophisticated, firmly verified laws connect scientific observations and conclusions. But the same sort of reasoning via lawlike generalizations marks communication whenever it has as its goal the bringing about of belief. If that is not the goal, then the reasoning model will not apply to nor adequately capture what is going on.

Critics themselves, says Isenberg, have misunderstood what they are about, and have wasted time and energy trying to discover the lawlike generalizations ("norms," he calls them) that would link factual observations and aesthetic judgments.[10] Critical communication, when properly understood, seeks rather to persuade hearers to notice or perceive something. Critics point to the suspenseful battle scenes or the white water not because they want you to believe that the novel is great or the river beautiful, but because they want you to notice or perceive these features. Many formalists share Isenberg's basic attitude: aesthetic experience is essentially a matter of reacting to what can be directly seen or heard; it is not a matter of forming judgments on the basis of extrinsic information, nor of coming to nonaesthetic beliefs about an object or event. It is the *how*, not the *what*, that matters.[11]

The insistence upon the primacy of formal or perceptual properties or upon the noncognitive nature of the aesthetic can lead to mistakes that we cannot ignore. But Isenberg and the formalists correctly agree that in aesthetic experience an individual's response is required before a description or judgment can be made. This is why the *particularity* that we discussed above is crucial; and it is why perceptual activity has so often been considered crucial to aesthetic experience. Critical communication, to use Isenberg's phrase, works only when a viewer actually perceives for oneself. Aesthetic features are those that can be delighted in only when an observer actually perceives the thing or event that they are features of. As David Pole writes, "Michelangelo indeed makes me see, but also feel; and the two things are hardly to be distinguished."[12]

This makes aesthetic features quite different from other sorts of features. I can delight that your behavior is good, that my bank account is growing, that a polio vaccine was discovered before my son was born, that the sum of the squares on the sides of a right triangle is equal to the square on the hypotenuse. But my delight is aesthetic only if I am actually in the presence of (and can actually perceive) the object of my delight. This is part of what it means to say that aesthetic features are *intrinsic*.[13]

I think Sibley was trying to get at this when he made such central use of 'taste'. The aesthetic is what must be perceived, although Sibley went astray when he went on to insist that the perception requires a special sense or sensitivity. On a March day, of what was clearly and depressingly not yet the end of a very bad Minnesota winter (the worst on record by many accounts), I looked out of a window and saw a male cardinal sitting in a leafless bush still half-buried by dirty white snow. The red was dazzling—and I am convinced that anyone who had spent that winter in Minnesota, not only those with special sensitivity, would have delighted in the sight. It was for me, and I am sure it would have been for others, a genuine aesthetic experience. Anyone with normal vision could have seen that bird against that background. What is required for aesthetic experience is not vision of a special kind, but a readiness or ability to stop and enjoy the sensation.

Reflection and Aesthetic Experience

As we have seen, the formalists insist on the exclusive relevance of properties like color, shape, sounds—essentially perceptual or sensuous qualities. The motivation for this is their fear that going outside a work will invariably result in a nonaesthetic experience, and since the perceptual qualities are located *in* the work, attention solely to these will prevent people from drifting into areas that are distracting. Sensual properties certainly are important: the red of the bird against the bleak, grey background, the play of light as it is reflected from the surface of a lake, harmonious progressions of chords, lush repetitions of soft consonants. We do delight in the arrangement of shapes or colors in Rembrandt's groups of people, or Cezanne's groups of apples, as well as in forests and mountains.

But undue and exclusive attention to perceptual properties can lead to a mistake. This mistake can be thought of as exaggerating the *in* in 'intrinsic'. We take aesthetic delight not only in things that we *perceive,* but also in things we *conceive;* it arises from *reflection* as well as from *perception.*

That this is true becomes obvious, I think, if we listen to what people say when they describe their aesthetic delight. (And one should be careful that refusal to listen is not due solely to arrogant confidence in the superiority or exclusive purity of one's own responses.) I have already quoted from a study for New Jersey pine barrens in which the people interviewed were unable to separate "what they saw from how they live."[14] Aesthetic response is much more complex than simple sensuous delight. A person who says, "It reminds me of the days when my grandmother took me berrypicking," does not necessarily prove that the speaker's reaction to the scene is nonaesthetic.

In another environmental study, the authors report that people say they like a *natural* scene. But what is natural differs for wildlands, rural areas, and urban scenes, and hence use of the term involves a conception as well as a perception of the object of attention.

> Naturalness is a concept which has no specific appearance in form; line, texture, and color or naturalness changes from place to place. These formal visual properties seem not to account for the power of naturalness as a predictor of visual preference. Because perception and cognition are not discrete events, landscape meaning may be more important than specific appearance in understanding people's visual preference for natural landscapes.[15]

This observation matches that of more recent aestheticians and critics who have increasingly rejected what they have come to consider the unduly restrictive nature of formalist theories. More and more attention is being given to the way in which the context of artistic or aesthetic objects affects our responses. Even a strong formalist like Birkhoff admitted that associative connotations are part of aesthetic response (although he ignored them in favor of what he apparently viewed as the more objective perceptual qualities of objects).[16] It is interesting to compare his *psychological* work of 1933 with E. H. Gombrich's of 1979, *The Sense of Order, A Study of the Psychology of Decorative Art*.[17] Both men are interested in the psychological foundations of preferences, but for Gombrich this demands attention to human experience per se, to habits, purposes, desires for information and order, and general interests that dominate our activities, such as interest in human form. Psychological studies of our delight in fairy tales, for example those done by Bruno Bettelheim, indicate how complex even the most apparently simple or childish pleasures in art works are.[18]

Since perception is often accompanied by cognitive knowledge, an adequate account of delight cannot be based exclusively on perception (the movement called "conceptual art" has stressed this point). Theories that attend solely to "constructions or arrangements which are primarily addressed to the eye and which are characterized by the structural features of unity with variety," as Roy R. Behrens defines "visual esthetic design,"[19] must be extended to include what we think. Objects can be addressed to the mind as well as to the eye (or other senses) and still be aesthetic. For example, one may need to think about color as well as to perceive particular colors in order to fully appreciate some paintings.

Much credit for drawing our attention to the role of context in aesthetic experience is due to Marxist theorists and art critics, who never accepted the formalist strictures. John Berger's fascinating essay on the growth of oil painting in the sixteenth and seventeenth centuries is one of the best examples of contextual criticism. He argues that what made the medium important cannot be separated from what made other things important for the audience and buyers of these paintings. As possessions become more and more important, it was essential that paintings take on tangibility—and oil served this need beautifully.[20] Berger may exaggerate the point, but certainly one cannot read his article without looking in a new way at the products of the period he discusses. Think, for example, about the function of the scores of second-rate paintings found in castles and manor houses.

"We only see what we look at. To look is an act of choice."[21] We will not see everything that's there to be seen in a work of art any

Figure 6. Frans Hals, *Regentesses of the Old Men's Alms House.* (Courtesy of the Frans Halsmuseum, Haarlem, The Netherlands.)

more than we will see everything that's there in the world. What we look at and for is directed by who we are and what we value and what our culture is and what it tells us to look at and for. Berger invites us to look at Frans Hals's representation of governesses of an alms' house as follows (see fig. 6): It was painted by "a destitute old painter who has lost his reputation and lives off public charity; he examines them through the eyes of a person who must nevertheless try to be objective, i.e. must try to surmount the way he sees as a pauper."[22] Here he is clearly *not* asking us to use our sensation alone, or our *taste*.

Kendall Walton has argued that we must know (and this entails having a conception of) the category (e.g., sonnet or lyric) to which a work belongs before we can judge or appreciate it.[23] Roger Scruton believes that this is particularly obvious in architecture, where the pleasure taken in an object depends on a description of it. As public objects, buildings become the loci of many meanings.[24] They display not just forms and patterns, but functions, political significance, attitudes toward human activity, and so on.

Similarly, deconstructionist theorists and critics have drawn attention to context—indeed, they believe not only that what is there to be sensed is insufficient to account for our responses, but that we do not even have enough if we add reflection. In addition to considering what is *there*, we have to sensitize ourselves to what is *not there*. "The work's insights . . . are deeply related to its blindnesses: what it does not say, and *how* it does not say it, may be as important as what it articulates; what seems absent, marginal or ambivalent about it may provide a central clue to its meanings."[25] Evasiveness, for example, can be important—as in *Sons and Lovers*, where Paul Morel never voices explicit, let alone bitter, criticism of his mother.

Aesthetic experience is as much a matter of reflection as perception. It may be that sometimes we just delight and perceive, for example, simply enjoy a particular shade of blue. But even this is not a pure physical pleasure; our eyes do not feel good the way our backs feel good when they are rubbed, for instance. A good symphony does not make our ears feel good the way a shrill sound makes them feel bad. For this reason I am inclined to think that conception is *always* involved in aesthetic pleasure. Sensuous pleasure of physical properties is important, but so is the pleasure taken in contemplation of what we might call abstract intellectual features—a building's function, a symphony's historic contribution to developments in techniques, a novel's effect on legislation. Paul Ziff has argued that only those things count as reasons in support of critical judgements that can be directly "contemplated," where contemplation is a kind of activity (to be distinguished from recognition, which is an event).[26] He stresses the role of perception, but for him contemplation becomes *directed perception*. Thus it must include thought as well as sensation.

Anthony Savile has made what I have called "reflection" the fulcrum of a theory of artistic evaluation. He reminds us that long ago Aristotle realized that learning is, fortunately, pleasant. A great work, Savile claims, "displays a deep understanding of its subject," and, thus, part of the pleasure is due to our learning from it.[27] His description of Massoccio's *Expulsion from Paradise* is a very nice example of what he means (as I do) by the reflective appreciation (one form of delight) of an abstract intellectual quality:

(W)e think of [*Expulsion from Paradise*] as a profound work because of the understanding it provides of the meaning for men of abandonment by God. What mediates this understanding is not just the despair of Adam and Eve stamped on their every limb and evident in their distraught gestures; more than that we are brought to realize how, in their despair, the world beyond the gates of Eden is bleak and unwelcoming to them. The painter has managed to intimate that the bleakness is not simply a feature the world has independently of them. In the absence of God's grace there is no other way in which they could see it. In their state, a state which we may also share, beauty and goodness have departed the world and departed it for reasons internal to those whose world it is.[28]

Perception of and Reflection upon Intrinsic Features

But surely, it will be objected, we have come a long way from *intrinsic* features.[29] A building's political role or a painting's statement about the Fall of Man are just not *in* works the way colors or pitches or rhymes are. Paul Morel's lack of criticism of his mother is not in the novel at all!

The answer is suggested, I think, by another of Savile's observations. We cannot teach people to have aesthetic responses. But, he says, "What we teach is how to see as an answer to a design," as a solution to a particular puzzle.[30] That is, not only does our perception depend upon our conception, but *in aesthetic experience we are conscious that our conception of something depends upon our perception of the thing.* When people reflect they are aware that the object being sensed is *necessary* to the conception. The delight that accompanies sensation or reflection is tied in clear ways to the particular object of attention. One may enjoy just thinking about the way some buildings express striving for democratic equality, but the enjoyment is aesthetic only when the delight arises from observing the way a particular building expresses such striving. The centrality of intrinsicness becomes clear when one realizes that delight accompanies *features in this particular thing*.

Critical communication of the sort Isenberg describes is obtained when conception and perception are one—when they are parts of the same phenomenon, and when appreciation is clearly rooted in features of the object or event. Critics invite people to perceive and reflect upon those features, and to delight in so doing. The aesthetic, then, is a combination of perceiving, conceiving, and delighting.

An example may help. Here are two descriptions of the Parthenon, one from the fifteenth and one from the seventeenth century:

The famous temple of Minerva, destroyed and crumbled by the bombs on account of all the grain and other food provisions that the enemy had stored in it, was composed of the finest marble and supported by thirty-two columns, and had already been converted by the Turks into a . . . mosque.[31]

But what I most wanted to do on revisiting that splendid citadel was more carefully to examine from every angle the most noble temple of the goddess Pallas, which is built of solid polished marble. . . . This excellent and marvelous temple survives to this day with fifty-eight columns, twelve on each front (so arranged that there are double rows of six in the middle at either end) and seventeen double each side outside the walls, all these columns being five feet in diameter. . . . Above the columns are epistyles one and a half feet long and four feet high, on which you see superbly carved sculptures of the Thessalian battles of the Centaurs and Lapiths, while on the frieze placed high on the inner walls about two cubits from the top, that great artist Phidias has magnificently represented the victories of Athens in the time of Pericles, each frieze being about the height of a ten-year old boy. . . . I have taken care to include a drawing as best I could, in the journals of my present travels through Greece.[32]

The first obviously refers to intrinsic properties, but not in a way that demands or invites reflection. The inclusion of reference to drawings in the second clearly shows that the author intended the audience to reflect upon—and delight in—the structure's properties. We are invited to think about the victories of Athens, to imagine what the city-state was like at the time of Pericles, indeed, to imagine whatever we might (to let our cognitive powers play freely, to use Kant's phrase, although not, I think, as he meant it), but these reflections remain rooted in the stone images. People do not just enjoy reflecting, they enjoy reflecting upon particular features via a particular thing.

Sometimes 'intrinsic' has been defined metaphysically. For example. R. M. Chisholm defines it (he uses the term *internal*) as describing a property that is "neither rooted outside times at which it is had nor outside the objects that have it."[33] First, an object's having an internal property does not require the prior or subsequent existence of another object. Being the third painting of Van Gogh or the next to the last poem read by Robert Frost at his last poetry reading is not internal. Second, there cannot be another object upon which having an internal property depends spatially. Being the left side of a triptych or above the west entrance of a cathedral are not internal properties.

Although this way of thinking of 'intrinsic' has some appeal, there are difficulties. For example, I believe the phrases, "is an early Rembrandt" and "is performed downstage while Lady Windermere is behind a screen upstage" refer to intrinsic features, for they are the sorts of things we can perceive and in which we can take aesthetic delight. For this reason, and because aesthetic experience involves a human response, I prefer an epistemological interpretation of 'intrinsic.'

In aesthetic experience a response is evoked by something, and one is aware that the response is due to that thing. In the absence of the object (or event or place or person) one cannot know whether one will be delighted by, repelled by, or indifferent to it. This is why perception of intrinsic features is central to a characterization of the aesthetic.

As I use the term, 'intrinsic' can be defined as follows:

F is an intrinsic feature of O if and only if direct inspection of O is a necessary condition for verifying the claim that O is F, and, if someone knows the meaning of 'F', then (under normal conditions) direct inspection of O is a sufficient condition for verifying the claim that O is F.

There are, admittedly, several problematic terms here—*meaning, normal,* and *verify,* particularly. But this definition captures the central point I want to utilize in my characterization: intrinsic features are those that require looking (listening, etc.); and looking—once we understand what we are looking for—is enough. One cannot know just by direct inspection that something was written in Poland, or led to reforms in the meat packing industry, or is where George Washington camped in the summer of 1778. These are extrinsic features. But looking or listening, if one understands how, will allow one to discover whether something is red, is unified by repetitions of a minor second, is written in iambic pentameter, is about meat packing, is in the Polish style, is on the left on a triptych, or is heavily treed. The phrases, "Is three feet square," "is about gamekeeping," "expresses love of nature," and "is unified by repetition of a minor second," are intrinsic. The phrases, "was composed in Vienna," "brought about improved working conditions in England," and "was painted in 1875," are not. The last three bits of information may *matter* aesthetically, but only if they direct our attention to intrinsic features.

Furthermore, since comparison and contrast are so much a part of criticism, one may have to inspect more than one work; being influenced by an earlier work is an intrinsic feature according to my view. For example, the subject matter and composition (intrinsic features) of Manet's painting, *Le Dejeuner sur L'Herbe,* can be directly perceived by just looking at his work. That these features are borrowed from Giorgione's *Concert Champetre* is also an intrinsic property, but this requires one to inspect both the Manet and the Giorgione works.

Practically, verification often involves more than just looking or listening. One may not immediately perceive a minor second or a complex rhyme scheme or even the subject matter (this is precisely why works of art bear repeated, sustained attention). One may need lots of extrinsic information before direct inspection allows him or her to perceive an intrinsic feature of a work; one may have to be told, for example, that a composition was written in Poland before the Polish style is perceived.

But *in theory* direct inspection is a necessary and sufficient condition for knowing that an object has an intrinsic feature.[34] That is, one must go directly to the object to determine whether a feature is present or absent. If going to the object or event is not required to settle the matter, then we are talking about something other than an intrinsic feature.

It does not follow that intrinsic features are *brute.* That is, that one must observe something for oneself to know if it possesses an intrinsic feature does not mean that observation is all that ever matters. People are permitted and sometimes required to have knowledge about extrinsic features in order to notice intrinsic features. Knowledge that a concerto was composed by Bach in the early eighteenth century (extrinsic feature) may bring one to notice the unusually dominant role of the harpsichord (intrinsic feature). Told that Dickens's novels contributed to improved working conditions in England (extrinsic) may result in one's noticing the special way he treats boss/worker relationships (intrinsic). "That a particular painting was done while the artist was in Rome may not per se be a reason why the painting is good, but a critic might well call attention to the fact in order to get his audience to see how well the artist has assimilated some aspect of style. . . . There is no quality that we can think of, in fact, that could not conceivably guide our contemplation of some painting or other."[35]

The formalists feared that audiences would lose sight of the object if they did not concentrate exclusively on formal properties. But as long as delight is tied to intrinsic features of the object, thinking about whatever one wants is permissible—an object's history as well as its color, what is unsaid as well as said. This is why specification of properties that are uniquely aesthetic is impossible. As long as one realizes that delight is possible only if and when one actually attends to the object or event, aesthetic and nonaesthetic pleasure will not be confused.

Carolyn Korsmeyer may have had something like this in mind when she tried to distinguish between the aesthetic and the artistic. The former consists of values that relate to the way things look, she says, the latter, to the value of art objects per se.[36] Only sometimes do they overlap; an object's educational or economic value may be part of the artistic, but not the aesthetic, value of it.

It is true that things other than art objects have aesthetic value, and that the value of art objects extends beyond intrinsic features. But, if I am right, the "way things look" tells only part of the aesthetic story.

A great deal of contemporary art seems to de-emphasize the object. The object even seems sometimes to disappear, as when Christo takes down his fence or a poet erases her poems. More emphasis is put on people doing things, or merely thinking about doing things. We seem no longer to be asked to look or listen for patterns, or to reflect at all; action is given priority. But I believe that good art demands reflection upon an object—and in conceptual art the concept itself, when publicly documented, becomes the object. We still have to ground reflection in a particular; it is the way Christo put up the running fence, the way (or context in which) a particular erasure is done, that matters. If reflection is missing, then, to use Anthony Powell's phrase, the experience is "exciting rather than interesting," and the aesthetic is undermined.

Aesthetic Laws

George Birkhoff (see sec. B above) believes—incorrectly, in my estimation—that natural laws connect the presence of certain perceptual or formal properties with favorable or unfavorable subjective responses in viewers. A better assessment of the relationship is made by Sibley and Isenberg, although Sibley fails to notice that lack of laws connecting one set of properties with another is not unique to aesthetic properties. He is correct, however, in maintaining that we cannot go from the claim that something is red or angular or rotationally symmetrical to a claim about beauty or vibrancy or excitability.

Arnold Isenberg, like Sibley, believes that we cannot go from formal properties to aesthetic properties, but he thinks this is not a distinguishing mark of the aesthetic. Indeed he compares aesthetic properties in this respect with nonaesthetic properties. His example of the latter is "paranoia."

> 'Paranoia is marked by a profound egocentricity and deep-seated feelings of insecurity'—the kind of statement which makes every student think he has the disease—is suitable for easy comparison of notes among clinicians, who know how to recognize the difference between paranoia and other conditions; but it does not explicitly set forth the criteria which they employ.[37]

Lack of criterial connectedness also attends aesthetic properties, he believes. Just as paranoia is not equivalent to inflated ego and insecurity, and hence not conclusively implied by their presence, so gracefulness is not equivalent to nor implied by fragility and delicacy and smooth lines.

Isenberg, like Sibley, was interested in how critics can communicate with their audience if there are no laws relating formal or nonaesthetic properties of an object or event to the aesthetic judgments that can or should be made about them. How, for example, can you go from a statement like "*War and Peace* has suspenseful battle scenes" to the statement, "*War and Peace* is a wonderful novel"? Or, to recall a previously cited case study, how can you go from assertions about the presence of white water along the Lower Devil to assertions about Lower Devil's beauty if there are not lawlike generalizations relating white water and beauty?

The problem is exacerbated by the fact that works of art are "replete."[38] Everything about them potentially contributes to the aesthetic appreciation of them. Stanley Fish has used this fact to try to distinguish aesthetic from nonaesthetic objects. In the former, he says, "Everything counts."[39] We expect that everything is a potential source of delight in aesthetic objects but not in nonaesthetic objects. I think we cannot use repleteness to make the distinction that Fish tries to make. (There may be other cases of repleteness; for example, in judging whether or not a person is healthy, perhaps nothing can be overlooked.) However, it is correct not to rule out anything a priori.[40] If anything is potentially a source of delight, how can there be any aesthetic laws?

Environmental case studies are valuable here because they show the *practical* problems that result if we abandon pursuit of laws. It is one thing to shrug one's shoulders and say, "Oh well, there's no accounting for taste,' if one's neighbors put a plastic pink flamingo in their front yard. Few people are seriously affected by such action. Perhaps the lack of normative generalizations is not terribly serious in decisions made by museum curators. Even if public funds support them, their choices are exhibited for the most part in places where people aren't required to look. But the kinds of decisions made by people who are charged with carrying out environmental aesthetic impact studies are far-reaching; we cannot look away from our environment.

There is a sense in which Isenberg places criticism outside the realm of *rationality* when he deprives it of a syllogistic basis and when he views critics as *pointers* not as *reason givers*. If we expect public policy to be rational, if we expect decision makers to justify their actions rationally, then we must somehow bring them back into the rational arena. Can we find anything in the aesthetic realm like the sort of lawlike statements that support our everyday reasoning?

If I am correct that what is aethetically valuable depends upon entrenchment within cultural traditions, then we can look to these traditions to see at least what people typically delight in when they attend to intrinsic features of objects and events. Even the activity of criticism as Isenberg explains it requires that critics choose some things rather than others to point to. They must have some *reason* for their choices. Studying our traditions uncovers a class of terms that refer to intrinsic features that are generally delightful. We use terms in this class when we point to anything aesthetic.

Why do I sometimes call my husband to the window to look at the sunset? It is because I believe that in our culture particularly vivid colors in the evening sky are worth pointing out. That is, we share a tradition in which sunsets are valued for their colors. (And I don't call him to the window at sunrise, precisely because I know that in our domestic "subculture" aesthetic delight is not forthcoming for him early in the day.) Something like the following syllogism holds:

1. A good sky is one with vivid colors.
2. That sky has vivid colors.
3. Therefore, that sky is good.

A reasonable translation of (1) is: "When there are vivid colors in the sky, it is worth pointing out." "Worth pointing out," is what we mean by 'delightful'. The same thing is true of suspenseful battle scenes, unifying minor seconds, rows of columns, deep understanding of the consequences of the absence of God's grace, white water, unusually dominant harpsichord parts, and so on. And when things have many features worth pointing out, they are very good.

G. E. Moore said that when things are intrinsically good, no external facts count for or against their goodness.[41] Sibley says the same thing about aesthetically valuable properties (see chap. 1). Nonetheless, Moore said, every argument supporting the notion that "Action A should be done" will include premises of two sorts: "A brings about B," and "B is intrinsically good." In spite of Isenberg's insistence that aesthetic criticism is not reason-giving, I believe that something like this also goes on in our aesthetic judgments. "A has B" and "B is delightful" entail "A deserves attention."

"B is delightful" is neither meaningless nor relative. It does not require that everyone be delighted, but it does require a positive response on the part of an identifiable segment of the population. It is shorthand for "B is traditionally delightful," where *traditionally* is timeless in the sense of being both a report on the past or present and a prediction about future individual responses. Clearly there are times when it will be straightforwardly false, because it fails either as a report on the past or present or as a prediction of the future.

We can also discover within our traditions the sorts of things that are *not* aesthetically delightful (or are aesthetically *undelightful* or repugnant) to us: intrinsic features that, when attended to and reflected upon (both sensual and abstract intellectual features), are accompanied by a negative reaction. Thus, critics and public policy makers can support negative, as well as positive, judgments. As was suggested earlier, we may even find that there is greater agreement about what is ugly or offensive than about what is beautiful.

It is not always going to be easy or even possible to separate distinctly the aesthetic from the nonaesthetic. Because of the complexity of objects and experiences with them, it may not always be clear that our delight is due to conceptions that result from attending to intrinsic features and not to merely thinking about something. It is interesting (hence delightful) to think about what the absence of God's grace implies—so interesting that one may forget entirely about Massoccio's painting. In theory it is only when the interest is conjoined with attention to intrinsic features that the delight is aesthetic. In practice we may not be certain that our pleasure is tied to intrinsic features. Probably, human attention span being what it is, aesthetic delight comes and goes (remember Kenneth Clark's observation that aesthetic attention does not last "longer than one can enjoy the smell of an orange, which in my case is less that two minutes.")[42]

In a wonderful book on the history of post office murals painted during the Great Depression of the '30s in the United States, Karal Ann Marling claims that aesthetic interests played a very small role. One of her reasons for saying so is that "although the people could be smitten en masse with an idiosyncratic fondness for garish hues and right angles," other interests dominated responses.[43] "Questions of art had little bearing. . . . The section was not an art program. It was, in the final analysis, a social program that employed artists."[44] Even if it was in the final analysis a project devoted to social interests, this in itself does not preclude the existence of genuinely aesthetic interests as well. But if Marling is correct about something else, then *aesthetic* features do disappear.

> Nor was it really necessary *to look* at paintings to discern their merits and defects. It was not in fact necessary to *look* at pictures in post offices either, since 'good' murals were always concealed in a sociable miasma of emotion emanating directly from the observing public. The cloud of belief floating over the post-office was the evanescent mirror in which the self-image of the public was truly reflected.[45] (My emphasis.)

If a "cloud of belief" does in fact keep one from looking and seeing what is *in* an object before us, then the experience is not aesthetic. In fact, as I tried to show in chapter 3, anything that prevents perception of or reflection upon features of an object or event prevents an aesthetic experience. This is why *control* is essential.

Characterization of 'Aesthetic'

A collection of the sundry points I have made may help us see what they jointly imply about the nature of the aesthetic.

1. There appears to be no perceptual, psychological, logical, or epistemological property that separates aesthetic objects or experiences from those that seem nonaesthetic. One must look elsewhere for the foundation of the distinction.

2. Control is a necessary, although not a sufficient, condition of delight. Only when we are *in control* can we attend to the object or event in the way that is required for aesthetic experience of it.
3. Features of objects and events referred to as 'aesthetic', or believed to contribute to a thing's aesthetic value, differ across time and culture, but have their locus in the object or event.
4. Consideration of practical aesthetic problems encountered in assessing scenic values shows that we can discover when assessment is aesthetic by seeing whether the given descriptions fit with traditions of art history and criticism—that is, whether they pick out things historically or traditionally considered delightful.
5. Aesthetic experiences are particular reactions to intrinsic features of objects and events.
6. Examination of traditions provides a basis for informed belief about which intrinsic features are delightful.

Using these points we can articulate a characterization of the aesthetic.

AN EXPERIENCE IS AESTHETIC IF THERE IS DELIGHT TAKEN IN AN INTRINSIC FEATURE OF AN OBJECT OR EVENT, AND THAT FEATURE IS TRADITIONALLY CONSIDERED WORTH ATTENDING TO, THAT IS, WORTH PERCEIVING OR REFLECTING UPON.

From this it follows that

AESTHETIC FEATURES OF OBJECTS OR EVENTS ARE THOSE INTRINSIC FEATURES TRADITIONALLY CONSIDERED WORTH ATTENDING TO, THAT IS, WORTH PERCEIVING OR REFLECTING UPON.

Ongoing traditions must exist in order for us to identify both the aesthetic and the artistic. Intrinsic features are aesthetic if they are the sorts of things people pick out when they discuss works of art, and vice versa. Works of art are to be distinguished from nonworks of art by the following definition.[46]

x is a work of art if and only if (1) x is an artifact, and (2) x is discussed in such a way that information about x directs the viewer's attention to features that are considered worthy of attending to in aesthetic traditions (history, criticism, and theory).

This is *not* a circle. At least in Western culture, the artistic is prior to the aesthetic. Aesthetic terms are terms that have been used in the past to discuss works of art. Thus, the characterization of 'aesthetic', to be stated precisely, must include time variables (t_n stands for a specific time).

> 'F' is an aesthetic term at t_n (names an aesthetic feature at t_n) if and only if F is an intrinsic feature of O at t_n and 'F' has been used to describe a work of art at t_m, and t_m is prior to t_n, and F is considered worth attending to, that is, worth perceiving or reflecting upon.

The terms we use to discuss works of art are also used to discuss other things—people and rivers and train rides, for example. When described in these terms, they become aesthetic objects or events. Members of the set change, but not all at once. A word like "masterpiece" becomes aesthetic when it is associated with obviously *artistic* terms—balance or composition, for example. A word like "elegant" loses its aesthetic function when it is no longer associated with *intrinsic* features. A term like "landscape," which was originally used only artistically, became aesthetic, and then took on other aspects as well—aspects in which extrinsic facts became as, if not more, important.

Suppose we stand looking at a stretch of road. "Sixteen tons of gravel were used in its construction," you tell me. "Wow!" I say. I am attending to and reflecting upon intrinsic features of the road. But the *weight* of gravel used is not a feature identified as delightful in our traditions. If you say while we are listening to a piece of music, "Sixteen bassoons are used in this passage," then my "Wow!" is aesthetic, for instrumentation does matter traditionally for us. Until feminists pointed them out to us, many intrinsic features of works—inadequate development of female characters in fiction, for example, or expression of sensitivity to color in textile design—did not matter. We certainly argue about whether an object or event *has* a particular intrinsic feature; but traditions tell us when our argument is aesthetic.

Applying the Characterization

Since a large portion of this book has dealt with assessing the environment, we should see just how helpful the characterization I have given of 'aesthetic' might be for our applied aestheticians. Remember that Richard Smardon said, "Courts feel uncomfortable administering a subjective standard relating to taste . . ."[47] Will my view of what is aesthetic make the courts feel any less uncomfortable? Suppose, for example, that a particular white water section of a river is to be eliminated by an electrical power station (as in the Jones & Jones study of the Upper Sisitna River). The law requires due attention to aesthetic amenities (it also requires due attention to cultural amenities; for me the two go together). Using my theory, the existence of aesthetic value would be presented in terms of the actual or potential delight that results from an area's intrinsic features, features that have been identified as worth perceiving and reflecting upon per se. People should be consulted (to make sure that the values are intact), but numerical studies are not necessary. If people *say* that they like to *look* at the water or that *listening* to the rush makes them *think* of the vastness of the universe, we have sufficient *objective* evidence that the river is aesthetically delightful. Further support is available from the presence of white water as a motif in paintings or in poetry, or as a feature pointed out in tourist advertisements.

On a recent trip to the Oregon coast, a friend observed that if Haystack Rock at Cannon Beach had received royalties every time someone photographed it, painted it, or put images of it on an ashtray or T-shirt, it would long ago have turned to gold. There exists a huge amount of objective evidence that places like this are valued aesthetically and culturally. Although the quantity of evidence is less for less well-known sites, objective evidence of similar sorts often can be found for their value as well. *Unquantified* evidence is nonetheless objective evidence to which rational decision makers can turn.

There is much in the Jones & Jones report discussed in chapter 4 that is praiseworthy. The authors obviously thought hard about and took seriously a difficult problem. They came up with assessments and predictions that do not jar most people's intuitions, and their inventories include items that spur people to think about contributions made by some features of the landscape that philosophical aestheticians might overlook. They also produced a report that is useful for making important environmental decisions. But it could be improved.

The greatest improvement would come, I believe, by providing more in the way of a theoretical foundation; and my characterization of the aesthetic provides this.

The first step—and the easiest—would be to show that the factors that they referred to and assessed are 'intrinsic' features. Landform spatial definition and vividness, for example, seem clearly intrinsic. Watershed features may not be, so they will have to be explained in such a way that direct inspection is emphasized.

The more difficult part of the task—showing that aesthetic amenities were indeed taken into account—involves showing that the intrinsic features assessed are traditionally considered delightful. Instead of apologizing for historical and cultural conditioning, the authors should relish it. This ensures, after all, that it is really the aesthetic that is captured while emphasizing cognizance of human values.

Historical and cultural conditioning—another way of saying *tradition*—accounts for the existence of values. Reference to unity in the report of Jones & Jones, for instance, can be justified because of its long history in artistic and aesthetic discussions. Nowhere is this discussed in the Jones & Jones report (indeed, it will be recalled that they wanted to *avoid* reference to landscape ideals).

By assessing physical features alone, the report leaves out something very important. Just as the formalists restrict and impoverish experience by limiting attention to formal properties, so Jones & Jones deny themselves access to features that enhance experience and support objective evaluation and prediction.

Many of these sorts of evidence were discussed in chapter 5—mystery, legibility, sense of place, prospect/refuge, historical values, and so forth. These come not from physical inventories, but from humanistic sources. Are there sketches and paintings of Lower Devil? Have sagas or epics been written in which it figures? Do letters or diaries report a rejoicing in it? What is its history? Does current usage suggest that it plays a role in the way the world is perceived? What legends, if any, are there about it? And if such sources are missing for this site in particular, what have people said, written, or painted about similar sites? A *humanistic* inventory would provide a fruitful source for assessment. It would be very interesting to see the result of coupling one with the physical inventories already available.

My characterization of the aesthetic does provide a method for investigating and verifying aesthetic value. It should thus be of help to people engaged in solving practical aesthetic problems. Even if my theory does not indicate how we prove or disprove that a particular landscape is unified, it does show that being unified is aesthetically relevant. It indicates that we must point to intrinsic features to support claims about unity—to organized patterns of color or textures, for instance. For these are the things to which art critics point when they discuss the unity of art works.

The characterization of the aesthetic that I have proposed does not show how we can compare or rank aesthetic value with other sorts of value. One attractive quality of assessment in financial terms, or in terms of capacity for generating kilowatt hours, is that such figures can be easily compared with one another. But the ease of comparison that such evaluations provide too often lulls us into thinking we have something that we do not have. The fact that a new dam will provide the local residents with 1,500,000 kilowatt hours if built at cite A, and only 1,000,000 if built at cite B, does *not* tell one how valuable the provision of electricity is. Such measures as "what people are willing to pay" do not ensure that we have measured delight in beauty either. And even if we have established that aesthetic amenities truly have been assessed, how are we to compare aesthetic and practical value?

But from the outset of this book I have explicitly and implicitly maintained that aesthetic experiences are an important part of human lives. Thus, I cannot avoid completely the question of how the aesthetic compares to other things that we value. To claim that one should seek the aesthetic is to say something about the meaning of life, and, hence, to make a kind of ethical judgment. Contemporary views of the aesthetic often separate the ethical and pragmatic from the aesthetic. Whether there are connections among pragmatic, ethical, and aesthetic values remains to be discussed. I believe that we learn something more about the natures of the aesthetic if we look at possible connections, particularly between aesthetic and ethical values.

7
The Aesthetic and the Ethical

The Gap Between Aesthetic and Ethical Value

Our culture assumes broadly that the ethical and aesthetic are separate. Most people would not hesitate to admit the possibility of graceful murders or amusing racist jokes or beautiful pornographic photographs or harmonically brilliant Nazi marches. In 1933 Nelson Rockefeller refused to allow installation of a mural that he commissioned Diego Rivera to paint in his center in New York City. He said he was afraid that a portrait of Lenin that the artist had included might offend people; but he insisted that the mural was beautifully painted.[1] Although Rockefeller's judgment might be questioned, the distinction between moral offense and positive aesthetic value makes perfectly good sense, at least on the face of it.

This popular attitude is also prevalent in contemporary moral philosophy, where many theorists argue that there are important theoretical differences between the ethical and the aesthetic. Stuart Hampshire argues that ". . . aesthetic judgements are not compatible with moral judgements, and that there are no problems of aesthetics comparable with the problems of ethics."[2] Artists' problems, he says, are their own problems—set for themselves by themselves. Moral problems, on the other hand, concern us all—are set for us from the outside, so to speak. The rational person looks for general principles that will help solve moral dilemmas, but artists (and their audiences) do not believe that there are general principles for preferring one aesthetic attitude or approach to another. People do not put themselves in an artist's shoes the way they try to imagine themselves in the position of a moral agent whose action they are judging.[3] "The spectator-critic in any of the arts needs gifts precisely the opposite of the moralists'; he needs to suspend his natural sense of purpose and significance. To hold attention still upon any particular thing is unnatural; normally we take objects—whether perceived by sight, touch, hearing, or by any combination of the senses—as signs of possible action and as instances of some usable kind; we look through them to their possible uses, and classify them by their uses rather than by sensuous similarities."[4]

Another philosopher, Philippa Foot, holds that aesthetic judgments wear their subjectivity on their sleeves, whereas ethical claims take the form of objective statement. ". . . We do maintain certain fictions about morality, and they are even reflected in the forms of language that we use, while there is no comparable lack of candour in what we say and think about works of art."[5]

Other writers have also distinguished ethical and aesthetic concerns. Rousseau observed in the *Essays on the Origin of Language* that "a man will weep at the sight of a tragic performance even though he never felt pity for a person in need." Henry James wrote a whole novel (*The Spoils of Poynton*) about a woman of impeccable aesthetic taste who comes as close as anyone in his novels to being thoroughly evil. Many plays and novels about the Nazis stress their delight in art. In one television play, *Playing for Time*, a prison camp commandant assures the conductor of an orchestra made up of women prisoners that listening to their music "helps us with our work." In Arthur Miller's *Incident at Vichy*, Prince von Berg asks, "Can people with a respect for art go about hounding Jews? Making a prison of Europe, pushing themselves forward as a race of policeman and brutes? Is that possible for artistic people?" Monceau (an actor) responds, "I'd like to agree with you, Prince von Berg, but I have to say that the German audiences—I've played there—no audience is as sensitive to the smallest nuance of a performance; they sit in the theater with respect, like in a church. And nobody listens to music like a German."[6] Thus it appears that the ethical and aesthetic compartments of human lives are separate, even conflicting.

'Delight' suggests another way of distinguishing aesthetic from ethical value. According to my theory, delight resides in and results from perception of and reflection upon intrinsic features of objects and events. But ethical delight (or satisfaction) has a different source. It is *action* (both of ourselves and others), not reflection, that counts ethically. In aesthetic situations controlled attention is directed at things; in ethical situations action is directed by the demands of everyday, practical concerns (see chap. 3). And extrinsic features like consequences or moral principles figure centrally in ethical deliberations. In one of Anthony Powell's novels, a character says, "Action is, after all, exciting rather than interesting."[7] The implication is that what is interesting, rather than exciting, is nonaction, that is, reflection. If reflection is characteristic of the aesthetic, and action of the ethical, then again we find a basic difference between these two areas of human experience.

There are, however, at least two reasons for my being reluctant to accept the view that aesthetic and ethical values are separate. First, in developing my characterization of the aesthetic I have insisted that the aesthetic is integrated with other kinds of concerns and values. Second, in making important decisions (such as whether to build a dam at a uniquely vivid site) it is often necessary to weigh aesthetic concerns against other kinds of concerns. Many of these are practical, but they may also involve ethical considerations. If the aesthetic were totally distinct from the ethical, there would be no way of comparing the two or of resolving conflicts short of deciding to ignore one or the other.

I believe that there is a way of relating aesthetic and ethical values (and ultimately of connecting all sorts of human values).

Closing the Gap

Support for the view that aesthetic and ethical value are distinct often comes from people who insist upon the primacy of the latter. They maintain that moral value always overrides aesthetic value when the two conflict. If the decision is between spending fifty thousand dollars on cosmetic plastic surgery or on helping the poor, then, based on such views, the latter action is always preferable. The trouble with such views is that they are ad hominem. We need to be able to convince those who place more value on cosmetic surgery that doing so is a value mistake—which, short of relying on intuitions or an already shared value system, is hard to do. It also begs the question under discussion, for it assumes that moral and aesthetic value are separate.

Another way of making aesthetic value separate and unequal is to identify it as *harmless* or *useless*. This has often been done in the history of Western thought.

> A man should endeavor to make the sphere of his innocent pleasures as wide as possible, that he may retire into them with safety, and find in them such a satisfaction as a wise man would not blush to take. Of this nature are those of the imagination, which do not require such a bent of thought as is necessary to our more serious employments, nor, at the same time suffer the mind to sink into that intelligence and

remissness, which are apt to accompany our more sensual delights, but, like a gentle exercise to the faculties, awaken them from sloth and idleness, without putting them upon any labor or difficulty. . . .[8]

It is difficult to convince someone who enjoys pictures of people being tortured, or of music being played by slaves, that their pleasures could not (by definition) be aesthetic because they were not harmless. Furthermore, it is too easy to slide from *harmless* or *innocent* pleasure to *trivial* pleasure; even if I am finally forced to separate aesthetic from moral value, I do not want to concede that aesthetics lies at best at the periphery of human life.

There are theorists who deny that aesthetic and moral value are separate. More and more people deny the possibility of *beautiful* photographs of women being tortured. Others think that there is an empirical connection between aesthetic preferences and moral concerns. One of the applied aestheticians whose work I cited earlier says, "People who take an interest in the special qualities of their community, in my experience, tend to take more concern in the qualities of their region and state and even of their nation."[9] Anthony Powell's novels contradict those of James, for in Powell's characters moral and aesthetic sensitivity go together.

At the very least, it is sometimes a surprise (as it was for Prince von Berg) to find artistic sensitivity combined with immorality. An interesting article by George Steiner on the infamous art historian-spy, Anthony Blunt, describes what Blunt did as evil. "Anthony Blunt was a K.G.B. minion whose treason over thirty years or more almost certainly did grave damage to his own country and may well have sent other men—Polish and Czech exiles, fellow intelligence agents—to abject deaths." Steiner asks how "a man who in the morning teaches his students that a false attribution of a Watteau drawing or an inaccurate transcription of a fourteenth-century epigraph is a sin against the spirit" could "in the afternoon or evening transmit to the agents of Soviet intelligence classified, perhaps vital information given to him in sworn trust by his countrymen and intimate colleagues."[10] If the morning and afternoon activities seem incongruous, then perhaps the separation between the moral and the aesthetic is not as definite as people accustomed to the expression of "art for art's sake" are initially ready to assert.

EQUATING THE GOOD AND THE BEAUTIFUL

Arthur Danto has been struck by the fact that from the very beginning, aesthetic questions have been central to Western philosophy.[11] The nature of beauty and artistic activity, for instance, were fundamental problems for Plato. Danto accounts for this on metaphysical grounds. He believes that as soon as we ask ourselves what is *real*, we are involved with paintings and plays, particularly when these are viewed, as they were by the Greeks, as *imitations of reality*.

Danto is surely right about the existence of such a connection. But I believe that the centrality of aesthetics depends on theories of value as well as theories of reality. For Plato, the Good, the Real, the True, and the Beautiful came together. In his views, it was because they did not present truth, or even attempt to produce it, that artists (at least most of them—some musicians were excepted) were not *valuable*. They were not only not good, but were also positively bad. For in addition to wasting their own time, they distracted others from the proper business of life—seeking knowledge. Value in general for Plato was ethically construed. Since only that which brought knowledge was good, artistic, and what is now called aesthetic, activity (the term 'aesthetic', it will be recalled, is a latecomer) could only be valuable if it too contributed to the search for the truth. For Plato, something evil yet beautiful is simply a contradiction.

What might Plato have said about Anthony Blunt? He would not have been at all surprised that someone who spent his mornings studying paintings (things "thrice removed from reality," as he put it in *The Republic*) would spend the rest of the day betraying friends and countrymen.

More recently in the history of Western thought, a similar view was expressed by Leo Tolstoy. Like Plato, his general theory of value dictated what the special nature of aesthetic value would be. In *What is Art?* he used a *food* analogy to clarify his position. What, he asked, is the value of food? This question can be answered only by considering its function; and once that is done the answer is simple: nutrition. Thus, food is to be assessed in terms of its relative contribution to bodily survival and health. Tolstoy chose food as his example because people are likely to think that what is *good* about food is the pleasure it gives. But even those who "live to eat" would finally be forced to admit that the real value of food is what it provides nutritionally, not how tasty it is.

For Tolstoy, it was no accident that people likely to confuse the value of food with its pleasure (compare the diets of nobility and the peasantry) are also those who are confused about the genuine value of artistic and aesthetic activity. In these areas, too, they mistakenly confuse value and pleasure. Here the pleasure is *beauty.* Art, like food, is accurately conceived only when its function is understood. As food is good when and only when it contributes to a healthy body, art is good when and only when it contributes to a healthy society. The aesthetic diet of the corrupt upper classes is as full of empty calories as the food they eat. It is the lower classes who, according to Tolstoy, best understand what is real and good art.

The function of art, in Tolstoy's view, is the transmission through words, shapes, sounds, movements, and so on of sincere human emotion that produces heightened feelings of *brotherhood*. Deeply feeling artists produce works that arouse those same feelings in the audience; thus all are united in mutual emotional experience. The assumption is that when this happens, we become *better* people; when we know how others feel—when we realize that they feel as we do—our treatment of one another will be more humane.

In a chapter on the pseudo or counterfeit art of the upper classes of his period, Tolstoy described a visit to an opera rehearsal in terms that suggest a descent into hell. The performers feign emotion, lack respect for one another, and produce something silly and utterly devoid of value. Tolstoy contrasted this with activity that is genuinely worth doing—harvesting hay, for instance. It is the lower classes who recognize what is genuinely important. Aesthetically they exemplify acquaintance with the real value of music; as an example, Tolstoy cited their deeply felt folk songs (throughout his discussion, Tolstoy assumed that peasants have a choice about what to do and what to eat!).

It would not have surprised Tolstoy (any more than it would Plato) that Blunt went astray. For Blunt's mornings were spent trafficking in counterfeit art. (The paintings of Watteau would have been exactly the sort of thing Tolstoy was criticizing.) Losing touch with fellow creatures, Blunt was bound finally to harm them.

AN EMPIRICAL CONNECTION

Yet another track has been taken by theorists who have tried to show that there is a kind of empirical connection between aesthetic delight and moral goodness. With Plato and Tolstoy, they have influenced our culture's views of morality and aesthetics in ways that contradict the separatist accounts.

Plato and Tolstoy were deeply suspicious of pleasure. They viewed it as distracting and corrupting, particularly when pursued for its own sake. Our culture shares this feeling to some extent. A life spent exclusively in the search for pleasures (especially bodily pleasures) is suspect.

Henry David Thoreau, for example, said that "the glory of the world is seen only by a chaste mind. To whomsoever this fact is not an awful but beautiful mystery, there are no flowers in nature."[12] A chaste mind, he wrote, is one that can rise above the trivial details of daily life to an elevation that characterizes both ethical and aesthetic outlooks (this has an obvious relation to what I said about *control* in chap. 2).

Another famous American, Thomas Jefferson, also believed that goodness and beauty are synergistic. He urged the beautification of cities and countryside on the grounds that it would improve the national character.[13] According to Eleanor D. Berman, he was greatly influenced by Lord Kames, who believed that moral sense and taste in and for the arts go together.[14]

Kames's view is most fully understood in his *Elements of Criticism* (1855) where he argues for a consequential connection between the aesthetic and the moral. Pleasures of the eye and ear revive and relax the spirits and "restore a proper tone of mind."[15]

> (A) taste in the fine arts goes hand in hand with the moral sense, to which indeed it is nearly allied: both of them discover what is right and what is wrong: fashion, temper, and education have an influence to vitiate both, or to preserve them pure and untainted: neither of them is local or arbitrary: being rooted in human nature, and governed by principles common to all men.[16]

Kames believes that delicacy of taste is related to ability to *sympathize* and is therefore connected with the tendency to behave morally.

> (N)o occupation attaches a man more to his duty, than that of cultivating a taste in the fine arts: a just relish of what is beautiful, proper, elegant, and ornamental, in writing or painting, in architecture or gardening, is a fine preparation for the same just relish of these qualities in character and behavior.[17]

Gardening is not only good for the soul; it inspires gaiety and benevolence. Beautiful gardens inspire goodness in others, whereas uncultivated ground "inspires peevishness and discontent."[18]

Consequentialist views of the relationship between enjoying the aesthetic life and practicing the moral life are still popular.

Even in as unexpected a place as the writings of the philosopher of science, Hilary Putnam, we find literature extolled for its contribution to moral life. Although novels do not provide knowledge in the sense of a body of verified or verifiable information, he says, they do help develop imagination, which leads to understanding of "moral perplexities."

> If I read Celine's *Journey to the End of the Night* I do not *learn* that love does not exist, that all human beings are hateful and hating (even if— and I am sure this is not the case—those propositions should be true). What I learn is to see the world as it looks to someone who is sure that hypothesis is correct. . . . But all this is not empirical knowledge at all; for being aware of a new interpretation of the facts, however repellent, of a construction that can—I now see—be put upon the facts, however perversely—is a kind of knowledge. It is knowledge of a possibility. It is *conceptual* knowledge.[19]

Putnam believes the ethical consequences of literature consist in its making people more perceptive. Anthony Savile has also pegged this as one of the valuable contributions that art makes to the human situation.

> We cannot give a coherent account of planning for the future unless we have available notions like 'desirable', 'valuable', or 'estimable'. . . . This can come about only if we find things in the world to be of value and to be worthy of our esteem, and that will happen only if we frame a vision of the world that sees it from a point of view that we share with others and that generates descriptions of it cast in terms of, and responsive to, our common interests.[20]

Art, he thinks, does this for us.

William James thought that art, by taking one step back from the world, as it were, offers the ethically necessary opportunity to attain "breadth of insight into the impersonal world of worths as such, to have any perception of life's meaning on a large objective scale."[21] Critics have said that his brother Henry believed that "fullest consciousness means maximum ability to do good; underdeveloped consciousness means maximum ability to do evil."[22] (This suggests that the aesthetically sensitive, morally insensitive character in *Spoils of Poynton* lacks full consciousness.)

The coming together of aesthetic and ethical outlooks, as I indicated above, is portrayed in the novels of Anthony Powell. I have detailed elsewhere Powell's presentation of "the aesthetic life" in his novels, especially in his twelve-volume work, *A Dance* *to the Music of Time.*²³ One of the things that marks the aesthetic life of the protagonist in these novels is that he sees the world as art. He compares things and events in the real world with works of art: skies are Baroque ceilings, people are described by comparison with characters from literary works, dinner parties are viewed as staged theatricals, and so on. Powell also organizes things and events according to the sorts of principles used to structure works of art. Instead of saying, for example, that someone looks like George Washington, his heroes would say that the person looks like Gilbert Stuart's portrait of George Washington. The difference lies in a special way of perceiving the world. Powell seems to suggest that those who view the world aesthetically treat one another better than those who do not. Those who lead a life in which reflection rather than action dominates are *better* people.

The consequentialist view of the connection between the moral and aesthetic life maintains that if people develop taste, they will become better human beings (or, perhaps, vice versa). The trouble with this view is that it seems obviously false, unless one seriously limits (as did Tolstoy, for instance) what counts as a genuine aesthetic experience. We would have to deny that the Nazis who hounded Jews really loved music or that Blunt really understood art, or deny that the Nazis were evil or Blunt despicable, or maintain that both were canny enough to use their aesthetic *pose* as a *cover*. Perhaps, however, a connection between the moral and the aesthetic is less direct.

A Deep Connection

THE ARISTOTLE/ MCDOWELL VIEW

A recurring strain in many of the thinkers we have looked at is the reference to a mutual development of moral and aesthetic *perception*. Moral behavior and aesthetic pursuits go hand in hand because people who see moral features in a situation are likely to see aesthetic features as well, and vice versa. To test this it is helpful, I think, to try to compare aesthetic seeing (both perceiving and reflecting) with moral seeing as it has been described by Aristotle and, more recently, by John McDowell.

Aristotle had a much higher opinion of the arts and artists than did Plato, largely because he believed that art could provide knowledge. But I am less interested here in his theories of art than I am with his ethical theories; less interested in the direct consequential connection that may exist between going to the theater and humane treatment of other people than in the indirect relationship between ways of looking at art and aesthetic objects and ways of looking at human behavior.

Aristotle believed that virtue is a habit.[24] We become virtuous by doing virtuous things, just as "we learn an art or craft by doing the things that we shall have to do when we have learnt it: for instance, men become builders by building houses, harpers by playing on the harp."[25] If people are virtuous they have a "settled disposition of mind," which leads to a consistent "observance of the mean."[26] The virtuous person "fixes his gaze" on some special thing, just as the aesthetic person seems to fix his or her gaze on special features identified traditionally as worthy of attention. As we've seen, the aesthetic person seems to fix his or her gaze on something special—features traditionally identified as delightful. Thus we have a possible connection: If people are virtuous they feel pleasure when they attend to the right features—those that bring them to do the right thing; if people are aesthetic they feel pleasure when they attend to the right features—those that reward sustained attention.

Although John McDowell takes a strictly ethical position, his Aristotelianism provides additional possible analogies between the moral and the aesthetic. It is interesting and informative to insert the possible aesthetic interpretations into his theories.

In a paper entitled "Virtue and Reason," McDowell says, "A kind person can be relied on to behave kindly when that is what the situation requires."[27] Perhaps an aesthetic person can be relied on to behave aesthetically when the situation requires (*requires* seems a bit strong here; it is probably better to speak of what the situation *permits;* I shall return to this below).

Recognition of what a situation requires is an act of reason and depends upon "reliable sensitivity . . . to requirements."[28] But the sort of sensitivity that McDowell has in mind is definitely not the same as that which we encountered in Sibley. McDowell views sensitivity as a kind of *knowledge*—a sensitivity to *facts* about the feelings and rights of others. An aesthetic analogy here might be the distinction between merely *seeing* a red patch next to a blue patch, and *seeing that* a red patch has been placed next to a blue patch—where delight arises from the later because such arrangements are valued in our culture.

Sometimes one person sees the requirements and another does not. Then the first can criticize the second for this failure. If you fail to notice that the circumstances call for charity, I can criticize you. An aesthetic analogy here might be your failure to see an object's gracefulness. Sometimes two people see different requirements: I see a call for honesty, you see a call for a white lie. Here it is not appropriate to say that only one of us is correct, but rather, "I can see that doing *x* is right for me, but doing *y* is right for you." Again we have an aesthetic analogy: Aesthetically I may see unity, where you see only boring repetition, in which case the appropriate observation would be, "I can see that you find the symphony not delightful, whereas I find it delightful."

Ethical and aesthetic *seeing* in this respect can be compared to aspect perception (see chap. 1). A person who sees only the duck in the duck-rabbit figure is not wrong; he or she has simply missed something. So people may miss some moral or aesthetic aspects. A person who sees a duck first may understand why or how another person tends to see the rabbit first, or to miss the duck completely. If I do not see a rabbit, but hear others describing the figure in terms of long ears, I may realize that I have missed something, and work to try to see more. Similarly, moral and aesthetic development is something like trying to learn to see more aspects.

McDowell believes (in agreement with many aestheticians) that general ethical principles are not formulable. But, he says,

> Now it is this misconception of the deductive paradigm which leads us to suppose that the operation of any specific conception of rationality in a particular area—any specific conception of what counts as doing the same thing—must be deductively explicable: that is, that there must be a formulable universal principle suited to serve as major premise in syllogistic explanations. . . .[29]

(McDowell would certainly criticize investigators who commit what I labeled the "quantitative/objective fallacy.")

Using an example of Wittgenstein's, McDowell believes that when given the series 2,4,6,8, . . . we simply see what needs to be done. We do not form a general principle, "Whenever you see 2,4,6,8, . . . keep adding 2." That principle may be wrong, and we know it may be wrong. Someone may be going on the principle, "Keep adding 2 until you reach 1000, and then start adding 4." What is going on is not capturable by a deductive model, but is provided by the context—a "form of life" (e.g., maximize the continuing regularity of the series) that helps us to know what is expected.

Ethics, according to McDowell, is like this. Aristotle's view of virtuous actions as explainable by a "virtuous person's conception of the sort of life a human being should lead" is not a major premise, and "a conception of how one should live is not simply an unorganized collection of propensities to action, on this or that occasion, in pursuit of this or that concern."[30] This *may* suggest why questionnaires about which specific things in the countryside should be preserved are so often misguided. A conception of what is valuable (the network of our goals, interests, delights, and so on) is required. "Occasion by occasion, one knows what to do, if one does, not by applying universal principles, but by being a certain kind of person: one who sees situations in a certain distinctive way."[31]

There may be aesthetically, as well as ethically, distinctive ways of seeing. Instead of applying aesthetic principles and deducing what is delightful, shared forms of life bring people to see and agree that white water or unity is valuable. Based on this view, aesthetic laws would not serve as deductive principles, but would be descriptions of what people in certain cultures find delightful. A correct description of what people do in one culture when confronted with the series 2, 4, 6, 8, . . . could be, "They continue to add 2 ad infinitum." In another it might be, "They add 2 until they reach 1000, and then begin adding 4." Similarly, one culture may see moral requirements primarily in terms of duty, another in terms of consequences. One culture may look for and find evidence of design, another may value color.

In another paper, McDowell says, "In moral upbringing what one learns is not to behave on conformity with rules of conduct, but to see situations in a special light, as constituting reasons for acting; this perceptual capacity, once acquired, can be exercised in complex novel circumstances, not necessarily capable of being foreseen and legislated for by a codifier of the conduct required by virtue, however wise and thoughtful he might be."[32] We do not learn first to see that something is a case of uttering deceptive statements, and then learn second that it is bad; we learn to see uttering deceptive statements as bad. Something like this seems to be true also of aesthetic upbringing. We do not learn to see the white water and then to see the river as beautiful; we learn to see and delight in the beauty of the white water at the same time; my son, for example, first called a Christmas tree, "the pretty."

A moral person, according to this view, sees what is required in the way of action. I have been suggesting that it is useful to view an aesthetic person as one who sees what is required in the way of attention and reflection. Is *required* too strong? Would it be preferable to speak of what a person is aesthetically *permitted*? It would be preferable, I think, if we misconstrue *requirement* as a demand that one set of features be the focus (colors, for instance). We will not construe *require* too strongly if we understand that the aesthetic person realizes that some features demand attention, and admits that these may vary from object to object, from person to person. Powell's hero, Nicholas Jenkins, time and again concentrates on what situations demand of him aesthetically—on what deserves aesthetically to be reflected upon and delighted in. But he sometimes misses moral demands.

> My own guilty feelings ... came back to me, those sudden awarenesses at military exercises of the kind that, instead of properly concentrating on tactical features, I was musing on pictorial or historical aspects of the landscape; what the place had seen in the past; how certain painters would deal with its physical features. That was just what was happening now. Instead of trying to comprehend in a practical manner the quarrymen's proposals, I was concentrating on The Devils Fingers themselves.[33]

There may be some contingent correlation between likelihood of seeing what is required ethically and what is required aesthetically, but conceptually the connection is not required.

THE PEIRCE/DAHL VIEW

Stuart Hampshire, it will be recalled, believes that there is something abnormal or atypical about fixing attention on objects in isolation from action—in thinking about them apart from their *uses*. He would surely think it a mistake to apply the Aristotle/McDowell view of moral attention to aesthetic attention. *Looking* has a goal outside of the situation perceived in the ethical case, whereas *reflection for its own sake,* or for the pleasure accompanying it, is the internal goal of aesthetic activity.

But even if being an aesthetic person does not make one a moral person, and if ethical attention is different from aesthetic attention, there is still a possible connection between the two, still an explanation for surprise that a man can be aesthetically scrupulous in the morning and ethically unscrupulous in the afternoon. This connection is suggested, I believe, if, instead of thinking about aesthetic people who are immoral, we look at the converse—moral people who are unaesthetic. Not *a*aesthetic, that is, not people who are too busy to engage in aesthetic activity, but people who make aesthetic mistakes comparable to the moral mistakes of Blunt and the music-loving Nazis. We are not going to look at people who put pink flamingoes on their lawn, or prefer Duran Duran to Pavarotti. What I want to consider are what I call *deep* aesthetic mistakes.

What would one think about a person who derived pleasure from the perception and contemplation of designs burned into human flesh (not as a part of a ritual, such as coming of age, but as a result of pain inflicted on persons against their will)? Wouldn't we believe that such a person is not, could not be, a *moral* person? An American president reputedly said, "If you've seen one tree, you've seen 'em all." Shouldn't such a shallow aesthetic judgment be a tip-off about corresponding inability to make wise choices in the arena of human action? It is one thing to fail to take the time to view sunsets, quite another to take the time and fail to respond. Surely there is something missing in the character and experience of a person who never delights in such things.

Dorothea Krook believes that Henry James wanted to suggest the following flaw in Isabel Archer, the heroine of his novel *Portrait of a Lady*.

> Aestheticism seeks always to substitute the appearance for the reality, the surface for the substance, the touchstone of taste for the touchstone of truth: the truth which in the life of man (Henry James comes more and more to insist) is in the first instance moral and only secondarily and derivatively aesthetic. Isabel Archer is too susceptible—just that shade too susceptible—to fine appearances, to a brilliant surface, to the appeal, in short, of the merely aesthetic, to be morally altogether sound.[34]

Clearly "aestheticism" here means a too shallow perception and reflection on particular relevant features of objects. Could it be that the Nazi and Blunt examples reveal attention to brilliant surfaces alone and betray a lack of *deeper* sensitivity that will not characterize the truly moral *nor* truly aesthetic life?

This sort of claim, I believe, says something in general about the meaning of life. Aristotle and McDowell believe that being able to make moral judgment demands being a certain kind of person. Being a certain kind of person entails a view about life's meaning. Perhaps at this *deep* level the two sorts of value begin to overlap. This possibility is the one I now wish to suggest and examine.

Charles S. Peirce believed that ultimate good (summum bonum) must be understood in 'aesthetic' terms—that ethics depends on aesthetics. Although here, as elsewhere, his writing tended to obscurity, Peirce's reason for so thinking seems to be his belief that aesthetics is the realm of *feeling* (this shows a Kantian influence) and that ultimately our choice about what is good depends on how we feel about what we choose. Like Tolstoy, he thought that aesthetic value determines what is beautiful rather than vice versa. But it also determines what is good (here, of course, he diverges radically from Tolstoy). "Ethics asks to what end all efforts shall be directed. That question obviously depends upon the question of what it would be that, independently of the effort, we should like to experience."[35] That is, how would the experience feel?

In Peirce's system, there is a parallel between truth and goodness. Truth is not in the world, but in human experience of the world. Ultimately, it depends upon the agreement of rational people. The question, "What is true?" means "What would a rational person believe?" Goodness is also based in human experience—but in feeling rather than belief. Ultimately, good depends upon how experience *feels*, not to *rational* minds, but to *cultured* minds. Agreement between cultured persons determines what is good and bad.

There is a connection between the cultured and the rational, however. It surfaces when one asks what the cultured mind feels good about. "The one thing whose admirableness is not due to an ulterior reason, is *Reason* itself comprehended in all its fulness, so far as we can comprehend it."[36] Thus, for Peirce, the meaning of life is rooted in rationality. *Rational* people will *feel* certain ways about certain sorts of things, will take delight in some things and not in others.

More recently, Norman Dahl has also argued for construing the meaningful as the rational life; and although his (like McDowell's) is the approach of a moral philosopher rather than an aesthetician, what he says can be extended to aesthetic concerns. "To ask whether life is meaningful is at least to ask whether there is a way of living one's life that will make it overall good. . . ."[37]

Dahl argues that an adequate characterization of the meaningful (and, hence, the rational) life must satisfy three conditions: an internalist, an objective, and an importance condition. The first stipulates that "this value is of the sort that when its nature is understood, a person will want to realize it."[38] This is a motivational requirement. The second condition demands the possibility of correct answers to disputes. The third necessitates that what matters *really matters*, that is, it will not depend upon idiosyncratic desires. Dahl's suggestion is that "life is meaningful if it exhibits moral behavior, where moral behavior is understood as a certain form of rational behavior. . . . There are certain desires or motives that a person will come to have if she exercises reason correctly."[39]

Perhaps the desire for aesthetic pleasure is one such desire. Perhaps, as Pierce suggested, the rational person will feel good about leading the rational life. Rationality surely involves, among other things, a balanced, inclusive view, and the ability to consider things that matter. Surely this last sentence can be read aesthetically as well as ethically. My own opinion is that a life in which one tree is enough is not "overall good." But before I present my own view fully there is another ethical theory that is suggestive for the task at hand.

THE WIGGINS VIEW

David Wiggins would warmly approve of Dahl's attention to the meaning of life, for he believes that this, and truth (which Dahl includes via his discussion of rationality and objectivity), are the central problems of moral philosophy. Otherwise, he says, it reduces to "the casuistry of emergencies." In a paper in which he attempts to relate "Truth, Convention and The Meaning of Life," Wiggins begins with a discussion of a suggestion made by Richard Taylor as to how one might make the life of Sisyphus meaningful.[40] According to mythology, Sisyphus was a poor wretch sentenced to spend eternity rolling a heavy stone up a steep hill, only to have it roll down again every time he reached the top. One way of making this existence meaningful, according to Taylor, would be to attach some *purpose* to getting the stone eventually to the top: the construction of a beautiful temple, for example. Another way would be to inject something into Sisyphus's veins—something that would make him feel good about what he is doing from the inside, as it were, independent of what happens on the outside (in the real world).

Although sympathetic to this "injection theory," Wiggins believes it is unacceptable. Such a noncognitive account of the meaning of life in which will is separated from intellect, value from fact, the subjective from the objective, is at bottom incoherent, he thinks. There is too little difference made between outcomes of different sorts of activities and the reasons given for engaging in them. Whether one spends a life pushing a stone or tending the sick, the reason given for doing it will be the same: "It makes me feel good." Differences in value that we may want to assign to different sorts of activity cannot come from the outside, for from there (independent of feeling) all forms of life are equally meaningless or full, based on the injection theory. We have no way of showing rationally that one life is preferable to another; all we can do is say that we *feel* it is.

Wiggins finds this unacceptable. "If we can project upon a form of life nothing but the pursuit of life itself, if we find there no non-instrumental concerns and no interest in the world considered as lasting longer than the animal in question will need the world to last to sustain the animal's own life, then the form of life must be to some considerable extent alien to us."[41]

Wiggins's suggested solution is to view claims about differences between forms of life as *assertable* rather than true, where *assertability* is to be understood in terms of what it makes sense for a rational person to assert in a particular situation.[42] We ascribe rationality to the speakers of a language "on the strength of their linguistic and other actions, an intelligible collection of beliefs, needs, and concerns. That is a collection which diminishes to the bare minimum the need (given the truth) to ascribe inexplicable error or inexplicable irrationality to them."[43]

For Wiggins, there is no theory of rationality independent of human ideals. The will and the intellect cannot be separated; in fact they can only be understood in terms of one another. The regular model of truth as that which is verifiable is very limited; it works for empirical claims, perhaps, but not even for such *objective* disciplines as mathematics or economics. Usually, as in these last two disciplines, what we find is "cognitive underdetermination." Assertability theories of truth have the advantage of realizing that we invent as well as discover meaning. But *invention* or *creation* should not be understood as added onto a form of life after the fact; our ideals permeate our lives. Value is not invented or created, but "lights up" a life "by the focus which the man who lives the life brings to the world. . . ."[44]

A HOLISTIC VIEW

In all three of these briefly described views (Aristotle/McDowell, Peirce/Dahl, and Wiggins) a *holistic* view of moral life is presented. The good life is the kind of life led by a certain kind of person. It is what makes a rational person feel good. When life has meaning, it ensures certain sorts of motives and desires. A meaningful life entails a whole view of the world; it "lights up" our activity. Although all of these writers are interested primarily in ethics, their claims have aesthetic applications. I have suggested what they are for Aristotle/McDowell and Peirce/Dahl. For Wiggins, Sisyphus's life will have meaning only if his feelings *and* beliefs about what he is doing reinforce one another. But Wiggins (as well as Taylor) overlooks a third alternative to the external goal and internal injection theories. Suppose someone points out to Sisyphus that there are intrinsic features of his activity that are worthy of attention—surfaces of the rock, the foliage on the hill, the rhythm of his own movements. If he begins to delight in such things, will not his life begin to take on meaning?

In chapter 5 I insisted that what is valued in the landscape cannot be separated from the whole network of human cultural values. When aesthetic and moral values are both seen as part of a more general value, construed as the overall meaning of life, then we begin to see how complicated the linkages of the network are. I want to bring together the loose and apparently disjointed strands of thought in earlier chapters via the basic idea that a rational life makes demands upon what we should like—what we should approve of and delight in, what we should disapprove and abhor.

Dahl says, "There are certain desires or motives that a person will come to have if she exercises reason correctly."[45] This can be extended to maintain that someone who is thinking or reasoning or reflecting properly would not take delight in all things. *Reflecting properly* entails noticing features of things and events that are relevant both morally and aesthetically. We should not enjoy pictures of women being tortured. Failure to perceive and reflect upon certain features is *reflecting improperly*.

There will be some things that can or should afford no aesthetic delight. This is consistent with what I have said earlier about *control*. There are some situations in which the inability to exercise control precludes our having an aesthetic experience. One kind of limit placed upon control will be set morally when rationality demands that we not take delight in what we perceive or reflect upon. Liking designs burned into human flesh is not part of a good, or rational, life. Realizing this, we will be unable to exercise the control necessary for aesthetic delight.

But, it might be objected, aesthetic delight is taken in *intrinsic* features. If all I look at is the designs themselves, surely I can be delighted. Lack of control is precluded by *extrinsic* information about how the marks were made. Isn't this the sort of consideration that should be put aside when something is approached aesthetically?

My answer is that at the meaning-of-life level, responses are not separable. Given my definition of 'intrinsic',

> F is an intrinsic feature of O if and only if direct inspection of O is a necessary condition for verifying the claim that O is F, and, if someone knows the meaning of F, then (under normal conditions) direct inspection of O is a sufficient condition for verifying the claim that O is F.

it is true that aesthetic features are intrinsic, and moral features are mainly extrinsic. That is, consideration of consequences or principles requires attention to extrinsic matters.

However, moral judgments are not made independently of attention to intrinsic features. Clearly we must know what is done; someone must directly inspect the action in order for us to know this. We are more willing to rely on others' reports in the moral case, but nonetheless the intrinsic features are relevant.

Similarly, in some instances aesthetic judgments are not made without attention to and reflection upon extrinsic matters. In contemporary Western culture, how marks get on a paper or canvas, for example, is relevant to the delight they generate. There is a difference between enjoying lines made by wind on sand and lines made by pen on paper. Both enjoyments are genuinely aesthetic. But in the second, *how* the marks got there matters. Judgment is influenced by learning that marks on a page were made not by a person with a pen but in fact by wind blowing dirty sand across a sheet of paper.

We might enjoy burn marks as we enjoy wind marks. But judgment will be influenced if one learns that they were made by a process of torture. The role of control is crucial. Usually pen marks and wind marks are compatible with exercising the sort of control necessary for aesthetic attention and reflection. However, burn marks and control usually are incompatible; it is difficult to put aside practical demands—the punishment of the *designer*, for instance. If the meaningful life is the sort of life it is rational to want, then one wants to be sensitive to both intrinsic and extrinsic features of a thing, because both are relevant.

Once the holistic nature of the meaningful life is recognized, it is possible to confront directly the question of primacy of value. Is it the case, as it seems to be in the burn-marks example, that moral considerations always override aesthetic considerations, and hence that moral value always matters more than aesthetic value?

These questions can be approached by considering an apparent divergence between moral and aesthetic judgments. If someone fails to consider the fact that designs are the result of torturing someone, it seems fair and reasonable to say that that person is bad. Thus:

I. If S fails to consider moral features, then S is *bad*.

But is the following statement true?

II. If S fails to consider aesthetic features, then S is *bad*.

Is it *wrong*, reprehensible not to look at the colors of a sunset or to consider it important to look at more than one tree? I believe that (II) will strike many readers as very odd, if not just plain false.

However, if moral value and aesthetic value really come together at the deep, meaning-of-life level, as I want to urge, then this divergence should not exist. I believe that much can be done to narrow the gap between (I) and (II). In particular, four "moves", each concentrating on different interpretations of 'bad' show that II is not as odd as it might at first seem.

1. Suppose we replace "is bad" in (II) with "leads a life that is not as valuable as it could or should be," or, to abbreviate, "leads an impoverished life."

IIa. If S fails to consider aesthetic features, then S leads an impoverished life.

(IIa) is clearly not strange, or false. The trouble is that some people might now think that the meaning of (I) has been drastically altered.

Ia. If S fails to consider moral features, then S leads an impoverished life.

If (I) is true, then S is open to criticism, or to moral censure, in a way that seems not applicable in (Ia).

2. The reason that (I) and (Ia) are different is that our moral actions affect others. Hence, being morally bad is not just a matter of one's life being impoverished. Aesthetic actions, on the other hand, seem only to involve oneself. (Actually I do not believe that this is true. We might censure someone who has it in her to be a great violinist but would rather lie on the beach than practice. More on this question below.) The unaesthetic, moral person

seems to hurt only himself or herself. That is why it does not seem *so bad* to neglect aesthetic features. Aesthetic, immoral people hurt others, but unaesthetic, moral people may not. If 'is bad' means or implies 'hurts others', then the unaesthetic moral person will not be bad. Thus,

> Ib. If S fails to notice moral features, then S hurts others.

is a reasonable translation of (I), but

> IIb. If S fails to notice aesthetic features, then S hurts others.

seems incorrect. If my theory about the connectedness of the two sorts of value is correct, then there must be another way of interpreting 'is bad' or of showing that hurting others is a consequence of the failure to notice aesthetic features.

3. Now look at another, a nonconsequentialist, way of interpreting 'is bad'. Here badness will be construed as failing to adhere to certain principles—not doing one's duty, or not being honorable, or not living according to a set of rules that one has determined should be followed. Now 'is bad' will turn out to mean something like 'will not do one's duty' or 'will not be honorable' or 'will not follow chosen principles'.

> Ic. If S fails to notice moral features, then S will fail to do one's duty (or be honorable or follow principles one should follow).

Considerations of honor strike many in contemporary society as rather odd—so odd that some people have even called them "more aesthetic than moral." Although (II) would no longer seem odd, formulation (I) might now be incomprehensible. The other nonconsequentialist translations—those in terms of duty or principle—are, perhaps, more helpful.

If one couches duties or principles in moral terms, then 'is bad' will, of course, retain the characteristics that make it unsuitable in (II). But if one believes it is a duty to lead as full and rich a life as possible, or holds the principle that one should always attempt to do so, we get this:

> Ic'. If S fails to notice moral features, then S does not lead as full and rich a life as possible, and hence S is bad.

And (II) interpreted this way is no longer odd.

> IIc. If S fails to consider aesthetic features, then S does not lead as full and rich a life as possible, and hence S is bad.

4. There is a way of understanding 'is bad' that will make (II) more attractive even to consequentialists, I think. It is suggested in an answer that Einstein is said to have given when he was asked, "Why would it be so bad if the world were destroyed?" He replied, "Because there would be no one around to listen to Mozart."

One of the reasons that moral values seem always to override aesthetic values is that in the examples typically given, one is always asked to weigh a lot of pain against a little delight. Someone must suffer a lot in order for someone else to delight in the designs on her back. Hundreds of people may be left sick and hungry during erection of public artworks enjoyed only by a few. Some of us spend money on entertaining movies and concerts when we could be giving it to a legal aid society.

In order *fairly* to test aesthetic against moral value, we must construct a situation in which the amounts of value are equal. (In the example that follows I might be accused of committing the quantitative/objective fallacy because I use numbers. I do this for the sake of simplicity and clarity—to present a case where equality of moral and aesthetic value is assured. That no such case exists in real life does not undermine the theoretical point.)

Suppose that we must decide whether to build a hydroelectric dam. If we do not build it, five hundred people will be deprived of cheap electricity and a more comfortable life than they would have without a dam (notice that this involves both moral and pragmatic considerations). They will suffer minor pain—they will have to keep thermostats lower, use lower-watt bulbs, and so forth. If we build the dam, those same five hundred people will be deprived of cheap beauty. Again, the suffering will not be major; they will not be able to see something beautiful as easily as they did before.

My inclination is to say that the dam should not be built, that here we have a case where aesthetic value outweighs moral value. Others may opt for the dam. The important point is not which decision should be made, but that it is no longer so obvious that aesthetic value is secondary. We now have an interpretation that makes both of the following meaningful and true:

Id. If S fails to consider the moral consequences of building a dam, then S is bad.

IId. If S fails to consider the aesthetic consequences of building a dam, then S is bad.

A similar way of seeing that aesthetic and moral value are equally deserving of consideration, as long as the amounts are kept comparable, is by returning to Dahl's view that the meaningful life is one that it is rational to want. He, of course, says that the moral life is the sort of life it is rational to want. But he leaves open the possibility of wanting other sorts of lives that will make a person's existence meaningful.

Suppose we are given a chance to be Bach or Madame Curie or Mother Teresa. Isn't it rational to want to be any of these? All are meaningful lives. If moral values always dominated, the decision would surely be easier.

Or suppose the choice is the following. Which would you choose to be?

a. a moderately good harpsichordist who is moderately moral
b. a moderately good harpsichordist who is a little immoral
c. a below average harpsichordist who is moderately moral
d. a wonderful harpsichordist who is a rotten person

I shall not give the answer. The fact, however, that there is a real choice here—that there are real questions to which the answers are not obvious—supports the view that moral value does not always outweigh aesthetic delight.

Considerations such as these also show how intricately connected and enmeshed our wants, desires, and values are. *Reflecting properly* involves paying attention to many sorts of things. The term *properly* may bother some people who see it as *elitist*. Having standards at all, however, necessitates remaining open to this charge. I find it unobjectionable to say, "If you were reflecting properly on that picture of a woman being tortured, you would not delight in it." It follows, then, that it must sometimes be unobjectionable to say, "If you were reflecting properly on the Upper Susitna River (or Bach's fifth *Brandenberg* Concerto or Michelangelo's *David*) you *would* delight in it." Having and applying standards is required for the first, and will result in the second as well.

This is related to Dahl's "importance condition." That is, aesthetic values and judgments and choices really matter. Decisions about the set of values one should adopt are not simply aesthetic. It is not like deciding what color to paint the bathroom or what sweater to wear.

You *should not* like to see designs burned on the backs of people, no matter how elegantly composed the designs are. The *should* here is neither just moral nor just aesthetic, it is the "meaning-of-life" *should*. Someone who says, "Of course, one does not want to cause people pain, but nonetheless the designs do have aesthetic value," simply gets *value* wrong. The way the designs are seen, the standards of judgment, cannot be compartmentalized in that way.

You *should* enjoy trees and sunsets and music, where again the *should* is the "meaning-of-life" *should*. There is a connection between being a person who has aesthetic experience and being a person who has sympathies and insights of a kind required for successful social interaction. This is not to say that the connection between leading an aesthetic life and leading a moral life is *direct*. We have considered too many counterexamples. But the person who hounded Jews probably experienced symphonies differently than the person did who protected Jews by hiding them in her attic. The man who says, "You've seen one tree, you've seen 'em all," will probably come up short when perceptivity with respect to human conduct is required.

The characterization I give of 'the aesthetic' (delight upon perceiving and reflecting upon intrinsic features of objects and events identified in our culture as valuable) does satisfy Dahl's three conditions of an adequate account of the meaning of life. A normal person wants to experience delight; it is possible to specify objectively what a culture identifies as valuable; and since the delight derives from what is culturally valuable, it will not depend on idiosyncratic quirks of individuals. (One can, from within a cultural value network, make judgments about the values of other cultures and subcultures. What is impossible is to step outside of *any* culture and make rankings. But this is contrary to the holistic view, and so not a problem.)

The theories considered above all make *rationality* central to the notion of a meaningful life. I have not attempted to define *rational* (nor does Dahl). I am not prepared to do so. Nor do I want to restrict it to any particular theory. As I intend it, it includes consideration of principles, striving for validity, consideration of means and ends, and concern for truth and consistency. Above all, it involves the demand one places upon oneself and others for *reasons*-as justification for beliefs and actions.

Nor do I want to confuse *rationality* with *objectivity* that is narrowly construed—in terms of quantifiability, for example. This is, I think, a point of agreement among the theories discussed above—including, particularly, my own. None of them forces one to ignore what is often called the *subjective* side of human experience—motives, desires, attitudes, wants, emotions: rather, they encompass them. If these views are extended to include my characterization of the aesthetic, then I must also speak of 'rational delight'. Some may object to this.

The noncognitivist distinctions between objective/subjective, intellectual/emotional, and fact/value keep coming back to haunt us, for there seems to be an important and fundamental asymmetry exemplified in the following pair:

1. That object cannot be beautiful; I don't like it.
2. That object cannot be a tomato; I don't like it.

A person who utters the first can be rational; a person who utters the second, it appears, cannot. One's likes seem to influence attribution of 'beauty' in a way that they do not affect attribution of 'tomato'.

Even if we admit that there is *something* lacking in people who do not like sunsets or cardinals or cathedrals, is it really *rationality* that is lacking? The *men* we have looked at might be accused of selling the emotional life short by their emphasis on the life of the mind. I do not think this a fair criticism.

There is something appealing about subjectivist theories of aesthetic value (I use 'beauty' here for simplicity's sake as a catch-all term for aesthetic value). Settling the facts is not enough to ensure aesthetic consensus in the way that it determines whether an object is or is not a tomato. It would be absurd to try to change someone's mind about whether or not something is a tomato by trying to persuade him or her to *like* it. Application of the concept of tomatoness does not depend upon the presence or absence of a special *attitude*. But it does not seem absurd to try to change people's minds about what is beautiful by trying to change their attitudes.

We can generalize about or predict what most people like. And we can make sense of the following statements:

1. I know the *Mona Lisa* is beautiful, but I don't like it.

2. I know the Upper Susitna River is beautiful, but it's too rough for me.

by interpreting them thus:

1. I know that most people find the *Mona Lisa* (Upper Susitna River) beautiful, but I don't.

or

2. I know that *Mona Lisa* (Upper Susitna River) has visual features that most people in our culture value, but I don't value them.

None of these seems irrational in the way their *tomato analogy* does.

I know that most people in our culture would consider things with these properties tomatoes, but I don't.

How can this difference be explained?
I suggest that it can be explained by interpreting *rational* more broadly than usual. (The broader interpretation *is* given by the men cited above. Certainly Dahl gives feeling a central place in his theory.) In Western thought, the emotions may have been given short shrift, but that must not lead to disregard of an intellectual or conceptual element of delight (and nondelight). Consider the following cases:

1. You are looking at, reflecting upon, and delighting in a geometric design. I tell you that it was made by burning the flesh of a child's back.
2. You are enjoying having your back rubbed with what you believe is a mink glove. I tell you that it is actually a rat skin.
3. My brother hates green beans. His wife used to enjoy disguising them in ways that would fool him into thinking they were something else. Once she battered and deep-fried them, and after he had yummed them up for a few minutes, she told him what he was eating. He spit them out. She was furious. "You loved them!" she screamed. "Yes," he replied, "but what would you do if someone told you that you had shit in your mouth?" (The story is crude, but it makes the point.)

The delight taken in things is directly dependent upon the concept of them. It is not irrational for my brother not to like green beans; it is irrational to conceive of them as he does, to confuse them with other things.

What I am suggesting (and this is not new) is that two people whose concepts of a thing are *identical* will have the same attitude. And it may be that it is not *always* irrational to say, "That cannot be a tomato, because I don't like it."

Conclusion

The deep connection between aesthetic and ethical value proposed in this chapter reinforces the claim I made in earlier chapters that the aesthetic cannot be understood in isolation from other human concerns and experiences. What delights or repels us aesthetically, what we believe, and what motivates or offends us morally influence and interfere with one another. Beliefs and moral and practical interests, although controlled, are never completely put aside in aesthetic experience.

Failure to connect the aesthetic with other human values results in policies and practices—environmental assessment and planning, for example—that are at best superficial and at worst pernicious. Even studies of environmental resources undertaken in the best of faith fail to give *due* consideration to aesthetic and cultural amenities when they lack grounding that allows for a thorough understanding of the preferences of human beings who share forms of life.

What puzzles one about the Blunt example is not merely *that* he separated the ethical and the aesthetic parts of his life. One also wonders *how* that separation can take place.

Perhaps an answer is suggested in the Nazi example. The rational life is marked by desires as well as beliefs of a certain sort. The Nazi belief in the superiority of the Aryan race was not just a belief about biology. Nazis often used aesthetic sensitivity to try to show that they were superior. They believed that the capacity to appreciate music, for instance, was a component of a meaningful life. The problem is that aesthetic experience for them became less an indication of a rational life and more an indication of a *rationalized* life. If one is engaged in morally reprehensible work, then one probably gives a rationalization, not a rationale, for doing it by pointing to the fact that listening to music "helps us with our work."

Someone who leads an immoral/aesthetic life harms others directly. Someone who leads a moral/unaesthetic life may also deprive others. He may litter streets or deface buildings. She may destroy beautiful buildings only after taking care that there are no people in them; but she fails to see that a world with fewer beautiful buildings is less worth inhabiting.

Failure to recognize the integration of the aesthetic with other aspects of human existence leads also to impoverished theory. Theories that keep the aesthetic separate from other areas of human life provide no way of resolving crucial conflicts. Once the aesthetic and the ethical (and the practical, etc.) are seen as contributing to an overall meaningful life, there is a way of inegrating them. If they cannot be directly compared, at least they can be seen as relevant to the same thing.

The problem is not primarily one of quantifying aesthetic value or of finding better methods for capturing aesthetic preferences. What is required is a way of showing how deep an impact decisions and policies have on the meaning of the lives of those affected. Delight taken in intrinsic features deemed worthy of attention and reflection is an important part of life. It contributes in crucial, primary ways to a good and rational life. Aesthetics is a matter of basics, not of frills. But it can only be justified as such— and our social and educational policies will only reflect this— when the aesthetic is characterized in such a way that its connection to our humanity is made manifest. I hope to have provided the beginnings of such an explanation in this book.

Notes

Chapter 1. Philosophical Approaches to the Aesthetic

1. Dennis D. Rooney, "Program Notes," for *Prelude,* Saint Paul Chamber Orchestra, Winter B series, 1982, p. 32.
2. Monroe Beardsley, "The Aesthetic Point of View," in *Contemporary Philosophic Thought,* vol. 3, ed. Howard E. Kiefer and Milton K. Munitz (Albany: State University of New York Press, 1970), pp. 219–37.
3. Jerome Stolnitz, *Aesthetics and the Philosophy of Art Criticism* (New York: Houghton Mifflin, 1960), p. 34.
4. J. O. Urmson, "What Makes a Situation Aesthetic?" *Proceedings of the Aristotelian Society,* suppl. vol. 31 (1957): p. 83.
5. Kendall Walton, "Categories of Art," *Philosophical Review* 79 (1970): p. 334.
6. Ibid., p. 339.
7. Ibid., p. 343.
8. Isabel Hungerland, "Once Again, Aesthetic and Non-Aesthetic," *Journal of Aesthetics and Art Criticism* 26 (1968): p. 285.
9. Ibid., p. 290.
10. Ibid., p. 290.
11. Frank Sibley, "Aesthetic Concepts," *Philosophical Review* 68 (1959): p. 421.
12. Ibid., p. 423.
13. Sibley does not carefully distinguish between 'property', 'term', and 'concept'. Again, I think I can present his view clearly enough in spite of this confusion.
14. Sibley, "Aesthetic Concepts," p. 423.
15. Frank Sibley, "Objectivity and Aesthetics," *Proceedings of the Aristotelian Society,* suppl. vol. 42 (1968): pp. 37–38.
16. Ibid., p. 49.
17. Peter Kivy, "Aesthetic Aspects and Aesthetic Qualities," *Journal of Philosophy* 65, no. 4 (February, 1968): p. 85.
18. Ibid., pp. 88–89.
19. Ibid., p. 92.
20. Ted Cohen, "Aesthetic/Nonaesthetic and the Concept of Taste," *Theoria* 39 (1973): p. 143.
21. Gary Stahl, "Sibley's 'Aesthetic Concepts': An Ontological Mistake," *Journal of Aesthetic and Art Criticism* 29 (Spring 1971): p. 386.
22. Ibid., p. 387.

Chapter 2. Locating the Aesthetic

1. Alan Tormey and Judith Farr Tormey, "Renaissance Intarsia: The Art of Geometry," *Scientific American,* vol. 247, no. 1, July 1982, pp. 136–43.
2. Linnea S. Dietrich, "The Subjective Vision of French Impressionism," catalog for show by same name (Tampa: The Tampa Museum, 1981) p. 8.
3. Elinor Fuchs, "The Death of Character," *Theatre Communications,* no. 2 (March 1983): p. 1.

4. Alan Trochtenburg, "Camera Work, Notes Toward an Investigation," *Massachusetts Review* (1978): pp. 838–39.

5. Richard Brettell et al., *A Day in the Country: Impressionism and the French Landscape* Exhibition Catalog (Los Angeles: Los Angeles County Museum of Art, 1984), p. 21.

6. John Berger, *Ways of Seeing* (London: Penguin Books, 1972), p. 166.

7. John Berger, "Lowry and the Industrial North," in *About Looking*, ed. Kenneth Clark (New York: Pantheon Books, 1980), p. 89.

8. Berger, *Ways of Seeing*, p. 166.

9. In what follows it must be remembered that historians are no more in possession of innocent eyes than are critics, philosophers, or audiences in general. A book such as the one by Arnold Hauser that I am about to discuss, for example, is decidedly a twentieth-century history, one that uses methods and exemplifies attitudes of contemporary historians who share a special ideology and values more universally held in current culture. Hauser shares this culture's sense of what's worth attending to. Nevertheless, bearing this in mind, one can draw from histories of art an idea of the ongoing changes in the things considered valuable.

10. Raymond Williams, *The Long Revolution* (New York: Columbia University Press, 1961) pp. 156–72.

11. Joseph Epstein, "Literary Biography," *New Criterion*, vol. 1, no. 9 (Massachusetts 1983): p. 27.

12. Arnold Hauser, *The Social History of Art and Literature* (New York: Vintage Books, 1951), p. 11.

13. William Fleming, *Art and Ideas* (New York: Holt, Rinehart and Winston, 1974), p. 74.

14. Ibid., p. 119.

15. Ibid., p. 210.

16. Ibid., p. 211.

17. Ibid., p. 262.

18. I do not mean in this discussion to imply that the contributions of individuals do not matter significantly in the history of art. Rembrandt's surely did. But he was also a member of a society and as such acted and reacted on its terms to a large degree. The relative weights of individuals and societies in the history of art are not something I wish to debate here. I only want to point to the importance of the latter.

19. The question of *why* changes takes place is, of course, beyond the scope of this book. I shall discuss some reasons for one kind of attitude change in chapter 5.

20. E. H. Gombrich preface to *Legend, Myth, and Magic in the Image of the Artist*, Ernst Kris and Otto Kurz (New Haven: Yale University Press, 1979), p. xii.

21. Ibid., p. 48.

22. David Summers, *Michelangelo and the Language of Art* (Princeton: Princeton University Press, 1981) p. 47.

23. Ibid., p. 48.

24. J. Overbeck, *Die Antiken Schriftquellen zur Geschicte der bildenen Kunste bei den Breichen*, quoted in Kris and Kurz, p. 82.

25. Edward Cahn, *Masterpieces, Chapters on the History of an Idea* (Princeton: Princeton University Press, 1979), p. 3.

26. Actually the term is still used in the original sense in some labor unions. A student told me that her husband, a pipe fitter, had a "masterpiece" in their

garage. And this, incidentally, shows that the contemporary non-aesthetic use is quite different from the contemporary aesthetic use. We do not stow masterpieces (understood A-ly).

27. Cahn, *Masterpieces*, p. 5.
28. Ibid., p. 75.
29. Ibid., p. 104.
30. Ibid., p. 79.
31. Ibid., p. 44.
32. Loren Partridge and Randolph Stern, *A Renaissance Likeness* (Berkeley: University of California Press, 1980), p. 19.
33. Jacob Burckhardt, quoted in Partridge and Stern, *A Renaissance Likeness*, p. 7.
34. Partridge and Stern, *A Renaissance Likeness*, p. 32.
35. Ibid., p. 18.
36. Ibid., p. 19.
37. Ibid., p. 37.
38. Wilhelm Voge, "Pioneers of the Study of Nature Around 1200," in *Chartres Cathedral*, ed. Robert Branner (New York: W. W. Norton & Company, Inc, 1969), p. 216.
39. Ibid., p. 105.
40. Ibid., p. 101.
41. Ibid., p. 102.

Chapter 3. A Necessary Feature of the Aesthetic

1. Marcia M. Eaton, "Strange Kind of Sadness," *Journal of Aesthetics and Art Criticism* 41, 1 (Fall 1982): pp. 51–63.
2. David Hume, "Of Tragedy," in *Of the Standard of Taste and Other Essays*, (1757; reprint, Indianapolis: Bobbs-Merrill, 1965), p. 29.
3. John Moreall, "Enjoying Negative Emotions in Fiction," *Philosophy and Literature*, vol. 9, no. 1 (1985): p. 95.
4. Edmund Burke, *A Philosophical Inquiry into the Origin of our Ideas of the Sublime and the Beautiful*, (1759, facsimile edition; Menston, England: Scolar Press Ltd, 1970), p. 55.
5. Ibid., p. 65.
6. Ibid., p. 76.
7. Ibid., pp. 76–7.
8. Edward Bullough, "Psychical Distance," in *A Modern Book of Aesthetics*, ed. Melvin Rader (New York: Holt, Rinehard & Winston, 1962), pp. 398–9.
9. Ibid., p. 398.
10. Ortega y Gasset, "The Dehumanization of Art," in Rader, p. 413.
11. Bullough, "Physical Distance," p. 395.
12. Gary Iseminger, "How Strange a Sadness," *Journal of Aesthetics and Art Criticism*, vol. 42 (Fall 1983): p. 81.
13. Lane Cooper, *Aristotle on the Art of Poetry, An Amplified Version with Supplementary Illustrations for Students of English* (New York, 1913) p. 17.
14. Ibid., p. 39.
15. Aristotle, *Politics*, Jowett translation, bk. 8, sec. 7.
16. Elizabeth Belfiore, "Pleasure, Tragedy, and Aristotelian Psychology," *Classical Quarterly* 35 (1985): pp. 349–61.

17. Donald Crawford; for more on Crawford's discussion of this issue, see "The Place of the Sublime in Kant's Aesthetic Theory," in *The Philosophy of Immanuel Kant*, ed. R. Kennington, *Studies in Philosophy of the History of Philosophy*, vol. 12 (Washington, D.C.: The Catholic University Press of America, 1985), pp. 161–183.

18. Susan Feagin, "The Pleasures of Tragedy," *American Philosophical Quarterly*, vol. 20, no. 1 (1983): pp. 95–104.

19. Colin Radford, "How Can We Be Moved By Anna Karenina?" *Proceedings of the Aristotelian Society*, supp. vol. 49 (1975): 67–93.

20. Ibid., p. 78.

21. Peter J. Lang, "Cognition in Emotion: Concept and Action," in *Emotion, Cognition, and Behavior* (New York: Cambridge University Press, 1983), p. 3.

22. Ibid., p. 10.

23. Ibid., p. 11.

24. Iseminger, "How Strange a Sadness," p. 32.

25. Quoted in Georges Clemenceau, *Claude Monet, The Water, Lilies* (New York, 1930), pp. 19–20.

26. John Stilgoe, *Common Landscapes of America, 1580–1845* (New Haven: Yale University Press, 1982), p. 11.

27. D. E. Berlyne, *Conflict, Arousal, and Curiosity* (New York: McGraw-Hill Book Company, 1960), p. 233.

28. Ibid., p. 233.

29. Kevin Lynch, "The Image of the Environment," in *Humanscape: Environments for People*, ed. Stephen Kaplan and Rachel Kaplan, (North Scituate, Mass: Duxbury Press, 1978), p. 154.

30. Jay Appleton, *The Experience of Landscape* (London: John Wiley & Sons, 1975).

31. Erving Goffman, *Asylums: Essays on the Social Situation of Mental Patients and Other Inmates* (Chicago: Aldine Publishing Company, 1961), p. 279.

Chapter 4. Applied Aesthetics

1. "An Inventory and Evaluation of the Environmental, Aesthetic, and Recreational Resources of the Upper Susitna River, Alaska," Jones & Jones, 105 South Main, Seattle, Washington, 98104, 14 March 1975. For Department of the Army, Alaska District, Contract DACW85-74-C-0057, P.V., p. v.

2. Ibid., p. 7.

3. Ibid., pp. 57–62.

4. Ibid., p. 78.

5. Ibid., p. 78.

6. Ibid., p. 79.

7. Ibid., p. 80.

8. Ibid., p. 80.

9. Ibid., p. 85.

10. Ibid., p. 137.

11. Ibid., p. 170.

12. M. Rupert Cutler, "Resource Policy and Esthetics; The Legal Landscape," in *Proceedings of Our National Landscape. A Conference on Applied Techniques for Analysis and Management of the Visual Resource*, April 23–25, 1979, Indian Village, Nevada. U. S. Department of Agriculture, Forest Service: Pacific Southwest

Forest and Range Experiment Station. Berkely California. General Technical Report PSW-35. p. 13 (hereafter cited as *PONL*).

13. Richard C. Smardon, "The Interface of Legal and Esthetic Considerations," in PONL, p. 677.

14. Ibid., p. 677.

15. C. D. Stone, *Should Trees Have Standing: Toward Legal Rights for Natural Objects* (Los Altos, Calif.: William Kaufman, 1973).

16. Smardon, "Interface," in PONL, p. 681.

17. Ibid., p. 681.

18. Ibid., p. 684.

19. Michael McCloskey, "Litigation and Landscape Esthetics," in *PONL*, p. 674.

20. Ibid., p. 675.

21. Robert W. Ross, Jr., "The Bureau of Land Management and Visual Resource Management—an Overview," in *PONL*, p. 668.

22. See, for example, Nelson Goodman, *Languages of Art* (Indianapolis, Indiana: Bobbs-Merrill Company, 1968), p. 2; and Stuart Hampshire, "Logic and Appreciation," in *Aesthetics and Language,* ed. William Elton (Oxford: Basil Blackwell, 1967), pp. 161–69.

23. Ibid., p. 668.

24. Bureau of Land Management, *Visual Resources Management Program Brochure*, 1980, p. 13.

25. Kenneth H. Craik, "Appraising the Objectivity of Landscape Dimensions," in *Natural Environment—Studies in Theoretical and Applied Analysis*, ed. John V. Krutella (Baltimore: The Johns Hopkins University Press, 1972), p. 302.

26. R. Burton Litton, "Descriptive Approaches to Landscape Analysis," in *PONL*, p. 77.

27. Ibid., p. 85.

28. William E. Hammet, "Measuring Familiarity for Natural Environments Through Visual Images," in *PONL*, p. 217.

29. Michael M. McCarthy, "Complexity and Valued Landscapes," in *PONL*, p. 235.

30. William G. E. Blair, Larry Isaacson, and Grant R. Jones, "A Comprehensive Approach to Visual Resource Management for Highway Agencies," in *PONL*, p. 367.

31. Michael Chubb, "River Recreation Potential Assessment: A Progress Report," in *Proceedings River Recreation Management and Research Symposium*, Minneapolis, Minnesota, 24–27 January 1977, p. 87 (hereafter cited as *PRRM*).

32. Thomas J. Nieman and Jane L. Futrell, "Projecting the Visual Carrying Capacity of Recreational Areas," in *PONL*, p. 420.

33. Peter J. Dooling and Stephen Shephard, *Recreation Land Use Review, Visual Resource Management and Visitor Reaction to Harvesting—A Bibliography with Abstracts* (Vancouver, B.C.: University of British Columbia, Park and Forest Recreation Resources, Faculty of Forestry, 1975).

34. Sarah Haskett, "Evaluating Visual Quality of the Coast Line: Some Significant Issues" (Working Paper no. 2, reprinted by the New York Sea Grant Institute, Albany, NY, 1975, p. 5.

35. Thomas W. Anderson, Ervin H. Zube, and William P. MacConnell, "Predicting Scenic Resource Values," in *Studies in Landscape Perception*, ed. Ervin H. Zube, pub. no. R-76-1 (Amherst: Institute for Man and Environment, March 1976), p. 14.

36. Gabriel J. Cherum and David E. Traweek, "Visitor Employed Photography: A Tool for Interpretive Planning on River Environments," in *PRRM*, p. 87.

37. Ibid., p. 87.

38. Rachel Kaplan, "The Green Experience," in *Humanscape: Environments for People*, ed. Stephen Kaplan and Rachel Kaplan (North Scituate, Mass.: Duxbury Press, 1978), p. 188.

39. Rachel Kaplan, "Preference and Everyday Nature: Method and Application," in *Perceptive on Environment and Behavior: Theory, Research, and Applications*, ed. Daniel Stokols (New York: Plenum Press, 1977), p. 243.

40. Elwood L. Shefer, Jr., John F. Hamilton, Jr., and Elizabeth A. Schmidt, "Natural Landscape Preference: A Pedictive Model," *Journal of Leisure Research*, 1 (1969): p. 1.

41. Ibid., p. 15.

42. *National Opinions Concerning the California Desert Conservation Area*, conducted for the Department of the Interior, Bureau of Land Management, The Gallup Organization, Inc., Princeton, N.J. January 1978.

43. Robert Kates, "The Pursuit of Beauty in the Environment," *Landscape*, vol. 12, no. 2 (Winter 1962–63): pp. 21–25.

44. William Edgar Hammet, "Visual and User Preference for a Bog Environment," (Ph.D., diss. University of Michigan, 1978), p. 11.

45. See William A. Gates, Bernard J. Nieman, Jr., and Robert H. Becker, "Obtaining Reliable User Assessment Measures of Riverway Landscapes: Methods for Obtaining and Applications of Publicly Ascertained Beauty Curves,: forthcoming, Department of Landscape Architecture, University of Wisconsin.

46. Herbert E. Echelberg, "The Visual Impact of Timber Harvest for Aesthetics," Ph.D. Diss., (Syracuse, NY: State University of New York, College of Environmental Science and Forestry, 1976), p. 125.

47. Gary D. Hampe and F. P. Noe, "Highway Attitudes and Levels of Roadside Maintenance," in *PONL*, pp. 373–79.

48. Stephen Kaplan, "Participation in the Design Process: A Cognitive Approach," in *Perspectives in Environment and Behavior: Theory, Research, and Applications* (New York: Plenum Press, 1977), pp. 223–24.

49. George H. Stankey, "A Strategy for the Definition and Management of Wilderness Quality," in *Natural Environments: Studies in Theoretical and Applied Analysis*, ed. John V. Krutella (Baltimore: The Johns Hopkins University Press, 1972), p. 95.

50. James F. Palmer, "Citizen Assessment of the Coastal Visual Resource," *Coastal Zone '78*, vol. 2, Symposium on Technical, Environmental, Socioeconomic, and Regulatory Aspects of Civil Engineers, 1978, pp. 1019–1037.

51. Robert E. Coughlin and Karen A. Goldstein, "The Extent of Agreement Among Observers on Environmental Attractiveness," Regional Science Institute paper no. 37 (Philadelphia: Regional Science Institute, 1970), p. 15.

52. Brian A. Gray, John Ady, and Grant R. Jones, "Evolution of a Visual Impact Model to Evaluate Nuclear Plant Siting and Design Option," in *PONL*, p. 49.

53. Roger de Piles, *Cours de peinture par principes* (Paris, 1708).

54. David W. Lime, "Research for River Recreation Planning and Management," in PRRM, pp. 202–9.

55. I am grateful to Morris L. Eaton for his help in the following discussion. The mistakes are mine.

56. Dennis B. Propst, "Policy Capturing with the Use of Visual Stimuli: A

Method for Quantifying the Determinants of Landscape Preference," Ph.D. diss., (Blacksburg, Va., VPI and SU, 1979), pp. 22–23.

57. Raymond E. Christal, "Selecting a Harem, and Other Applications of the Policy Capturing Model," *Journal of Experimental Education*, vol. 36, no. 4 (1968): pp. 35–41.

58. Propst, *Policy Capturing*, p. 108.

59. Ibid., p. 127.

60. Ibid., p. 132.

61. Hampe and Noe, "Highway Attitudes," p. 373.

62. R. Kaplan, "The Green Experience," p. 193.

63. David A. King, "Economic Evaluation of Alternative Uses of Rivers," in *PRRM*, p. 66.

64. See Anthony C. Fisher and John V. Krutella, "Termination of Optimal Capacity of Resource-Based Recreation Facilities," in *Natural Environments: Studies in Theoretical and Applied Analysis* ed. John V. Krutella (Baltimore: The Johns Hopkins University Press, 1972), p. 117.

65. Hugh A. Johnson and Jesse R. Russell, "Economics of Natural Beauty," USAA Economic Research Service, 1967, p. 17.

66. Nicholas H. Coomber and Asit K. Biswas, *Evaluation of Environmental Intangibles* (Bronxville, N.Y.: Genera Press, 1973), p. 32.

67. See Barrie B. Greenbie, "Problems of Scale and Context in Assessing a Generalized Landscape for Particular Persons," in Zube, Brush, and Fabos, *Landscape Assessment: Values, Perception and Resources*, ed. Ervin H. Zube, Robert O. Brush, and Julius Fabos (Stroudsburg, Pa.: Dowden, Hutchinson & Rose, 1975), pp. 65–91.

68. See Guy Thomas Briswell, *How People Look At Pictures, A Study of the Psychology of Perception in Art* (Chicago: University of Chicago Press, 1935), pp. 1–7.

69. Maitland Graves, *The Art of Color and Design* (New York: McGraw-Hill Book Company, 1941), p. vii.

70. Ibid., pp. 71–72.

71. Gyorgy Kepes, *Language of Vision* (Chicago: Paul Theobald and Company, 1959), p. 44.

72. D. E. Berlyne, *Conflict, Arousal, and Curiosity* (New York: McGraw-Hill Book Company, 1960), p. 232.

73. Kevin Lynch, "The Image of the Environment," in Kaplan and Kaplan, *Humanscope*, p. 151.

74. Ibid., p. 153.

75. Stephen Kaplan, "Perception and Landscape, Conceptions and Misconceptions," in PONL, pp. 241–48.

76. Hammett, "Visual and User Preference," p. 121.

77. Ibid., p. 121.

78. For more on some of the unresolved issues in motivational studies, see Joachim F. Wolhwill, "Environmental Aesthetics," in *Human Behavior and Environment, Advances in Theory and Research*, vol. 1, ed. Irvin Altman and Joachim F. Wohlwill (New York: Plenum Press, 1976), pp. 37–86.

79. Lewis Thomas, "Humanities and Science," in *Late Night Thoughts On Listening to Mahler's Ninth Sympony* (New York: Bantam Books, 1983), p. 144.

Chapter 5. Measuring What Matters

1. William G. Lycan and Peter K. Machamer, "A Theory of Critical Reason," in *Language and Aesthetic*, ed. B. R. Tilghman (Lawrence: University of Kansas Press, 1973), pp. 87–112.

2. Kenneth Clark, *Landscapes into Art* (London: John Murray, 1949), p. xvii.

3. John Dewey, *Reconstruction in Philosophy* (Boston: Beacon Press, 1957), p. 85.

4. Quoted in John Opie, "Seeing Desert as Wilderness and as Landscape—An Exercise in Visual Thinking," in *PONL*, p. 10).

5. Robert G. Heady, "Land Use and the States: A Variety of Discontents," in *Land in America: Commodity or Natural Resource*, ed. Richard N. L. Andrew (Lexington, Mass: Lexington Books, 1978), p. 12.

6. Ada House Huxtable, "Water, the Wine of Architecture," *Horizon*, vol. 4, no. 5 (May 1969): p. 12.

7. Ibid., p. 15.

8. Edgar Anderson, "Horse-and-Buggy Countryside," in *Landscapes: Selected Writings of J. B. Jackson*, ed. Ervin H. Zube (Amherst: University of Massachusetts Press, 1970), p. 126.

9. J. B. Jackson, "The Abstract World of the Hot-Rodder," in Zube, *Landscapes*, p. 147.

10. Ervin H. Zube, "The Natural History of Trees," in Kaplan and Kaplan, *Humanscape*, p. 181.

11. For more on this change in attitude, see Paul Shephard, Jr., "They Painted What They Saw.' *Landscape*, 3, 1953–54, pp. 6–12.

12. See, for example, Andrew Wilton, *Turner and the Sublime* (Chicago; University of Chicago Press, 1980), p. 9.

13. John Ruskin, "The Novelty of Landscape," in *Modern Painters, Volume 3,* reprinted in John Ruskin, *Selections and Essays* (New York: Charles Scribners' Sons, 1918), p. 108.

14. Ibid., p. 108.

15. Clark, *Landscapes into Art*, pp. 2–3.

16. Clarence Glacken, *Traces on the Rhodian Shore, Nature and Culture in Western Thought From Ancient Times to the End of the Eighteenth Century* (Berkely: University of California Press, 1967), p. vii.

17. Ibid., pp. 491–2.

18. See J. B. Jackson, "The Necessity for Ruins," in *The Necessity for Ruins*, ed. J. B. Jackson (Amherst: University of Massachusetts Press, 1980), p. 21.

19. See John R. Stilgoe, *Common Landscapes of America, 1580 to 1845* (New Haven: Yale University Press, 1982); see also Kenneth Clark, *Landscapes into Art*, p. 10.

20. Wilton, *Turner and the Sublime*, p. 69.

21. Ibid., p. 69.

22. Stilgoe, *Common Landscapes of America*, p. 11.

23. Peter Carroll, *Puritans and the Wilderness* (New York: Columbia University Press, 1969), pp. 2–5.

24. Carroll, *Puritans*, p. 9.

25. Ibid., p. 11.

26. Stilgoe, *Common Landscapes of America*, pp. 51–2.

27. Carroll, *Puritans*, p. 61.

28. Stilgoe, *Common Landscapes of America*, pp. 58–63.

29. J. B. Jackson, "Several American Landscapes," in Zube, *Landscapes*, p. 48.

30. Clark, *Landscapes into Art*, p. 74.

31. Ibid., p. 132.

32. Ibid., p. 140.

33. Ibid., p. 66ff.

34. David Lowenthal, quoted in Zube, *Landscapes*, p. 123.
35. Philip Wagner, "America Emerging," in Zube, *Landscapes*, p. 19.
36. Ibid., p. 20.
37. John Kenneth Galbraith, "Economics and the Quality of Life," *Science*, vol. 145, no. 3628, 10 July 1964, pp. 117–23.
38. See Fred P. Bosselman and David Callies, "The Quiet Revolution in Land Use Control," in *Land Use in America: Commodity or Natural Resource*, ed. Richard N. L. Andrews (Lexington, Mass: Lexington Books, 1978), pp. 41–3.
39. See Daniel R. Fusfield, "Next Stages in Land Policy," in Andrews, *Land Use in America*, pp. 55–59.
40. J. B. Jackson, "The New American Countryside," in Zube, *Landscapes*, p. 35.
41. Ibid., p. 38.
42. J. B. Jackson, "Ghosts at the Door," in Zube, *Landscapes*, p. 51.
43. Gyorgy Kepes, *The New Landscape in Art and Science* (Chicago: Paul Theobald, 1956), p. 19.
44. J. B. Jackson, "Jefferson, Thoreau and After," in Zube, *Landscapes*, p. 5.
45. J. B. Jackson, *The Necessity for Ruins*, p. 16.
46. John W. Sinton and Geraldine Gender, "Visual Resources of the New Jersey Pine Barrens," in *PONL*, p. 456.
47. William James, "On a Certain Blindness in Human Beings", 1911, in *Essays on Faith and Morals*, ed. Ralph Barton Perry (New York: Longmans, Green & Co., 1943), p. 259.
48. Jay Appleton, *The Experience of Landscape* (London: John Wiley & Sons, 1975), p. 15.
49. Ibid., p. 74.
50. Ibid., p. 80.
51. Ibid., p. 105.
52. Ibid., p. 237.
53. Ibid., p. 246.
54. Yi-Fu Tuan, *Topophilia: A Study of Environmental Perception, Attitudes and Value* (Englewood Cliffs, NJ: Prentice-Hall, 1974).
55. Ibid., p. 69.
56. Kenneth Clark, *Looking at Pictures* (London: John Murray, 1960), p. 16.
57. Tuan, *Topophilia*, p. 94.
58. Ibid., pp. 96–7.
59. Ibid., p. 60.
60. Ibid., p. 120.
61. Ibid., p. 257.
62. See Paul Ziff, "Reasons in Criticism," in Israel Scheffer ed., *Philosophy and Education* (Boston, 1958); and Arnold Isenberg, "Critical Communication," *Philosophical Review*, vol. 58 (July 1949): pp. 330–344.
63. See Richard N. L. Andrews, "Landscape Values in Public Decisions, in *PONL*, pp. 686–692.
64. John Ruskin, "The Skies of Nature, Morning, Noon, Sunset, Sunrise," *Modern Painters, Vol. I, Part 2*, p. 32. in Scribner, 1918.
65. Wilton, *Turner and the Sublime*, p. 80.
66. Fred P. Bosselman, "The World as a Park?" in *Land Use in America*, p. 80.
67. Henry James, *The American Scene* (London: Rupert Hart-Davis, 1968, written in 1905), p. 32.

68. Arnold Berleant, "Toward a Phenomenological Aesthetics of the Environment," draft, p. 17.
69. Ibid., p. 21.
70. Ibid., p. 23.
71. Paul Shephard, "The Cross Valley Syndrome," *Landscape* 10, no. 3 (1961): p. 7.
72. J. B. Jackson, *The Necessity for Ruins*, p. 16.
73. Henry James, *The American Scene*, p. 11.
74. Ibid., p. 77.
75. Ibid., p. 87.
76. Christopher Lunnard, *A World With A View: An Inquiry Into the Nature of Scenic Values* (New Haven: Yale University Press, 1978), p. 55.
77. Ibid., p. 109.
78. Gyorgy Kepes, "Art and Ecological Consciousness," in *Arts of the Environment*, ed. Kepes (New York: George Braziller, 1972), p. 1.
79. David Pitt, "Physical Dimensions of Scenic Quality in Streams," in *Studies in Landscape Perception*, ed. Ervin H. Zube, Pub. no. R-6-76-1 (Amherst, Mass.: Institute for Man and Environment, March 1976), pp. 147–8.
80. Anthony Savile, *The Test of Time* (Oxford: The Clarendon Press, 1982), p. 89.
81. Ibid., p. 178.
82. William G. Lycan and Peter K. Machamer, "A Theory of Critical Reasons," in *Language and Aesthetics*, ed. B. R. Tilghman, (Lawrence: University of Kansas Press, 1979), pp. 87–112.
83. James Burke, "Excellence in Biography: Rambler No. 60 and Johnson's Early Biography," *South Atlantic Bulletin* 44, no. 2 (1979): pp. 16–17.
84. Clark, *Landscape into Art*, p. 3.
85. R. J. Tetlow and S. R. J. Sheppard, "Visual Resources of the Northeast Coal Area Study," Victoria, British Columbia, Ministry of the Environment, Sept. 1977, Appendix, p. 7.
86. R. Burton Litton et al, *Water and Landscape; An Aesthetic Overview of the Role of Water in the Landscape* (Port Washington, NY: Water Information Center, 1974).
87. Ibid., p. 104.
88. Ian C. Laurie, "Aesthetic Factors in Visual Evaluation," in Zube, Brush, and Fabos, *Landscape Assessment*, pp. 102–117.
89. Herbert E. Echelberg, "The Visual Impact of Timber Harvest on Forest Aesthetics" (Ph.D. diss., Syracuse, NY: State University of New York College of Environmental Science and Forestry, 1976), pp. 180–83.
90. Colin Stillman, "This Fair Land," in Zube, Brush, and Fabos, *Landscape Assessment*, p. 24.
91. For other studies in which explicit reference is made to aesthetic traditions, see Kenneth J. Polakowski, "Landscape Assessment of the Upper Great Lakes Basin Resources: A Macro-Geomorphic and Micro-Composition Analysis," in Zube, Brush, and Fabos, *Landscape Assessment*, pp. 203–19; and *A Planning Classification of Scottish Landscape Resources*, Battleby, Scotland, County Commission for Scotland, 1971.
92. Clark, *Landscape into Art*, p. 125.
93. Max Friedland, *Landscape—Portrait—Still-Life: Their Origin and Development* (New York, 1965), p. 21.
94. *Scottish Landscape Resources*, p. 2.
95. E. H. Gombrich, *Art and Illusion* (New York: Pantheon Books, 1960), p. 134.

96. Adelheid Fischer, "The Lure of Flight," *Arts,* August 1986, p. 29.

Chapter 6. A Characterization of 'the Aesthetic'

1. A. G. Baumgarten, *Aesthetica,* 1750.
2. Immanuel Kant, *Critique of Judgment,* 1790.
3. Ruby Meager, "Aesthetic Ranking," (unpublished).
4. Roy R. Behrens, *Design in the Visual Arts* (Englewood-Cliffs, NJ: Prentice Hall, 1984), p. 8.
5. Marcia M. Eaton, "Aesthetic Pleasure and Aesthetic Pain," *Journal of Aesthetics and Art Criticism* (Summer 1973): pp. 481–85.
6. I am going to use the term 'feature' for the most part because 'property' may too easily be confused with something physical, and, as we shall see, this must not happen.
7. Roger Fry, "The Artist and Psychoanalysis," in *The Hogarth Essays,* ed. Leonard S. Woolf and Virginia Woolf (1924; reprint, Freeport, NY: Books for Libraries Reprint Series, 1970), p. 297.
8. Murray Krieger, *Arts on the Level, The Fall of the Elite Object* (Knoxville: University of Kentucky Press, 1981, pp. 1–13.
9. George Birkhoff, *Aesthetic Measure* (Cambridge: Harvard University Press, 1933), p. 42.
10. Arnold Isenberg, "Critical Communication," *Philosophical Review,* vol. 58 (July 1949): pp. 330–44.
11. A related stance has been taken by philosophers and art theorists who argue that aesthetic experience is essentially noncognitive. George Dickie ("Evaluating Art," *British Journal of Aesthetics,* vol. 25, no. 1 [Winter 1985]: pp. 3–16) has recently discussed a controversy between Monroe Beardsley and Nelson Goodman on precisely this issue. Beardsley favors an experiential approach to the aesthetic, whereas Goodman believes that aesthetic value is fundamentally cognitive.
12. David Pole, "Presentational Objects and Their Interpretation," in *Philosophy and the Arts,* Royal Institute of Philosophy Lectures, vol. 6, 1971–72 (London: MacMillan, 1973), p. 155.
13. Alan Tormey argues for a similar position. Whenever we offer a critical judgment, he says, it presupposes acquaintance with the object. Using Hintikka's distinction between self-sustaining propositions (If I know that you know that p, then it follows that I know that p) and indefensible propositions (such as, "if I believe that you believe that p then I believe that p"), Tormey investigates propositions like, "If I know that you judge that p, then I judge that p." The latter is not true because judging requires an eye-witness account, he argues. Although I disagree in some points with Tormey, as shall later be seen, I do think he is correct that our aesthetic judgments are nontransmissible.
14. John W. Sinton and Geraldine Gender, "Visual Resources of the New Jersey Pine Barrens," in *PONL,* p. 456.
15. Joan Nassauer, "Managing Naturalness in Wildland and Agricultural Landscapes," in *PONL,* p. 447.
16. Birkhoff, *Aesthetic Measure,* p. 9.
17. E. H. Gombrich, *The Sense of Order, A Study in the Psychology of Decorative Art* (Ithaca: Cornell University Press, 1979).

18. Bruno Bettelheim, *The Uses of Enchantment* (New York: Alfred A. Knopf, 1976).
19. Roy R. Behrens, *Design in the Visual Arts*, p. 8.
20. John Berger, *Ways of Seeing* (London: Penguin Books, 1972), pp. 83–112.
21. Ibid., p. 8.
22. Ibid., p. 15.
23. Kendall Walton, "Categories of Art," *Philosophical Review* 79 (1970): pp. 334–67.
24. Roger Scruton, *The Aesthetics of Architecture* (Princeton: Princeton University Press, 1979), p. 73ff.
25. Terry Eagleton, *Literary Theory* (Minneapolis: University of Minnesota Press, 1983), p. 178.
26. Paul Ziff, "Reasons in Art Criticism," in *Philosophy and Education*, ed. Israel Scheffler (Boston: 1958), p. 222.
27. Anthony Savile, *The Test of Time* (Oxford: Clarendon Press, 1982), p. 141.
28. Ibid., p. 145.
29. Some readers may wonder why I am not relating this discussion to Locke's primary/secondary quality distinction. I would if that distinction were clear and/or if everyone interpreted it in the same way. Since it is not and they do not, I prefer to avoid the quagmire. Those who find it helpful are cordially invited to translate my remarks into the Lockian vocabulary.
30. Savile, *The Test of Time*, p. 173.
31. Christopher Ivanovich, "An Eyewitness Account of the Bombardment of the Acropolis—1687–1688," in *The Parthenon*, ed. Vincent J. Bruno (New York: W. W. Norton & Company, 1974), p. 128.
32. Fifteenth-century traveller's description of the Parthenon, in Bruno, *The Parthenon*, pp. 114–16.
33. R. M. Chisholm, *Person and Object* (LaSalle, Ill.: Open Court, 1976) p. 127. In this discussion I am indebted to Joseph Owens.
34. A true aesthetic claim may appear as the conclusion of a deductive argument; hence, it would appear that direct inspection is not always required for verification. For example, if I know that all of Smith's symphonies are unified via repetitions of minor seconds and that the Saint Paul Chamber Orchestra will perform Smith's Second Symphony on August 15, 2001, then I know (without necessarily being there) that the Saint Paul Chamber Orchestra will play a symphony unified via repetitions of minor seconds on August 15, 2001. However, verification of the major or minor premises in such a deductive argument will require direct inspection. Hence, verification of claims about the presence of intrinsic features at least indirectly requires direct inspection. I am grateful to Inkyo Chung for this point.

Some people say that they have aesthetic experiences through memory or imagination. Like dreams (mentioned in chap. 3) memories or images should not be ruled out of hand as objects of aesthetic experience. But if one has an aesthetic experience remembering, say, St. Paul's Cathedral, the object (and the thing to be directly inspected) must be the image, not the cathedral itself.

35. William G. Lycan and Peter K. Machamer, "A Theory of Critical Reasons," in *Language and Aesthetics*, ed. B. R. Tilghman (Lawrence: University of Kansas Press, 1973), p. 90.
36. Carolyn Korsmeyer, "On Distinguishing 'Aesthetic' and 'Artistic'," *Journal of Aesthetic Education* (1977): pp. 45–57.
37. Isenberg, "Critical Communication," p. 337.

38. For a discussion of repleteness, see Nelson Goodman, *Languages of Art* (Indianapolis: Bobbs-Merrill Company, 1968), p. 230ff.

39. Stanley Fish, *Is There a Text in This Class?: The Authority of Interpretive Communities* (Cambridge: Harvard University Press, 1980), p. 330.

40. We may hope that certain features will not delight us, for example violent treatment of human beings or callous disregard of servants. Unfortunately we cannot be certain that our responses will be what we hope for. More on this topic will be said in the next chapter where I discuss the connection between ethical and aesthetic value.

41. G. E. Moore, *Principia Ethica* (Cambridge: Cambridge University Press, 1903), pp. 1–36.

42. Kenneth Clark, *Looking at Pictures* (London: John Murray, 1960), pp. 16–17.

43. Karal Ann Marling, *Wall-to-Wall America, A Cultural History of Post-Office Murals in the Great Depression* (Minneapolis: University of Minnesota Press, 1982), p. 16.

44. Ibid., p. 19.

45. Ibid., p. 17.

46. This theory has been fully elaborated on in my book, *Art and Nonart: Reflections on an Orange Crate and a Moose Call* (New Brunswick, N.J.: Fairleigh Dickinson University Press, 1983).

47. Richard Smardon, "The Interface of Legal and Esthetic Considerations," in PONL, p. 677.

Chapter 7. The Aesthetic and the Ethical

1. For a discussion of this episode, see Karal Ann Marling, *Wall-to-Wall America* (Minneapolis: University of Minnesota Press, 1982), p. 31.

2. Stuart Hampshire, "Logic and Appreciation," in *Aesthetics and Language*, ed. William Elton (Oxford: Basil Blackwell, 1959), p. 162.

3. Ibid., p. 164.

4. Ibid., p. 166.

5. Philippa Foot, "Morality and Art," *Proceedings of the British Academy*, 1970, p. 3.

6. Arthur Miller, *The Incident at Vichy* in *The Portable Arthur Miller*, ed. Harold Clurman (New York: Penguin Books, 1977), p. 304.

7. Anthony Powell, *The Valley of Bones* (1964; reprint New York: Popular Library, 1976), p. 107.

8. Joseph Addison, *The Spectator* (1811), 4:335–66.

9. Fred P. Bosselman, "The World as a Park," in *Land in America: Commodity or Natural Resource*, ed. Richard N. L. Andrews (Lexington, Mass.: Lexington Books, 1978), p. 80.

10. George Steiner, "The Cleric of Treason," *New Yorker*, 8 Dec. 1980, p. 158ff.

11. Arthur Danto, *Transfigurations of the Commonplace* (Cambridge: Harvard University Press, 1981), p. 20ff.

12. Henry David Thoreau, *Journal* 4:185; I am grateful to Rutherford Aris for this point.

13. See letter to James Madison, 20 Sept. 1785, in *The Portable Thomas Jefferson*, ed. Merrill D. Peterson (New York: Viking Press, 1975), pp. 389–99. I am grateful to John Howe for this source.

14. Eleanor D. Berman, *Thomas Jefferson Among the Arts* (New York: Philosophical Library, 1947), p. 389.
15. Lord Henry Kames, *Elements of Criticism*, ed. Rev. James R. Boyd (New York: A. S. Barnes, 1855), p. 25.
16. Ibid., p. 15.
17. Ibid., p. 28.
18. Ibid., p. 472.
19. Hilary Putnam, "Literature, Science, and Reflection," in *Meaning and the Moral Sciences* (Boston: Routledge & Kegan Paul, 1978), pp. 87–90.
20. Anthony Savile, *The Test of Time* (Oxford: Clarendon Press, 1982), p. 93.
21. Henry James, "On a Certain Blindness in Human Beings," in *Essays on Faith and Morals*, ed. Ralph Barton Perry (New York: Longmans, Green and Co., 1943), p. 272.
22. Ross Labrie, "The Morality of Consciousness in Henry James," *Colby Library Quarterly* (9 Sept. 1970–72): pp. 409–10. I am grateful to Cindy Carlton-Ford for this point.
23. Marcia M. Eaton, "Anthony Powell and the Aesthetic Life," *Philosophy and Literature* (1984): pp. 166–83.
24. Aristotle, *Nichomecean Ethics* bk. 2.
25. Ibid. Translated by H. Richkam (Cambridge: Harvard University Press, Loew Classical Library, 1926) p. 73.
26. Ibid. Book 6.
27. John McDowell, "Virtue and Reason," *Monist*, vol. 62, no. 3 (1980): p. 331.
28. Ibid., p. 331.
29. Ibid., p. 339.
30. Ibid., p. 343.
31. Ibid., p. 347.
32. John McDowell, "Are Moral Requirements Hypothetical Imperatives," *Proceedings of the Aristotelian Society*, suppl. vol. 52 (1978): p. 21.
33. Anthony Powell, *Hearing Secret Harmonies* (New York, Popular Library, 1976), p. 161.
34. Dorothea Krook, *The Ordeal of Consciousness in Henry James* (New York: Cambridge University Press, 1962; reprinted in Norton Critical Edition), p. 729.
35. C. S. Pierce, *Collected Papers* (Cambridge: Harvard University Press, 1931–35), 2.199.
36. Ibid., 1.615.
37. Norman Dahl, "Morality and the Meaning of Life: Some First Thoughts," forthcoming, *Canadian Journal of Philosophy*, p. 4 in typescript.
38. Ibid., p. 6.
39. Ibid., p. 14.
40. Richard Taylor, *Good and Evil* (New York: Macmillan, 1970), p. 113.
41. David Wiggins, "Truth, Invention and The Meaning of Life," *Proceedings of the British Academy*, 1976, p. 344.
42. Wiggins adheres to an assertibility view of truth. Based on this view, a proposition is true not if it is verifiable, as many have insisted, but if it can rationally be asserted. For a discussion of this theory, see, for example, Michael Dummet.
43. Wiggins, "Truth," p. 354.
44. Ibid., p. 378.
45. Dahl, "Morality and The Meaning of Life," p. 14.

Works Cited

Addison, Joseph. *The Spectator.* Vol. 4. 1711.

Anderson, Edgar. "Horse-and-Buggy Countryside." In *Landscapes: Selected Writings of J. B. Jackson,* edited by Ervin H. Zube, 125–28. Amherst: University of Massachusetts Press, 1970.

Anderson, Thomas, Ervin H. Zube, and William P. MacConnell. "Predicting Scenic Resource Values." In *Studies in Landscape Perception,* edited by Ervin H. Zube. Amherst: Institute for Man and Environment, pub. no. R-76-1, March 1976.

Andrews, Richard N. L., ed. *Land in America: Commodity or Natural Resource.* Lexington, Ky: Lexington Books, 1978.

———. "Landscape Values in Public Decisions." In *PONL,* 686–92. *See* U. S. Department of Agriculture.

Appleton, Jay. *The Experience of Landscape.* London: John Wiley & Sons, 1975.

Aristotle. *Nicomachean Ethics.* Book 2. Translated by H. Richkam. Loeb Classical Library. Cambridge: Harvard University Press, 1926.

———. *Politics.* Jowett trans.

Baumgarten, A. G. *Aesthetica.* 1750.

Beardsley, Monroe. "The Aesthetic Point of View." In *Contemporary Philosophic Thought,* edited by Howard E. Kiefer and Milton K. Munitz, vol. 3. Albany: State University of New York Press, 1970.

Behrens, Roy R. *Design in the Visual Arts.* Englewood-Cliffs, N.J.: Prentice Hall, 1984.

Belfiore, Elizabeth. "Pleasure, Tragedy, and Aristotelian Psychology." *Classical Quarterly* 35 (1985): 349–61.

Berger, John. *Looking at Art.* New York: Pantheon Books, 1980.

———. "Lowry and the Industrial North." In *About Looking,* by Kenneth Clark. New York: Pantheon Books, 1980.

———. *Ways of Seeing.* London: Penguin Books, 1972.

Berleant, Arnold. "Toward a Phenomenological Aesthetics of the Environment." Typescript.

Berlyne, D. E. *Conflict, Arousal, and Curiosity.* New York: McGraw-Hill, 1960.

Berman, Eleanor D. *Thomas Jefferson among the Arts.* New York: Philosophical Library, 1947.

Bettelheim, Bruno. *The Uses of Enchantment.* New York: Alfred A. Knopf, 1976.

Birkhoff, George. *Aesthetic Measure.* Cambridge: Harvard University Press, 1933.

Blair, William G. E., Larry Isaacson, and Grant R. Jones. "A Comprehensive Approach to Visual Resource Management for Highway Agencies." In *PONL,* 365–72. *See* U. S. Department of Agriculture.

Bosselman, Fred P. "The World as a Park." In *Land in America: Commodity or Natural Resource. See* Andrews, Richard N. L.

Bosselman, Fred P. and David Callies. "The Quiet Revolution in Land Use

Control." In *Land in America: Commodity or Natural Resource*, 41–53. *See* Andrews, Richard N. L.

Brettell Richard, Sylvie Gache-Patin, Francoise Heilbrun, and Scott Schaeffer. *A Day in the Country: Impressionism and the French Landscape.* Exhibition catalog. Los Angeles: Los Angeles County Museum of Art, 1984.

Briswell, Guy Thomas. *How People Look at Pictures: A Study of the Psychology of Perception in Art.* Chicago: University of Chicago Press, 1935.

Bullough, Edward. "Psychical Distance." In *A Modern Book of Aesthetics*, edited by Melvin Rader, 394–410. New York: Holt, Rinehart & Winston, 1962.

Burke, Edmund. "A Philosophical Inquiry into the Origin of our Ideas of the Sublime and the Beautiful. 1759. Facsimile edition. Menston, England: Scholar Press, 1970.

Burke, James. "Excellence in Biography: *Rambler* No. 60 and Johnson's Early Biography." *South Atlantic Bulletin* 44, no. 2 (1979): 16–17.

Cahn, Edward. *Masterpieces: Chapters on the History of an Idea.* Princeton: Princeton University Press, 1979.

Carroll, Peter. *Puritans and the Wilderness.* New York: Columbia University Press, 1969.

Cherum, Gabriel J. and David E. Traweek. "Visitor Employed Photography: A Tool for Interpretive Planning on River Environments." In *PRRM*, 236–44. *See Proceedings*.

Chisholm, R. M. *Person and Object.* LaSalle, Illinois: Open Court, 1976.

Christal, Raymond E. "Selecting a Harem, and Other Applications of the Policy Capturing Model." *Journal of Experimental Education* 36, no. 4 (1968): 35–41.

Chubb, Michael. "River Recreation Potential Assessment: A Progress Report." In *PRRM*, 83–90. *See Proceedings*.

Clark, Kenneth. *Landscape into Art.* London: John Murray, 1949.

———. *Looking at Pictures.* London: John Murray, 1960.

Clemenceau, Georges. *Claude Monet: The Water Lilies.* Garden City, New York: Doubleday, Doran & Company, 1938.

Cohen, Ted. "Aesthetic/Nonaesthetic and the Concept of Taste." *Theoria* 39 (1973): 113–152.

Coomber, Nicholas H. and Asit K. Biswas. *Evaluation of Environmental Intangibles.* Bronxville, N. Y.: Genera Press, 1973.

Cooper, Lane. *Aristotle on the Art of Poetry: An Amplified Version with Supplementary Illustrations for Students of English.* New York: Ginn & Company, 1913.

Coughlin, Robert E. and Karen A. Goldstein. *The Extent of Agreement among Observers on Environmental Attractiveness.* Regional Science Institute Paper no. 37. Philadelphia: Regional Science Institute, 1970.

County Commission for Scotland. *A Planning Classification of Scottish Landscape Resources.* Battleby, Scotland: 1971.

Craik, Kenneth H. "Appraising the Objectivity of Landscape Dimensions." In *Natural Environment—Studies in Theoretical and Applied Analysis*, edited by John V. Krutella. Baltimore: Johns Hopkins University Press, 1972.

Crawford, Donald. "The Place of the Sublime in Kant's Aesthetic Theory." In *The Philosophy of Immanuel Kant*, edited by R. Kennington, 161–83. Vol. 12 of *Studies in Philosophy of the History of Philosophy.* Washington, D.C.: The Catholic University Press of America, 1985.

Cutler, M. Rupert. "Resource Policy and Esthetics: The Legal Landscape." In *PONL*, 12–15. *See* U. S. Department of Agriculture.

Dahl, Norman. "Morality and the Meaning of Life: Some First Thoughts." *Canadian Journal of Philosophy.* Forthcoming.

Danto, Arthur. *Transfigurations of the Commonplace.* Cambridge: Harvard University Press, 1981.

Dewey, John. *Reconstruction in Philosophy.* Boston: Beacon Press, 1957.

Dickie, George. "Evaluating Art." *British Journal of Aesthetics* 25 (Winter 1985): 3–16.

Dietrich, Linnea S. "The Subjective Vision of French Impressionism." Exhibition catalog. Tampa, Fla.: The Tampa Museum, 1981.

Dooling, Peter J. and Stephen Shephard. *Recreation Land Use Review, Visual Resource Management and Visitor Reaction to Harvesting—A Bibliography with Abstracts.* Vancouver: University of British Columbia, Park and Forest Recreation Resources, Faculty of Forestry, 1975.

Eagleton, Terry. *Literary Theory.* Minneapolis: University of Minnesota Press, 1983.

Eaton, Marcia M. "Aesthetic Pleasure and Aesthetic Pain." *Journal of Aesthetics and Art Criticism* 31 (Summer 1973): 481–85.

———. "Anthony Powell and the Aesthetic Life." *Philosophy and Literature* 8 (1984): 166–83.

———. *Art and Nonart: Reflections on an Orange Crate and a Moose Call.* New Brunswick, N.J.: Fairleigh Dickinson University Press, 1983.

———. "Strange Kind of Sadness." *Journal of Aesthetics and Art Criticism* 41(Fall 1982): 51–63.

Echelberg, Herbert E. "The Visual Impact of Timber Harvest for Aesthetics." Ph.D. diss., State University of New York, College of Environmental Science and Forestry, 1976.

Epstein, Joseph. "Literary Biography." *New Criterion* 1(May 1983): 27–37.

Feagin, Susan. "The Pleasures of Tragedy." *American Philosophical Quarterly* 20, no. 1(1983): 95–104.

Fischer, Adelheid. "The Lure of Flight." *Arts,* August 1986, 28.

Fish, Stanley. *Is There a Text in this Class?: The Authority of Interpretive Communities.* Cambridge: Harvard University Press, 1980.

Fisher, Anthony C. and John V. Drutella. "Termination of Optimal Capacity of Resource-Based Recreation Facilities." In *Natural Environments: Studies in Theoretical and Applied Analysis,* edited by John V. Krutella, 115–41. Baltimore: Johns-Hopkins University Press, 1972.

Fleming, William. *Art and Ideas.* New York: Holt, Rinehart & Winston, 1974.

Foot, Philippa. "Morality and Art." *Proceedings of the British Academy,* 1970.

Friedland, Max. *Landscape—Portrait—Still-Life: Their Origin and Development.* New York: Philosophical Library, 1965.

Fry, Roger. "The Artist and Psychoanalysis." In *The Hogarth Essays,* edited by Leonard S. Woolf and Virginia Woolf. 1924. Freeport, N. Y.: Books for Libraries Reprint Series, 1970.

Fuchs, Elinor. "The Death of Character." *Theatre Communications* 5 (March 1983): 1–6.

Fusfield, Daniel R. "Next Stages in Land Policy." *Science* 145 (July 1964): 55–59.

Galbraith, John Kenneth. "Economics and the Quality of Life." *Science* 145 (July 1964): 117–23.

Gates, William A., Bernard J. Nieman, Jr., and Robert H. Becker. "Obtaining Reliable User Assessment Measures of Riverway Landscapes: Methods for Obtaining and Applications of Publicly Ascertained Beauty Curves." Dept. of Landscape Architecture: University of Wisconsin. Forthcoming.

Glacken, Clarence. *Traces on the Rhodian Shore: Nature and Culture in Western Thought from Ancient Times to the End of the Eighteenth Century.* Berkeley: University of California Press, 1967.

Goffman, Erving. *Asylums: Essays on the Social Situation of Mental Patients and Other Inmates.* Chicago: Aldine Publishing Company, 1961.

Gombrich, E. H. *Art and Illusion.* New York: Pantheon Books, 1960.

———. Preface to *Legend, Myth, and Magic in the Image of the Artist,* by Ernst Kris and Otto Kurz. New Haven: Yale University Press, 1979.

———. *The Sense of Order: A Study in the Psychology of Decorative Art.* Ithaca: Cornell University Press, 1979.

Goodman, Nelson. *Languages of Art.* Indianapolis, Ind.: Bobbs-Merrill Company, 1968.

Graves, Maitland. *The Art of Color and Design.* New York: McGraw-Hill, 1941.

Gray, Brian A., John Ady, and Grant R. Jones. "Evolution of a Visual Impact Model to Evaluate Nuclear Plant Siting and Design Option." In *PONL,* 491–98. *See* U. S. Department of Agriculture.

Greenbie, Barrie B. "Problems of Scale and Context in Assessing a Generalized Landscape for Particular Persons." In *Landscape Assessment: Values, Perception and Resources,* 65–91. *See* Zube, Brush, and Fabos, eds.

Hammet, William E. "Measuring Familiarity for Natural Environments through Visual Images." In *PONL,* 217–26. *See* U. S. Department of Agriculture.

———. "Visual and User Preference for a Bog Environment." Ph.D. diss., University of Michigan, 1978.

Hampe, Gary D. and F. P. Noe. "Highway Attitudes and Levels of Roadside Maintenance." In *PONL,* 373–79. *See* U.S. Department of Agriculture.

Hampshire, Stuart. "Logic and Appreciation." In *Aesthetics and Language,* edited by William Elton. Oxford: Basil Blackwell, 1959.

Haskett, Sarah. "Evaluating Visual Quality of the Coast Line: Some Significant Issues." Working paper no. 2, Albany, N.Y.: New York Sea Grant Institute, 1975.

Hauser, Arnold. *The Social History of Art and Literature.* New York: Vintage Books, 1951.

Heady, Robert G. "Land Use and the States: A Variety of Discontents." In *Land in America. See* Andrews, Richard N. L.

Hume, David. "Of Tragedy." In *Of the Standard of Taste and Other Essays.* 1757. Indianapolis, Indiana: Bobbs-Merrill Company, 1965.

Hungerland, Isabel. "Once Again, Aesthetic and Non-Aesthetic." *Journal of Aesthetics and Art Criticism* 26 (1968): 285–96.

Huxtable, Ada House. "Water, the Wine of Architecture." *Horizon*, May 1969, p. 12.

Iseminger, Gary. "How Strange a Sadness." *Journal of Aesthetics and Art Criticism* 42 (Fall 1983): 81–82.

Isenberg, Arnold. "Critical Communication." *Philosophical Review* 58 (July 1949): 330–44.

Ivanovich, Christopher. "An Eyewitness Account of the Bombardment of the Acropolis—1687–88." In *The Parthenon*, edited by Vincent J. Bruno. New York: W. W. Norton & Company, 1974.

Jackson, J. B. "The Abstract World of the Hot-Rodder." In *Changing Rural Landscapes*, 140–51. *See* Zube and Zube, eds.

———. "Ghosts at the Door." In *Changing Rural Landscapes*, 41–52. *See* Zube and Zube, eds.

———. "Jefferson, Thoreau and After." In *Landscapes: Selected Writings of J. B. Jackson*, 5–9. *See* Zube, Ervin H., ed.

———, ed. *The Necessity for Ruins*. Amherst: University of Massachusetts Press, 1980.

———. "The New American Countryside." In *Changing Rural Landscapes*, 27–38. *See* Zube and Zube, eds.

———. "Several American Landscapes." In *Landscapes: Selected Writings of J. B. Jackson*, 43–63. *See* Zube, Ervin H., ed.

James, Henry. *The American Scene*. 1905. London: Rupert Hart-Davis, 1968.

James, William. "On a Certain Blindness in Human Beings." 1911. In *Essays on Faith and Morals*, edited by Ralph Barton Perry. New York: Longmans, Green & Company, 1943.

Jefferson, Thomas. Letter to James Madison, 20 September 1785. In *The Portable Thomas Jefferson*, edited by Merrill D. Peterson, 389–99. New York: Viking Press, 1975.

Johnson, Hugh A. and Jesse R. Russell. "Economics of Natural Beauty." USAA Economic Research Service, 1967, 13–19.

Jones & Jones. "An Inventory and Evaluation of the Environmental, Aesthetic, and Recreational Resources of the Upper Susitna River, Alaska." Report prepared for U. S. Dept. of the Army, Alaska District, Contract DACW85-74-C-0057.

Kames, Lord Henry. *Elements of Criticism*. 1755. Edited by Rev. James R. Boyd. New York: A. S. Barnes & Company, 1972.

Kant, Immanuel. *Critique of Judgment*. 1790. Translated by J. H. Bernard. London, 1892. Reprint. New York: Hafner Library of Classics, 1963.

Kaplan, Rachel. "The Green Experience." In *Humanscape: Environments for People*. *See* Kaplan and Kaplan, eds.

———. "Preference and Everyday Nature: Method and Application." In *Perspectives on Environment and Behavior: Theory, Research, and Applications*. *See* Stokols, Daniel, ed.

Kaplan, Stephen. "Participation in the Design Process: A Cognitive Approach." In *Perspectives on Environment and Behavior: Theory, Research and Applications*. *See* Stokols, Daniel, ed.

———. "Perception and Landscape, Conceptions and Misconceptions." In *PONL*, 241–48. *See* U. S. Department of Agriculture.

Kaplan, Stephen and Rachel Kaplan, eds. *Humanscape: Environments for People*. North Scituate, Mass.: Duxbury Press, 1978.

Kates, Robert. "The Pursuit of Beauty in the Environment." *Landscape* 12 (Winter 1962–63): 21–25.

Kepes, Gyorgy. "Art and Ecological Consciousness." In *Arts of the Environment*, edited by Gyorgy Kepes. New York: George Braziller, 1972.

———. *Language of Vision*. Chicago: Paul Theobald & Company, 1959.

———. *The New Landscape in Art and Science*. Chicago: Paul Theobald & Company, 1956.

King, David A. "Economic Evaluation of Alternative Uses of Rivers." In *PRRM*, 60–66. *See Proceedings*.

Kivy, Peter. "Aesthetic Aspects and Aesthetic Qualities." *Journal of Philosophy* 65 (February 1968): 86–93.

Korsmeyer, Carolyn. "On Distinguishing 'Aesthetic' and 'Artistic'." *Journal of Aesthetic Education* 11(1977): 45–57.

Krieger, Murray. *Arts on the Level: The Fall of the Elite Object*. Knoxville: University of Kentucky Press, 1981.

Krook, Dorothea. *The Ordeal of Consciousness in Henry James*. New York: Cambridge University Press, 1962.

Labrie, Ross. "The Morality of Consciousness in Henry James." *Colby Library Quarterly* 9 (September 1970–72): 409–10.

Lang, Peter J. "Cognition in Emotion: Concept and Action." In *Emotions, Cognition, and Behavior*, edited by Carroll E. Izard, Jerome Kagan, and Robert B. Zajone. New York: Cambridge University Press, 1984.

Laurie, Ian C. "Aesthetic Factors in Visual Evaluation." In *Landscape Assessment: Values, Perception and Resources*, 102–17. *See* Zube, Brush, and Fabos, eds.

Lime, David W. "Research for River Recreation Planning and Management." In *PRRM*, 202–9. *See Proceedings*.

Litton, R. Burton. "Descriptive Approaches to Landscape Analysis." In *PONL*, 77–87. *See* U.S. Department of Agriculture.

Litton, R. Burton, Robert J. Tetlow, Jens Sorensen and Russell A. Beatty. *Water and Landscape: An Aesthetic Overview of the Role of Water in the Landscape*. Port Washington, N.Y.: Water Information Center, 1974.

Lunnard, Christopher. *A World with a View: An Inquiry into the Nature of Scenic Values*. New Haven: Yale University Press, 1978.

Lycan, William G. and Peter K. Machamer. "A Theory of Critical Reasons." In *Language and Aesthetics*, edited by B. R. Tilghman, 87–112. Lawrence: University of Kansas Press, 1973.

Lynch, Kevin. "The Image of the Environment." In *Humanscape: Environments for People*. *See* Kaplan and Kaplan, eds.

McCarthy, Michael M. "Complexity and Valued Landscapes." In *PONL*, 235–40. *See* U. S. Department of Agriculture.

McCloskey, Michael. "Litigation and Landscape Esthetics." In *PONL*, 674–75. *See* U. S. Department of Agriculture.

McDowell, John. "Are Moral Requirements Hypothetical Imperatives?" *Proceedings of the Aristotelian Society*, suppl. vol. 52 (1978): 13–30.

———. "Virtue and Reason." *Monist* 62, no. 3 (1980) 331–50.

Marling, Karal Ann. *Wall-to-Wall America: A Cultural History of Post-Office Murals in the Great Depression.* Minneapolis: University of Minnesota Press, 1982.

Meager, Ruby. "Aesthetic Ranking." Unpublished.

Miller, Arthur. *The Incident at Vichy.* In *The Portable Arthur Miller*, edited by Harold Clurman. New York: Penguin Books, 1977.

Moore, G. E. *Principia Ethica.* Cambridge: Cambridge University Press, 1903.

Moreall, John. "Enjoying Negative Emotions in Fiction." *Philosophy and Literature* 9, no. 1(1985): 95–103.

Nassauer, Joan. "Managing Naturalness in Wildland and Agriclutural Landscapes." In *PONL*, 447–53. See U.S. Department of Agriculture.

National Opinions Concerning the California Desert Conservation Area. Study conducted for the U. S. Department of the Interior, Bureau of Land Management. Princeton, N.J.: The Gallup Organization, January 1978.

Nieman, Thomas and Jane L. Futrell. "Projecting the Visual Carrying Capacity of Recreational Areas." In *PONL,* 420–27. *See* U.S. Department of Agriculture.

Opie, John. "Seeing Desert as Wilderness and as Landscape—An Exercise in Visual Thinking." In *PONL,* 101–08. See U. S. Department of Agriculture.

Ortega y Gasset, Jose. "The Dehumanization of Art." In *A Modern Book of Aesthetics*, edited by Melvin Rader, 394–410. New York: Holt, Rinehart & Winston, 1960.

Palmer, James F. "Citizen Assessment of the Coastal Visual Resource." *Coastal Zone '78.* Vol. 2 of the Symposium on Technical, Environmental Socioeconomic, and Regulatory Aspects of Civil Engineers, 1978: 1019–37.

Partridge, Loren and Randolph Stern. *A Renaissance Likeness.* Berkeley: University of California Press, 1980.

Peirce, C. S. *Collected Papers.* Cambridge: Harvard University Press, 1931–35.

Piles, Roger de. *Cours de peinture par principes.* Paris, 1708.

Pitt, David. "Physical Dimensions of Scenic Quality in Streams." In *Studies in Landscape Perception,* 147–65. *See* Zube, Ervin H., ed.

Polakowski, Kenneth J. "Landscape Assessment of the Upper Great Lakes Basin Resources: A Macro-Geomorphic and Micro-Composition Analysis." In *Landscape Assessment: Values, Perception and Resources,* 203–19. *See* Zube, Brush, and Fabos, eds.

Pole, David. "Presentational Objects and Their Interpretation." In *Philosophy and the Arts.* Vol. 6 of Royal Institute of Philosophy Lectures, 1971–72. London: Macmillan, 1973.

PONL. See U. S. Department of Agriculture, Forest Service: Pacific Southwest Forest and Range Experiment Station.

Powell, Anthony. *Hearing Secret Harmonies.* New York: Popular Library, 1976.

———. *The Valley of Bones.* 1964. New York: Popular Library, 1976.

Proceedings: River Recreation Management and Research Symposium. Minneapolis, Minnesota, 24–27 January 1977.

Propst, Dennis B. "Policy Capturing with the Use of Visual Stimuli: A Method for Quantifying the Determinants of Landscape Preference." Ph.D. diss., Virginia Polytechnical Institute and Southern University, 1979.

PRRM. See Proceedings: River Recreation Management and Research Symposium.
Putnam, Hilary. "Literature, Science, and Reflection." In *Meaning and the Moral Sciences*, edited by Hilary Putnam. Boston: Routledge & Kegan Paul, 1978.
Radford, Colin. "How Can We Be Moved by Anna Karenina?" *Proceedings of the Aristotelian Society*, suppl. vol. 49 (1975): 67–93.
Rooney, Dennis D. *Prelude*. Program notes to Saint Paul Chamber Orchestra Concerts, Winter B series, 1982.
Ross, Robert W., Jr. "The Bureau of Land Management and Visual Resource Management—An Overview." In *PONL*, 666–70. *See* U.S. Department of Agriculture.
Ruskin, John. "The Novelty of Landscape." In *Modern Painters, Vol. 3*, reprinted in *Selections and Essays* by John Ruskin. New York: Charles Scribners' Sons, 1918.
———. "The Skies of Nature, Morning, Noon, Sunset, Sunrise." In *Modern Painters, Vol. 1, Part 2*. Charles Scribners' Sons, 1918. *See* above.
Savile, Anthony. *The Test of Time*. Oxford: The Clarendon Press, 1982.
Scruton, Roger. *The Aesthetics of Architecture*. Princeton: Princeton University Press, 1979.
Shefer, Elwood L., Jr., John F. Hamilton, Jr., and Elizabeth A. Schmidt. "Natural Landscape Preference: A Predictive Model." *Journal of Leisure Research* 1 (1969): 1–19.
Shephard, Paul [Jr.]. "The Cross Valley Syndrome." *Landscape* 10, no. 3 (1961): 4–8.
———. "They Painted What They Saw." *Landscape* 3 (1953–54): 6–12.
Sibley, Frank. "Aesthetic Concepts." *Philosophical Review* 68 (1959): 421–50.
———. "Objectivity and Aesthetics." *Proceedings of the Aristotelian Society*, suppl. vol. 42 (1968): 31–54.
Sinton, John W. and Geraldine Gender. "Visual Resources of the New Jersey Pine Barrens." In *PONL*, 454–61. *See* U.S. Department of Agriculture.
Smardon, Richard C. "The Interface of Legal and Esthetic Considerations." In *PONL*, 676–85. *See* U.S. Department of Agriculture.
Stahl, Gary. "Sibley's 'Aesthetic Concepts': An Ontological Mistake." *Journal of Aesthetics and Art Criticism* 29 (Spring 1971): 385–90.
Stankey, George H. "A Strategy for the Definition and Management of Wilderness Quality." In *Natural Environments: Studies in Theoretical and Applied Analysis*, edited by John V. Krutella, 88–114. Baltimore: Johns Hopkins University Press, 1972.
Steiner, George. "The Cleric of Treason." *New Yorker*, 8 December 1980.
Stilgoe, John R. *Common Landscapes of America, 1580 to 1845*. New Haven: Yale University Press, 1982.
Stillman, Colin. "This Fair Land." In *Landscape Assessment: Values, Perception and Resource*, 18–30. *See* Zube, Brush, and Fabos, eds.
Stokols, Daniel, ed. *Perspectives on Environment and Behavior: Theory, Research, and Applications*. New York: Plenum Press, 1977.
Stolnitz, Jerome. *Aesthetics and the Philosophy of Art Criticism*. New York: Houghton Mifflin, 1960.
Stone, C. D. "Should Trees Have Standing?" In *Toward Legal Rights for Natural Objects*. Los Altos, Calif.: William Kaufman, 1973.

Summers, David. *Michelangelo and the Language of Art*. Princeton: University of Princeton Press, 1981.

Taylor, Richard. *Good and Evil*. New York: Macmillan, 1970.

Tetlow, R. J. and S. R. J. Sheppard. "Visual Resources of the Northeast Coal Area Study." Victoria, British Columbia: Ministry of the Environment, September 1977.

Thomas, Lewis. "Humanities and Science." In *Late Night Thoughts on Listening to Mahler's Ninth Symphony*, by Lewis Thomas. New York: Bantam Books, 1983.

Thoreau, Henry David. *Journal*, 4.

Tormey, Alan and Judith Farr Tormey. "Renaissance Intarsia: The Art of Geometry." *Scientific American* 247 (July 1982): 136–43.

Trochtenburg, Alan. "Camera Work, Notes Toward an Investigation." *Massachusetts Review* (1978): 838–39.

Tuan, Yi-Fu. *Topophilia: A Study of Environmental Perception, Attitudes and Value*. Englewood Cliffs, N. J. Prentice-Hall, 1974.

U.S. Bureau of Land Management. *Visual Resources Management Program Brochure*. 1980.

U.S. Department of Agriculture, Forest Service: Pacific Southwest Forest and Range Experiment Station. *Proceedings of our National Landscape. A Conference on Applied Techniques for Analysis and Management of the Visual Resource*. [PONL] General Technical Report PSW-35, Indian Village, Nevada: 23–25 April 1979.

Urmson, J. O. "What Makes a Situation Aesthetic?" *Proceedings of the Aristotelian Society*, suppl. vol. 31(1957): 75–92.

Voge, Wilhelm. "Pioneers of the Study of Nature around 1200." In *Chartres Cathedral*, edited by Robert Branner. New York: W.W. Norton & Company, 1969.

Wagner, Philip. "America Emerging." In *Landscapes: Selected Writings of J. B. Jackson*, 16–26. See Zube, Ervin H., ed.

Walton, Kendall. "Categories of Art." *Philosophical Review* 79 (1970): 334–67.

Wiggins, David. "Truth, Invention and the Meaning of Life." *Proceedings of the British Academy*, 1976, 331–378.

Williams, Raymond. *The Long Revolution*. New York: Columbia University Press, 1961.

Wilton, Andrew. *Turner and the Sublime*. Chicago: University of Chicago Press, 1980.

Wohlwill, Joachim F. "Environmental Aesthetics." In *Human Behavior and Environment, Advances in Theory and Research*. Vol. 1, edited by Irvin Altman and Joachim F. Wohlwill. New York: Plenum Press, 1976.

Ziff, Paul. "Reasons in Art Criticism." In *Philosophy and Education*, edited by Israel Scheffler, 219–36. Boston, 1958.

Zube, Ervin H. "The Natural History of Trees." In *Humanscape: Environments for People*. See Kaplan and Kaplan, eds.

Zube, Ervin H., ed. *Landscapes: Selected Writings of J. B. Jackson*. Amherst: University of Massachusetts Press, 1970.

———. *Studies in Landscape Perception*. Amherst: Institute for Man and Environment, pub. no. R-6-76-1, March 1976: 147–48.

Zube, Ervin H., Robert O. Brush, and Julius Fabos, eds. *Landscape Assessment:*

Values, Perception and Resources. Stroudsburg, Pa.: Dowden, Hutchinson & Rose, 1975.

Zube, Ervin H., and Margaret J. Zube, eds. *Changing Rural Landscapes.* Amherst: University of Massachusetts Press, 1977.

Index

Abstract properties, 137
Action, 153
Addison, Joseph, 192 n.8
Ady, John, 185 n.52
Aesthetic amenities, 77, 94, 127, 148, 178
Agreement, 21, 81, 166
Anderson, Edgar, 98, 187 n.8
Anderson, Thomas W., 184 n.35
Andrews, Richard N. L., 188 n.38
Appleton, Jay, 63, 107–9, 114, 119, 183 n.30, 188 n.48
Aquinas, Thomas, 39
Aristotle, 33, 54–56, 120, 137, 160–64, 165, 168, 182 n.15, 193 n.24
Artists, 28, 33, 122, 142, 148, 152
Assertability, 168
Attention, 15, 28, 33, 35, 40, 47, 61, 110, 116, 124, 130, 164, 170, 179
Attitude, 15, 31, 111, 136, 176

Baumgarten, A. G., 129, 190 n.1
Beardsley, Monroe, 14
Beauty, 155–58
Becker, Robert H., 185 n.45
Behrens, Ray R., 129, 135, 191 n.19
Belfiore, Elizabeth, 56, 182 n.16
Belief, 132, 146, 178
Berger, John, 30, 103, 135–36, 181 n.6, 191 n.20
Berleant, Arnold, 114, 118, 189 n.68
Berlyne, D. E., 63, 183 n.27, 186 n.72
Berman, Eleanor D., 158, 193 n.14
Bettelheim, Bruno, 135, 191 n.18
Biewas, Asit K., 186 n.66
Biology, 92
Birkhoff, George, 131, 135, 142, 190 n.9
Blair, William G. E., 184 n.30
Blunt, Anthony, 155, 157, 165, 178
Bosselman, Fred, 112, 188 n.38, 192 n.9
Brettel, Richard, 181 n.5
Briswell, Guy Thomas, 186 n.68
Brueler, Thomas, 97
Bullough, Edward, 52, 63, 182 n.8
Burckhardt, Jacob, 42, 182 n.33

Bureau of Land Management, 77, 184 nn. 21 and 24
Burke, Edmund, 50–52, 99, 103
Burke, John, 120, 189 n.83

Cahn, Edward, 37–41, 181 n.25, 182 n.27
Callies, David, 188 n.38
Carroll, Peter, 187 nn. 23, 24, and 27
Catharsis, 55
Cherum, Gabriel J., 185 n.36
Chisholm, R. M. 139, 191 n.33
Christal, Raymond E., 186 n.57
Chubb, Michael, 184 n.31
Clark, Kenneth, 100, 104, 110, 187 nn. 2, 15, and 30, 188 n.56, 192 n.42
Clemenceau, Georges, 183 n.25
Cognitive knowledge, 135
Cognitive mapping, 84
Cohen, Ted, 24–25
Conceptualization, 122, 134, 138, 164, 178
Conditions: governing, 20, 22, 24; necessary, 18, 31, 138, 147; sufficient, 18, 31, 138, 147
Contemplation, 137, 165
Context, 14, 43, 94, 106, 135, 137
Control, 59–62, 130, 146, 147, 153, 158, 169
Coomber, Nicholas, 186 n.66
Cooper, Lane, 182 n.13
Coughlin, Robert E., 185 n.51
Craft, 36
Craik, Kenneth, 77–78, 184 n.25
Crawford, Donald, 56, 63, 183 n.17
Critics, 22, 122, 130, 132, 135, 138, 159
Culture, 70, 127, 147, 150, 178
Cutler, M. Rupert, 183 n.12

Dahl, Norman, 164–67, 168, 174, 177, 193 nn. 37 and 45
Danto, Arthur, 155, 192 n.11
Defeasibility, 20
Delight, 28, 33, 47, 51–52, 64, 106, 110, 122, 129, 130, 133, 135, 138, 140, 141,

205

145, 148, 149, 150, 153, 161, 162, 169, 173, 175, 176, 178, 179
de Piles, Roger, 88, 185 n.53
Description, 13, 77–81, 95, 120, 133
Dewey, John, 96, 187 n.3
Dietrich, Linnea S., 180 n.2
Disagreement, 81
Dooling, Peter J., 79

Eagleton, Terry, 191 n.25
Eakins, Thomas, 97
Eaton, Marcia Muelder, 182 n.1, 190 n.5, 193 n.23
Eaton, Morris L., 185 n.55
Echelberg, Herbert E., 121, 189 n.89
Economic theories, 89–90, 105, 118
Elitism, 124
Emotion, 14, 90, 176, 177
Environment, 60–93, 134, 143, 148, 178
Environmental Policy Act (1969), 73, 100
Epistemological theories, 14, 15–17, 140, 146
Epstein, Joseph, 31, 181 n.11
Ethics, 151, 152–79
Evaluation, 42, 69, 71, 76, 84, 89, 90, 95, 110, 137, 178
Experts, 85
Extrinsic, 130, 153, 169

Facts, 161, 76
Feagin, Susan, 57, 183 n.18
Fischer, Adelheid, 190 n.96
Fish, Stanley, 143, 192 n.39
Fisher, Anthony C., 186 n.64
Fleming, William, 31, 181 n.13
Foot, Philippa, 153, 192 n.5
Formalism, 15, 29, 30, 130, 133, 134, 141, 150
Formula, 80
Form of life, 94, 162, 167
Friedland, Max, 189 n.93
Fry, Roger, 190 n.7
Fuchs, Elinor, 29, 180 n.3
Function, 157
Fusfield, Daniel R., 188 n.39
Futrell, Jane L., 184 n.32

Galbraith, John Kenneth, 104, 188 n.37
Gallup polls, 83, 185
Gates, William A., 185 n.45

Gender, Geraldine, 107, 188 n.46, 190 n.14
Gibson, J. J., 92
Glacken, Clarence, 100, 187 n.16
Goffman, Erving, 64, 183 n.31
Goldstein, Karen A., 185 n.51
Gombrich, E. H., 33, 123, 135, 181 n.20, 189 n.95, 190 n.17
Good, 155–79
Goodman, Nelson, 184 n.22, 190 n.11, 192 n.38
Graves, Maitland, 90
Gray, Brian A., 185 n.52
Greenbie, Barrie B., 186 n.67

Habit, 161
Hamilton, John F., Jr., 185 n.40
Hammett, William, 92, 184 n.28, 185 n.44, 186 n.76
Hampe, Gary D., 185 n.47
Hampshire, Stuart, 152, 164, 184 n.22, 192 nn. 2, 3, and 4
Haskett, Sarah, 79, 184 n.34
Hauser, Arnold, 31, 181 n.12
Heady, Robert G., 187 n.5
History, 16, 70, 94, 96–106, 116, 122, 124, 130, 137, 141, 147, 150
Holistic view, 168
Human need, 107, 111, 116
Humanistic theories, 106–11, 119, 150
Humanities, 94, 111, 150
Hume, David, 39, 48, 182 n.2
Hungerland, Isabel, 17, 23, 26, 180 n.8
Huxley, Aldous, 119
Huxtable, Ada, 187 n.6

Ideals, 70, 71, 109, 124, 168
Ideology, 30
Imagination, 35, 36
Imitation, 56
Intrinsic, 31, 35, 40, 61, 106, 130, 133, 134, 138–41, 145, 147, 148, 149, 153, 169, 179
Inventories, 77, 111, 119, 149, 150
Isaacson, Larry, 184 n.30
Iseminger, Gary, 54, 59, 182 n.12
Isenberg, Arnold, 132, 143, 190 n.10, 191 n.37

Jackson, J. B., 98, 105, 106, 116,

187 n.9, 188 nn. 42, 44, and 45, 189 n.72
James, Henry, 113, 117, 153, 155, 165, 189, 193
James, William, 107, 159, 188 n.47
Jefferson, Thomas, 158, 193 n.14
Johnson, Hugh A., 186 n.65
Jones, Grant R., 184 n.30, 185 n.52
Jones & Jones study, 67–72, 128, 149, 150

Kames, Lord Henry, 158, 193 nn. 15, 16, 17 and 18
Kant, Immanuel, 129, 190 n.2
Kaplan, Rachel, 82, 185 nn. 38 and 39, 186 n.62
Kaplan, Stephen, 85, 92, 185 n.48, 186 n.75
Kates, Robert, 83, 185 n.43
Kepes, Gyorgy, 91, 186 n.71, 188 n.43, 189 n.78
King, David A., 186 n.63
Kivy, Peter, 22–24, 180 nn. 17, 18, and 19
Knowledge, 141, 159
Korsmeyer, Carolyn, 142, 191 n.36
Krieger, Murray, 130, 190 n.8
Kris, Ernst, 33–35
Krook, Dorothea, 165, 193 n.34
Krutella, John V., 186 n.64
Kury, Otto, 33–35

Labrie, Ross, 193 n.22
Lang, Peter J., 58, 60, 183 n.21
Language, 28, 35–42, 95–96, 113, 116, 168
Laws: aesthetic, 132, 142–46; legal, 66, 72–76, 120, 149; natural, 92, 96, 142
Laurie, Ian C., 121, 189 n.88
Lime, David W., 87, 185 n.54
Linear regression techniques, 87
Litton, R. Burton, 78, 184, 189 n.86
Logical theories, 14, 17–18
Lowenthal, David, 188 n.34
Lunnard, Christopher, 118, 189 n.76
Lycan, William G., 95, 120, 186 n.1, 189 n.82, 191 n.35
Lynch, Kevin, 183 n.29, 186 n.73

McCarthy, Michael M., 184 n.29
McCloskey, Michael, 75, 184 n.19

MacConnell, William P., 184 n.35
McDowell, John, 160–64, 165, 169, 193 n.32
Machamer, Peter K., 95, 120, 186 n.1, 189 n.82, 191 n.35
Marling, Karal Ann, 146, 192 n.43
Masterpiece, 37–41
Meager, Ruby, 129, 190 n.3
Meaning of life, 166–79
Miller, Arthur, 153, 192 n.6
Moore, G. E., 145, 192 n.41
Moreall, John, 48, 182 n.3
Motivation, 92

Nassauer, Joan, 190 n.15
Nieman, Bernard J., Jr., 185 n.45
Niewman, Thomas J., 184 n.32
Noe, F. P., 185 n.47
Numeric scores, 84, 86, 89, 94, 149

Objectivity, 19, 21, 22, 69, 70, 80, 81, 86, 119, 121, 149, 150, 166, 168
Opie, John, 187 n.4
Ortega y Gasset, José, 52, 63, 182 n.10
Overbeck, J., 181 n.24

Pain, 48–58, 129, 173
Palmer, James F., 185 n.50
Particularity, 111, 133, 147
Partridge, Loren, 43, 182 nn. 32, 33, 34, 35, 36, and 37
Peirce, Charles, 164–67, 168, 193 n.35
Perception, 18, 19, 21, 23, 70, 90–91, 99, 109, 110, 122, 129–42, 146, 149, 153, 159, 160, 165
Photographic studies, 81–83
Physiology, 21, 90
Pitt, David, 119, 189 n.79
Plato, 155, 157
Pleasure, 48
Polakowski, Kenneth J., 189 n.91
Pole, David, 133, 190 n.12
Powell, Anthony, 142, 153, 155, 159, 164, 192, 193 n.33
Pragmatic, 151
Preferences, 69, 77, 82, 84, 85, 88, 90, 93, 94, 106, 107, 122, 179
Propst, Dennis, 88, 185 n.56
Prospect, 108, 114, 150
Psychoanalytic theories, 31

Psychological theories, 14, 18, 90–93, 106, 135
Public policy, 84, 144
Putnam, Hilary, 159, 193 n.19

Qualitative methods, 74
Quantification, 71, 74, 80, 83–88, 90, 112, 119, 131, 149, 179
Quantitative/objective fallacy, 80, 86, 94, 119, 162, 173
Questionnaires, 83, 88, 89
Quine, W. V. O., 26

Radford, Colin, 57, 183 n.19
Rationality, 144, 149, 152, 166, 168, 169, 174, 175, 176, 179
Reasons, 137, 144, 166
Reflection, 28, 35, 40, 47, 61, 130, 134–42, 146, 153, 164, 165, 169, 170, 174, 179
Refuge, 114, 150
Regional qualities, 15
Rooney, Dennis D., 180 n.1
Ross, Robert W., Jr., 77, 184 n.21
Roulliard, Sebastien, 46
Rousseau, Jean Jacque, 153
Ruskin, John, 100, 103, 112, 187 n.13, 188 n.64
Russell, Jesse R., 186 n.65

Savile, Anthony, 119, 137, 138, 159, 189 n.80, 193 n.20
Scales, ranking, 70
Science, 68, 79, 94, 106, 130–31
Scruton, Roger, 136, 191 n.24
Sense of place, 107, 112, 150
Sense properties, 134
Sensitivity, 161
Shefer, Elwood L., Jr., 185 n.40
Shephard, Stephen, 79, 184 n.33
Shephard, Paul, Jr., 118, 187 n.11, 189 n.71
Sheppard, S. R. J., 120, 189 n.85
Sibley, Frank, 18–22, 44, 46, 133, 145, 161
Sinton, John W., 107, 188 n.46, 190 n.14
Smardon, Richard C., 73–76, 148, 184 n.13, 192 n.47
Smith, John, 102
Social change, 31
Social needs, 94

Stahl, Gary, 25, 180 n.21
Stankey, George H., 185 n.49
Statistics, 85
Steiner, George, 155, 192 n.10
Stern, Randolph, 43, 182 nn. 32, 33, 34, 35, 36, and 37
Stevin, Simon, 103
Stilgoe, John, 63, 183 n.26, 187 n.26
Stillman, Colin, 121, 189 n.90
Stolnitz, Jerome, 15, 180 n.3
Stone, C. D., 184 n.15
Strawson, P. F., 26
Subjectivity, 119, 129, 153, 167, 176
Summers, David, 35–36, 181 n.22
Surveys, 83

Taste, 18, 19, 21, 22, 23, 31, 110, 111, 136, 148, 158, 160
Taylor, Richard, 167, 169, 193 n.40
Technology, 98
Tetlow, R. J., 120, 189 n.85
Theoretical foundations, 76, 78, 79, 89, 106, 149
Thomas, Lewis, 93, 186 n.79
Thoreau, Henry David, 157, 192 n.12
Tolstoy, Leo, 156, 157, 160
Tormey, Alan, 28, 180, 190
Tormey, Judith Farr, 28, 180 n.13
Traditions, 94, 95, 106, 113, 116–120, 122, 130, 144, 145, 147, 150, 161
Traweek, David E., 185 n.36
Trochtenberg, Alan, 29, 181 n.4
Truth, 166, 168
Tuan, Yi-Fu, 109–11, 119, 188 n.54

Unity, 15
Universality, 111
Urmson, J. O., 15, 180 n.4

Values, 94, 122, 142, 151, 154, 169, 174
Virtue, 161
Vocabulary, 122
Voge, Wilhelm, 182 n.38

Wagner, Philip, 104, 188 n.35
Walton, Kendall, 16, 136, 180, 191 n.23

Wiggins, David, 167–68, 193nn. 41, 42, 43, and 44
Wilderness, 102
Williams, Raymond, 31, 181 n.10
Wilton, Andrew, 112, 187 n.12, 188 n.65

Wittgenstein, Ludwig, 18, 23, 95
Wordsworth, William, 112

Ziff, Paul, 188 n.62, 191 n.26
Zube, Ervin H., 184 n.35, 187 n.10

3 1543 50141 0932

111.85
E14ae

DATE DUE

Cressman Library
Cedar Crest College
Allentown, Pa. 18104

DEMCO